A PALI GRAMMAR FOR STUDENTS

A PALI GRAMMAR FOR STUDENTS

by

Steven Collins

Silkworm Books

ISBN 978-974-9575-69-7

First edition published in 2006, Second edition 2009 by
Silkworm Books
6 Sukkasem Road, T. Suthep, Chiang Mai 50200, Thailand
E-mail: info@silkwormbooks.com
www.silkwormbooks.com

Front cover graphic: Umaporn Soetphunnuek
Set in HP-Janson Text 10 pt. by Silk Type

This book is dedicated to HRH Princess Sirindhorn of Thailand,
in honor of the completion of her 4th cycle, 2548 / 2004

CONTENTS

Preface *vii*

Grammar:

1. *akkharā padāni ca māgadhabhāsāya*, Letters and Words in Pali *1*
    - 1.1 *sara* Vowels, *vyañjana* Consonants *1*
    - 1.2 *akkharānaṃ sannipāta*, When Letters Meet *3*
    - 1.3 *vyāya* (Change), Inflection *12*

2. *nāma*, Nouns, Adjectives, Pronouns and Pronominal Adjectives, Numerals *17*
    - 2.1 *nāmanāma, guṇanāma* (Nouns substantive, Nouns adjective) *17*
        - 2.1.1 *vibhatti*, Case-Endings *18*
        - 2.1.2 *kāraka*, Factors of Action *42*
        - 2.1.3 Nominal Paradigms *52*
    - 2.2 *sabbanāma*, Pronouns and Pronominal Adjectives *61*
    - 2.3 *saṃkhyā*, Numerals *70*

3. *ākhyāta*, Verbs *75*
    - 3.1 Introduction *75*
    - 3.2 *tyādi vibhatti*, Endings such as *ti* (i.e Conjugations) *79*
    - 3.3 *kitanta*, Words Ending in *-kit*, etc. (Participles), *tvādiyanta*, Words Ending in *-tvā*, etc. (Absolutives), *tumanta*, Words Ending in *-tum* (Infinitives) *102*

4. *nipāta*, Particles, Adverbs *121*
4.1 *samuccaya-vikappanādi*, Particles (Effecting) Conjunction, Disjunction, etc. *121*
4.2 *bhāvanapuṃsaka*, a Neuter (Commenting on) the Verb, *kriyāvisesaṇa* (Specifying the Action of the Verb), Adverbs *124*

5. *upasagga*, Prepositions and Verbal Prefixes *125*
5.1 *vīsati upasagga*, Twenty Prepositions and Verbal Prefixes *125*
5.2 *nāma-*, *tvādiyanta-upasagga*, Nouns and Absolutives Used as Prepositions *126*

6. *samāsa*, Compounds *129*
6.1 *samāsapada*, Compound Words *129*
6.2 *samāsavidha*, Categories of Compound *131*

7. *iti-sadda*, Direct and Indirect Speech *141*

Appendix 1: Pali Grammatical Terms *143*

Appendix 2: English Grammatical Terms *149*

Appendix 3: Meter *188*

Appendix 4: Bibliographical Essay *195*

Preface

This book is intended to be a work of reference and not a primer, as was MacDonnell's *Sanskrit Grammar* on which my title is modeled. It grew out of my teaching at the University of Chicago, where students beginning Pali have always done at least a year of Sanskrit. Although no knowledge of Sanskrit is strictly necessary to use this book, beyond perhaps familiarity with its alphabet, no serious understanding of Pali is possible without it, and I have written in that light. Many good primers and grammars of Pali already exist (see the Bibliographical Essay, Appendix 4). Geiger's *Pāli Grammar* is irreplaceable, but its layout can create difficulties for students, and it is presented solely in terms of European grammar. This book is, to my knowledge, the first to use both western and Pali grammatical categories. Pali and Sanskrit grammar recognize four kinds of word: *nāma* (nouns, adjectives, pronouns, numerals), *ākhyāta* (verbs), *upasagga* (prepositions, prefixes), and *nipāta* (particles, conjunctions, adverbs), and the book is organized in those terms. It uses and translates passages from the only traditional Pali grammar yet available in a good European edition, Aggavaṃsa's *Saddanīti*. Paradigms are given in full, regardless of whether every single form has been cited from a Pali text. There are two reasons for this: first, by no means all Pali texts have been sifted for linguistic data of this kind, and second, Pali remains a living medium in Theravāda Buddhist countries, and if a form is linguistically possible, then perhaps tomorrow someone will use it. All examples given are taken, however, from the Canonical texts, save a few given by Aggavaṃsa. This has been done for convenient reference to existing texts and secondary materials. But the study of Pali has for far too long been restricted to the Canon and commentaries, and it is high time that more use was made of later texts, especially the many from Southeast Asia which are not available in western editions.

Since many contemporary students of Sanskrit and Pali have not been trained in classical languages, nor in English grammar, Appendix 2 explains the major categories of English grammar with their classical derivation, arranged alphabetically.

I would be grateful if users of these book would point out typographical or other errors, and suggestions for improvement in the second edition, to me at: Department of South Asian Languages and Civilizations, University of Chicago, Chicago, IL 60637, USA.

I would like to thank Peter Skilling, Ven. Nanatusita, and an anonymous reader for Silkworm Books for helpful comments on an earlier draft. I also thank the Humanities Division of the University of Chicago, and former Dean Janel Mueller, for help with publication costs. It is my hope that this book may help people learn Pali, and also stimulate interest in the Pali grammatical tradition.

Chiang Mai, July 2003

The Second Edition has corrected the unfortunately large number of typographical errors (spelling, punctuation) in the First Edition. For help with these I am grateful to Sonam Kachru and Peter Skilling. There are also some minor points of substantial content, for which I am grateful to my colleague in Chicago Gary Tubb.

Bourbouloux, July 2009

1 *akkharā padāni ca māgadhabhāsāya*
Letters and Words in Pali

1.1 *sara* (Vowels), *vyañjana* (Consonants)

Pali has eight vowels, three of which can be nasalized, and thirty-two consonants, three of which are semivowels.

A. The eight vowels are *a ā i ī u ū e o*, plus the nasalization of *a*, *i*, and *u* represented by *ṃ*.

e and *o* are usually long, but can be short when followed by a double consonant.

aṃ, *iṃ*, and *uṃ* are written with what Pali grammarians call *niggahīta* (Sanskrit *anusvāra*), now represented in western editions always as *ṃ*, in some older texts as *ŋ*. It is not a consonant, but a sign of the nasalization and hence lengthening of the preceding vowel, and is pronounced either as the labial consonant *m*, or as *ng*. It is called *niggahīta* because the preceding vowel sound is nasalized and prolonged (√*ni-gṛh*) at its place of articulation, with the mouth closed. According to Aggavaṃsa the Sanskrit term *anusvāra*, Pali *anussāra*, is found in grammatical treatises (*saddasattha*) but not in those of the Teaching (*sāsana*).

The Sanskrit vowels *ṛ*, *ṝ* and *ḷ* are replaced in Pali either by expansion into *ăr/ăl*, or by the substitution of *ă*, *ĭ*, or *ŭ*. There is no rule to predict when one or the other will be chosen, though there is a tendency for a consonant to influence the choice in favor of the vowel of its own class; that is, a guttural, palatal, or labial preceding or following *ṛ* might change it → *ă*, *ĭ* or *ŭ* respectively:

kṛta → *kata*, *kṛśa* → *kisa*, *pṛcchati* → *pucchati*, *hṛdaya* → *hadaya*, *dṛṣṭi* → *diṭṭhi*, *mṛṣā* → *musā*, √*kḷp* → *kalpate* → *kappati/kappeti*, (but *kḷpta* → *kutta*).

The Sanskrit internal sandhi rule by which *ṛ*, *r* and *ṣ* change *n* → *ṇ* often leaves its trace in Pali: *śramaṇa* → *samaṇa*, *gṛhṇāti* → *gaṇhāti* (with metathesis), *prakīrṇa* → *pakiṇṇa*.

B. The thirty-two consonants are: *k kh g gh ṅ* | *c ch j jh ñ* | *ṭ ṭh ḍ ḍh ṇ* | *t th d dh n* | *p ph b bh m* | *y r l v s* | *h ḷ*

The semi-vowels *y*, *r*, and *v* correspond to and are sometimes interchanged with *i*, Sanskrit *ṛ*, and *u* respectively.

The three Sanskrit sibilants *ś*, *ṣ*, and *s* all appear in Pali as dental *s*.

The intervocalic *ḷ*, which is a feature of Vedic Sanskrit, usually represents *ḍ* (and rarely *ḷh* for *ḍh*). There is also confusion in manuscripts between *l* and *ḷ*: thus *Pāli* or *Pāḷi*.

Consonants are ordered according to:

(i) their place of articulation in the mouth
(ii) whether they are voiceless (unsounded, surd) or voiced (sounded, sonant), and
(iii) whether they are aspirated or non-aspirated.

Gutturals are pronounced in the throat.
Palatals are pronounced in the palate.
Cerebrals/Retroflexes are pronounced with the tongue curled round, touching the top of the mouth.
Dentals are pronounced with the teeth.
Labials are pronounced with the lips.

place of articulation → manner of articulation ↓	*kaṇṭhaja* guttural	*tāluja* palatal	*muddhaja* cerebral, retroflex	*dantaja* dental	*oṭṭhaja* labial
aghosa sithila voiceless unaspirated	*k*	*c*	*ṭ*	*t*	*p*
aghosa dhanita voiceless aspirated	*kh*	*ch*	*ṭh*	*th*	*ph*
ghosavat sithila voiced unaspirated	*g*	*j*	*ḍ*	*d*	*b*

ghosavat dhanita voiced aspirated	*gh*	*jh*	*ḍh*	*dh*	*bh*
nāsikā nasal	*ṅ*	*ñ*	*ṇ*	*n*	*m*
antaṭṭha semivowel		*y*	*r, ḷ [ḷh]*	*l*	*v**
hakāra/sakāra spirant / sibilant	*h*	*[ś]*	*[ṣ]*	*s*	
sara corresponding vowels	*ā, ĕ**	*ĭ*	*[ṛ ṝ]*		*ŭ, ŏ**

* *v* is dental-labial, *dantoṭṭhaja*, *e* is guttural-palatal, *kaṇṭhatāluja*, *o* is guttural-labial, *kaṇṭhoṭṭhaja*.

1.2 *akkharānaṃ sannipāta*, When letters meet

With rare exceptions:

Words must begin with a single vowel or single consonant, e.g. the Sanskrit prefixes *pra* and *prati* become *pa* and *paṭi* (with cerebralization), *pramāda* → *pamāda*, *skandha* → *khandha*. But double consonants return when not initial, as in compounds and after verbal prefixes: Sanskrit *pramāda* → Pali *pamāda* → *appamāda*; Sanskrit *skandha* → Pali *khandha* → *upādānakkhandha*.

They must end in a vowel, thus Sanskrit ablative *lokāt* → *lokā*.

At any point in a word or compound there cannot be more than two consonants together, e.g. *matsya* → *maccha*, *ūrdhvaṃ* → *uddhaṃ*.

An aspirated consonant cannot be followed by another consonant, *budh* + *ta* → *buddha*. This is important in changes involving *s*, *puṣpa* → *puppha*, *dṛṣṭa* → *diṭṭha*, *strī* → *itthĭ*.

A long vowel cannot be followed by a double consonant. This is known in western scholarship as the Law of Mora. *Mora* is Latin for a measure of time, and is used to translate Pali *mattā* (Sanskrit *mātrā*). One *mattā/mora* is the length of time it takes to pronounce a short vowel; two *mattā/mora* are required for a long vowel. The crucial restriction is that no vowel can be long and followed by a double consonant. So only the following possibilities exist:

vowel	followed by	*matta*	examples
short	nothing	1	*atha*
	single consonant	1	*sara*
	double consonant	2	*patta*
long or nasalized	nothing	2	*kātuṃ, tadā*
	single consonant	2	*vaṃsa, nipāta*

Because of this restriction, vowel length in many places has to be shortened: for example, Sanskrit feminine accusative singular *-ām* → *-aṃ*, alternative first person ending *-āmi* → **-āṃ* → *-aṃ*. Partly as a result of this, there are very many forms in Pali ending in *-aṃ*. There are numerous other examples: *prāpta* → *patta*, *māṃsa* → *maṃsa*, etc.

A short vowel followed by a double consonant is equivalent to a long vowel followed by a single consonant, so many words can be spelled in two ways: *śrūyate* → *sūyati* or *suyyati*, *kṣīyate* → *khīyati* or *khiyyati*, *hīyate* → *hīyati* or *hiyyati*.

The very rare examples where the Law of Mora is broken either involve a semi-vowel, so that there are one and a half consonants and not two (*vākya*, *bhūtvā*), or are an unusual result of combining vowels, e.g. *te* + *assa* → *tyāssa*. This happens sometimes with the prefix *sa-*, with, *sa* + *aṭṭhakathā* → *sāṭṭhakathā*.

Understanding how words are formed and what happens to them when they are put together in sentences and compounds depends on the two principles of vowel gradation and consonant strength. Such processes depend on internal and external sandhi (putting-together, junction).

Vowel Gradation and Sandhi

Grammarians use Pali versions of the Sanskrit terms familiar to all students of Sanskrit, *guṇa* and *vṛddhi* → *vuddhi*. *Guṇa* and *vuddhi* are, with the exception of short *a*, the addition of one *a* strength:

[zero strength]	*guṇa* strength	*vuddhi* strength
a	*a*	*[a + a] ā*
i ī y	*[a + i/y] = ay or ĕ*	*[a + a + i/y] = āy or ē*
u ū v	*[a + u/v] = av or ŏ*	*[a + a+ ŭ/v] = āv or ō*

Items in brackets are not in order of appearance in words, but elements of the grade which appear in words and sandhi in any order. Thus *ĕ* = *ay* or *ya*, *ō* = *āv* or *ava* or *vā*. The sandhi *yo* + *assa* → *yvāssa* is to be explained as [*a* + *v*] + *a* = *vā*, and *te* + *assa* → *tyāssa* as [*a* + *y*] + *a* = *yā*. The verbal affixes -*aya*- and -*ē* are interchangeable. The Sanskrit prefix *ava*- standardly appears as *o* (= *ō*), although *ava*- can be retained (*ŏ*- can also be a development from *apa*-, *u*-, *ut*-, *upa*-, etc.). The prefixes *vi*- and *ava*- together can → *vō*, *vyavahāra* → *vohāra*, *vyavasthāna* → *votthāna*/*vavatthana* (*voṭṭhāna*/*vavaṭṭhāna*).

When vowels meet as final + initial of two words or within a compound, five things can happen:

(i) They stay the same, with hiatus (mostly with *a* + *a*), *jayamaṅgala-aṭṭhagāthā*, *upāsika-adinna*.
(ii) One is elided (often marked by an apostrophe in E[e]), *kilanto+asmi* → *kilanto 'smi*.
(iii) They undergo sandhi, as in Sanskrit, *mahā+udadhi* → *mahodadhi*
(iv) The former is turned into a semivowel, *api+etaṃ* → *apyetaṃ*, *su+akkhāta* → *svakkhāta*.
(v) A consonant is inserted, *atta-d-atthaṃ*, *cha-ḷ-abhiññā*, *na-y-idaṃ*, *ajja-t-agge* or *ajja-d-agge*.

It is not necessary to know the full gamut of theoretically possible sandhis. The common ones are:

ā̆	+	*ā̆*	=	*ā*
ī̆	+	*ī̆*	=	*ī*
ū̆	+	*ū̆*	=	*ū*
ā̆	+	*ī̆*	=	*e*
ā̆	+	*ū̆*	=	*o*
ā̆	+	*e*	=	*e*
ā̆	+	*o*	=	*o*

Nasalized vowels, especially *aṃ*, can be treated as long vowels, e.g. *idam* + *ahaṃ* → *idāhaṃ*.

e or *o* + vowel can change into *y* and *v*, can be elided, or can cause elision of the following vowel.

When vowels meet within words, and when they are changed by the rules of word-formation, the same rules apply:

√*nī* (present) → *ne/ay* + *ati* → *neti* or *nayati*
ati + *ī̆ta* (past passive participle of √*ī*) → *atīta*
√*bhū* in the present tense is *bhavati* [*bh* →*h*, and *ava* → *o*] → *hoti*; in the future can be *bhavissati* → [*v* lost] *bha* + *issati* → **bhessati* [*bh* → *h*] → *hessati*.

√*śru* → Pali √*su*
causative *sāveti*
future passive participle (i) + *tabba* √ *sotabba*, (ii) + *anīya* → *savaṇīya*
passive (root vowel lengthened) *sūyati* or *suyyati*; future *sossati*
aorist Sanskrit *aśrauṣīt* → *assosi*.

From √*ī* or √*yā*
present tenses *ayati*, *eti*, *yāti*, *yāyati*
future tenses *issati*, *essati*
past passive participle -*ī̆ta*
absolutive (after prefix) -*icca*
action nouns *aya*, *ayana*
causative *yāpeti*.

From √*vṛ*
present tenses *-varati*, *vuṇāti*, *vuṇoti*
aorist *avāri*
past passive participle *–vuṭa*, *-vaṭa*
causative *vāreti*.

From √*duṣ*
present *dussati*
past passive participle *duṭṭha*
causatives *dūseti*, *doseti*
future passive participles *dosanīya*, *dosaneyya*

From √*bhī*
present tenses: *bhāyati*, *-bheti*
past passive participle *bhīta*
causatives *bhāyayati*, *bhiṃsāpeti*.

From √*pā*
present *pivati* (irregular)
future *pivissati*
aorists *pivi*, *apāyi*
past passive participle *pīta*
future passive participle *pātabba*, *pānīya*, *peyya*
causative *pāyeti*.

Consonant strength

In descending order of strength [◆] the consonant groups are:

◆◆◆◆ mutes*: surd/unvoiced, sonant/voiced, non-aspirate and aspirate, in guttural, palatal, cerebral/ retroflex, dental and labial consonant groups = *k*, *kh*, *g*, *gh*, *c*, *ch*, *j*, *jh*, *ṭ*, *ṭh*, *ḍ*, *ḍh*, *t*, *th*, *d*, *dh*, *p*, *ph*, *b*, *bh*.
◆◆◆ sibilant, spirant = *s*, *h*
◆◆ nasals = *ṅ*, *ñ*, *ṇ*, *n*, *m*
◆ semivowels = *y*, *r*, *l*, *v*

* "Mute" because they require closure or contact (*phassa*) in their place of articulation (*ṭhāna-karaṇa*), and stopping of the breath. This use of the term should not be confused with that which refers to surd, unvoiced consonants.

1. When two consonants are juxtaposed, three things can happen:
a) if one consonant (usually the second) is a nasal or semivowel, an epenthetic/*svarabhakti* vowel can be inserted, *sūrya* → *suriya* (with shortened -*u*), *caitya* → *cetiya*, *sūkṣma* → *sukhuma*, *kleśa* → *kilesa*, *sve* → *suve*, *padma* → *paduma*
b) if they are identical (with or without aspiration), they stay the same, √*ud-dhṛ* → *uddharati*
c) if they are different, one or both changes, in one of three ways:
   - the second is assimilated to the first: √*pūj* + *ya* → *pujja*, √-*spṛś* + *ya* → -*spṛśya* → *phussa*
   - the first is assimilated to the second: √*sat* + *kāra* → *sakkāra*, *nir* + *vāṇa* → *nibbāna* (*nibbāṇa*)
   - they alter each other: √*budh* + *y* + *ati* → *bujjhati*, *rāj* + *nā* → *raññā*, *mṛtyu* → *maccu*

2. General rules for instances where one or both of the consonants change are:
a) when both consonants are the same strength, the first is assimilated to the second, *śikta* → *sitta*, *sat* + *purisa* → *sappurisa*, *khadga* → *khagga*, *prāpta* → *patta*, *śabda* → *sadda*, *prāgbhāra* → *pabbhāra*.
b) weaker consonants are assimilated to stronger: √*kṛ* → *kar* + *tum* → *kattuṃ*, *ṛdra* → *udda*, *vaiśya* → *vessa*, *drakṣyati* → *dakkhati* (also *dakkhiti*)
c) Specific instances or exceptions are:

(i) mute first:

(a) mute ◆◆◆◆ + mute ◆◆◆◆

- [*c* + *t*] *c* → *k*, then *kt* → *tt*, √*muc* + *ta* → *mukta* → *mutta*, √*vac* + *ta* → *ukta* → *vutta* [The initial *v*- here is euphonic, not from the root. Pali preserves the Sanskrit weakening *vac* → *uc*.]
- [*ch in* √*pṛch*] + *ta*, *pṛṣṭa* [→ *puch*] → *puṭṭha*

• in past passive participles *j* → *g* before *na*, √*bhañj* + *na* → *bhagna* → *bhagga*, *j* → *k* before *ta*, √*bhuj* + *ta* → *bhukta* → *bhutta*. In some instances, *t* → *ṭh*, with *j* assimilated, √*maj* + *ta* → *maṭṭha*, *avasṛj* + *ta* → √*o-(s)saj* + *ta* → *os(s) aṭṭha*.

• *j* sometimes → *ṣ*, *rāj* + *tra* → *rāṣṭra* → *raṭṭha*.

• [*dh* or *bh* + *t*] *t* → *d* and the previous consonant is assimilated, √*labh* + *ta* → *labdha* → *laddha*, √*vṛdh* + *ta* → *vaḍḍha/vuḍḍha*, √*vyadh* + *ta* → *viddha*.

(b) mute ◆◆◆◆ + sibilant ◆◆◆

• [*k* or *c* or *j* + *s*] → *kkh*, *dakṣina* → *dakkhiṇa*, √*vac* (fut.) *vakṣyate* → *vakkhati*, √*bhuj* (fut.) *bhokṣyate* → *bhokkhati*.

• [*t* or *p* + *s*] → *cch: vicikitsā* → *vicikicchā*, √*labh* (future) *lapsyate* → *lacchati*.

• [*ut* + *s*] → either *cch* or *ss: utsṛṣṭa* → *ucchiṭṭha*, *utsāha* → *ussāha*.

(c) mute ◆◆◆◆ + nasal ◆◆

• [*j* + nasal] *j* → *g*, and nasal is assimilated, √*sam-vij* + *na* → *saṃvigga*.

• [*d* + nasal] *d* is assimilated, √*chid* + *na* → *chinna*, √*bhid* + *na* → *bhinna*.

(d) mute ◆◆◆◆ + semivowel ◆◆

• [*k* + *y*] → *kk* usually, *Śakya* → *Sakka*, but cp. *vākya* → *vākya*.

• [dental + *y*] dental → palatal, then palatal doubled:

[*t* + *y*] → *cc*, *atyanta* → *accanta*, *jātiyā* → (**jātya*) → *jaccā*.

[*d* + *y*] → *jj*, *nadiyā* → (**nadyā*) → *najjā*.

[*dh* + *y*] → *jjh*, √*budh* + *yati* → *bujjhati*.

[prefix *ud-* + *y*] → *yy*, *udyāna* → *uyyāna*.

(ii) sibilant, spirant first

(a) sibilant ◆◆◆ + mute ◆◆◆◆

• sibilant assimilates, with aspiration of the second consonant, *asti* → *atthi*, *puraskaroti* → *purakkharoti*, *āścariya* → *acchariya*.

• the prefixes *nis* and *dus* are special cases:

neither cerebralizes a following dental: *nis* + *tarati* → *nittharati*.

dus does not cause aspiration of a following mute: → *dus* + *tara* → *duttara*.

nis can cause aspiration of a following palatal: *nis* + *carati* → *niccharati*, but also *nis* + *cal* → *niccala*.

(b) sibilant ◆◆◆ + sibilant ◆◆◆

• [*s* + *s*] → *kkh* or *cch*. These cases occur with the future tense of some verbs, and they preserve the Sanskrit internal sandhi which removes one sibilant:

[*ś* or ṣ] + *-sya-* → *-kṣy-*: √*pra-viṣ* → *pravekṣati* → *pavekkhati*, √*dṛś* → *drakṣyati* → *dakkhati*, √*śus* → *śokṣyati* → *sokkhati*.

s + *-sya-* → *-tsya-*: √*vas* → *vatsyati* → *vacchati*, √*ghas* (desiderative) → *jigitsati* → *jighacchati*.

(c) sibilant ◆◆◆ + nasal ◆◆

• sibilant → h with metathesis, *-asmā/-amhā*, *-asmiṃ/-amhi*, (ablative/locative case endings), *praśna* → *pañha*, *uṣna* → *uṇha*, *snāna* → *nhāna* or *nahāna*, *yuṣmākaṃ* → *tumhākaṃ*, *vismaya* → *vimhaya*.

(d) spirant h

• [+ mute] *h* usually assimilates, with surds → sonants, and aspiration of the second consonant, sometimes with cerebralization, √*nah* + *ta* → *naddha*, √*dah* + *ta* → *daḍḍha*.

• [+ t] can → *ḷh*, with lengthening of previous vowel, √*muh* + *ta* → *mūḷha*, √*vah* + *ta* → *vūḷha* [n.b. this is √*vah* +*ta* → *ūḷha* (cf. Sanskrit *ūḍha*) → *vūḷha*; the v is euphonic, not from the verb].

• [+ nasal or *y* or *v*] metathesis, √*gṛh* → √*gah* + *nā* + *ti* → *gaṇhāti*, *jihma* → *jimha*, √*ava-ruh* → √*o-ruh* + *ya* → *oruyha*, *jihvā* → *jivhā*. [Note *brāhmaṇa* → Prakrit *bamha*, but → Pali *brāhmaṇa*].

(iii) nasal first

In all instances a nasal can appear as *-ṃ-*, but it can also appear as the nasal of its class, *sam* + *gaha* → *saṃgaha* or *saṅgaha*.

(a) nasal ◆◆ + mute ◆◆◆◆

• √*kṛ* + prefix *sam-* inserts *-s-*, *saṃskaroti* → *saṅkharoti* (*saṃkharoti*), *saṃskāra* → *saṅkhāra* (*saṃkhāra*).

(b) nasal ◆◆ + sibilant ◆◆◆

nasal → *ṃ*.

(c) nasal ◆◆ + nasal ◆◆
• first assimilates to second, *sam* + *nisīdati* → *sannisīdati*, [*ut* →] *un+mūlyati* → *ummūleti*.

(d) nasal ◆◆ + semivowel ◆
• [*n* + *y*] → *ññ*, *kanyā* → *kaññā*, *manyate* → *maññati*.
• [*n* + *u*] → *nv* or *nn*, *anu* + *eti* → *anveti*, *sam-anu-ā-gata* → *samannāgata*.
• [*m* + *y*] → *mm* or *ṃy or ññ*, *āgamya* → *āgamma*, *saṃyojana* → *saṃyojana* or *saññojana*.
• [*m* + *r* or *s* or *h*] → *ṃr* or *m* dropped and preceding vowel lengthened, √*sam-ruh* → *saṃruhati* or → *sāruhati*, *saṃrāga* → *sārāga*, *viṃṣati* → *vīsati*.
• [*m* + *l*] → *ll*, *sam* + *lāpa* → *sallāpa*.

(iv) semivowel first

(a) semivowel ◆ + nasal ◆◆
• [*r* + *m*] → *mm*, *karma* → *kamma*, *dharma* → *dhamma*.
• *dur* + *n* does not cause cerebralization, *dur* + *niggaha* → *dunniggaha*.

(b) semivowel ◆ + semivowel ◆
• [*r* + *y*] either remains with *svarabhakti* vowel, *vīrya* → *viriya*, or → *yy*, √*mṛ* → *miyyati (= mīyati)*, or → *ll*, *viparyāsa* → *vipallāsa* [n.b. *ārya* → *ariya* or *ayya*].
• [*r* + *r*] → r with preceding vowel lengthened, *dur+rakkha* → *dūrakkha*.
• [*r* + *l*] → *ll*, *durlabha* → *dullabha*.
• [*r* + *v*] → *vv* → *bb*, *kurvanti* → *kubbanti*.
• [*l* + *y*] → *ly* or *ll*, *kalyāṇa* → *kalyāṇa*, *kalya* → *kalla*.
• [*v* + *y*] → *vy* / *by* at the start of words, *vyañjana* / *byañjana*; but elsewhere → *bb*, *udayavyaya* → *udayabbaya*.
• [*v* + *r*] → *vv* → *bb*, *pravrajyā* → *pabbajjā*.

d) Here are two examples of important words in Sanskrit Buddhism misunderstood through not knowing these Sanskrit ↔ Pali correspondences:

(i) *bodhisattva*. This word has traditionally been analysed as *bodhi* + *sattva*, enlightenment-being, which makes no grammatical sense. What seems to have happened is that the Pali (or related MIA) word *satta* has been re-

Sanskritized as *sattva*. This is a possible correspondence, but *satta* in Pali can be equivalent to two other words in Sanskrit, both of which make better sense than *sattva*. From √*sañj*, to adhere to, be intent on, the past passive participle is *sakta*, which → *satta* in Pali. From √*śak*, to be able to, be capable of, the past passive participle is *śakta*, which also → *satta* in Pali. Intent on enlightenment or capable of enlightenment are both more à propos than enlightenment-being, so it is likely one of these two senses of *bodhisatta* was the original.

(ii) In the compound *saṃvṛti-satya*, conventional truth, *samvṛti* was derived by some Buddhists in India, and by some modern scholars, from √*saṃ-vṛ*, (cl.5) to cover, whereas the correct derivation is from √*sam-man* (cl. 4), to think together, agree on. The term must originally have been Pali, or a similar form of MIA: from √*sam-man* is derived the noun *sammati* or *sammuti*, agreement. (The *u* in *sammuti* is an example of what is called the labialization of vowels). The latter was Sanskritized as *saṃvṛti*, which would be possible from Pali √*sam-var*, cover, instead of the correct *sammati*.

1.3 *vyaya* (Change), Inflection

- *vācogadhapada*, Words Contained in Language, are of four kinds:

nāma	noun, adjective, pronoun, numeral
ākhyāta	verb
upasagga	preposition, verbal prefix
nipāta	particle, conjunction, adverb

nāma and *ākhyāta* are subject to inflection, i.e. they end in a variable suffix (*vibhatti*, *vibhatyanta*), but *upasagga* and *nipāta* are not, being *avyaya* and *avibhatyanta*. The most fundamental level of linguistic analysis is the verbal root, *dhātu*. Verbs, and thence almost all nouns, are derived from roots, with the exception of Denominative verbs, which are derived from nouns. In the declension of nouns, adjectives and pronouns the basic unit of analysis is the stem (*pātipadika*, *liṅga*, *sadda*) to which endings are added. Neither roots nor stems are actual words, and cannot appear in themselves in sentences, but the stem form is used in English when citing Pali words and Proper Names.

- English nouns and pronouns have three cases (i) subject, (ii) object [which has three forms, direct object, indirect object, object of a preposition], and (iii) possessive. Western scholarly tradition has seen eight cases in Pali, and given them names taken from Latin tradition. Pali grammar recognizes eight "divisions," *vibhatti*, which correspond to the eight cases, but only six "factors of action," *kāraka*. The cases can be seen analytically, though not historically, as an expansion of the three cases of English:

ENGLISH CASE	PALI CASE	PREPOSITIONS COMMONLY USED IN TRANSLATION	OED DESCRIPTION: 'THE CASE...'
SUBJECT	nominative		of nouns, adjectives, and pronouns, which is, or is connected with, the subject of a verb
DIRECT OBJECT	accusative	[to]	expressing destination or goal of motion; the case which follows prepositions implying motion towards; the object of transitive verbs, i.e. the destination of the verbal action
OBJECT OF A PREPOSITION	instrumental	by, with, through	denoting that with or by which something is done
OBJECT OF A PREPOSITION	dative	to, for	which denotes the indirect or remote object of the action of a verb, that to or for whom or which we do a thing, or to whom we give a thing
OBJECT OF A PREPOSITION	ablative	from	expressing direction from a place or time; the source whence action proceeds; the cause or ideal source of an event, the instrument and agent or material sources of an action
POSSESSIVE	genitive	apostrophe and /or -s, of	chiefly used to denote that the person or thing signified is related to another as source, possessor, or the like, but also employed in a variety of idiomatic usages
OBJECT OF A PREPOSITION	locative	at, in	which denotes 'place where'
SUBJECT	vocative		of nouns, adjectives, or pronouns, used to express address or invocation

The prepositions here are those standardly used, but they should only be taken as a guide to meaning. The following sentence uses all the cases:

Sir, that man gave his girlfriend a necklace, obtained through a friend at the market the previous Sunday from a suspicious character.

Sir (VOCATIVE), that man [subject, NOMINATIVE] gave to his [possessive, GENITIVE] girlfriend [indirect object, DATIVE] a necklace [direct object, ACCUSATIVE], obtained through a friend [means, INSTRUMENTAL] at the market [place, LOCATIVE] the previous Sunday [time, LOCATIVE] from a suspicious character (source, ABLATIVE).

The term oblique is used to refer to cases other than the nominative and vocative, and sometimes also accusative. The latter usage is followed here.

English verbs are understood in terms of tense and mood, with aspect as an additional interpretative category. Pali terminology for verbs was taken from Sanskrit, Pāṇinian grammar, and ordered its categories as follows, assigning each a syllable beginning with *l*-. (The Vedic subjunctive is omitted here.)

syllable		Sanskrit name	Pali name	meaning	English term
1	*laṭ*	*vartamānā*	*vattamānā*	occurring	present
2	*liṭ*	*parokṣā*	*parokkhā*	past before today, action out of sight	perfect
3	*luṭ*	*śvastanī*	*[svatanī]*	future beyond today	periphrastic future
4	*lṛṭ*	*bhaviṣyantī*	*bhavissanti*	general and immediate future	future
5	*loṭ*	*pañcamī*		fifth	imperative
6	*laṅ*	*anadyatanī*	*hiyyatanī, anajjatanī*	past before today, can have been seen by speaker	imperfect
7	*liṅ*	*saptamī*	*sattamī*	seventh	optative
8	*luṅ*	*adyatanī*	*ajjatanī*	past earlier today	aorist
9	*lṛṅ*	*kālātipatti*		non-realization of an action	*conditional*

Pali has 1 present, 4 future, 5 imperative, 7 optative, 8 aorist, 9 conditional.

Some characteristics of conjugated verbal forms in Pali:

TERM	TRANSLATION	COMMENTS
dhātu	root	can denote an activity (*kiriyā*) or a condition (*bhāva*)
paccaya, vibhatti	ending	used to refer to both verbal and nominal endings
(no)vikaraṇa(-paccaya)	suffix, infix	can be placed after or in the root before an ending
akārāgama	augment	applies to some aorists and the conditional
abbhāsa	reduplication	applies to verbs such as √*dā* → *dadāti*, √*hā* → *jahāti*, and derivative forms such as Desideratives and Intensives

They can have:

tikāla: atīta, anāgata, paccuppanna	three times: past, future, present	conjugated, finite forms express tense, whereas declined participial forms express aspect
anutta-, aniyatakāla	time unexpressed, not restricted to a specific time	applies to fifth (imperative) and seventh (optative)
tipurisa	three persons	first = he/she/it/they, second = you, third = I/we
tikāraka: kattā, kamma, bhāva	three factors of action: agent/ subject, object, state	this is not the same as kāraka applied to nouns
dvivacana: ekavacana, bahuvacana	two numbers: singular, plural	i.e. no dual
attiliṅga	none of the three genders	participles do have gender, because they behave, and decline, as adjectives

In giving paradigms, Pali grammar uses different terms from Western grammar, and a different order:

ekavacana	word for one	singular
bahuvacana	word for many	plural

paṭhama	first = he/she/it, they	first person
majjhima	middle = you	second person
uttama	last = I/we	third person

Paradigms have been learned traditionally in the order: *ekavacana paṭhama*, *bahuvacana paṭhama*, *ekavacana majjhima*, etc. Thus Aggavaṃsa lists the twelve endings of the present tense:

ti anti si tha mi ma; te ante se vhe e mhe

In this book, however, paradigms are given in the usual Western order: first person = I/we, second person = you, third person = he/she/it, they.

2 *nāma*

Nouns, Adjectives, Pronouns and Pronominal Adjectives, Numerals

2.1 *nāmanāma, guṇanāma,* Nouns substantive, Nouns adjective

Pali grammarians distinguished between nouns and adjectives in two ways:
(i) by the fact that adjectives must take the gender of the nouns they qualify
(ii) by the difference between a quality or attribute and that which has the quality or attribute.

A noun is	An adjective is
guṇi-pada, a word for that which has qualities	*guṇa-pada,* word for a quality
abhidheyya-liṅga, whose gender is that which it signifies	*vācca-liṅga,* whose gender is that of the word which it qualifies
padhāna-linga, whose gender is superordinate	*appadhāna-liṅga,* whose gender is subordinate

As single words, nouns have one gender and adjectives three, but as the final member in compounds where they act as adjectives nouns can also have three. Nouns in Pali can be used adjectivally in three ways:
(i) as the final member of a bahuvrīhi compound: *putta*, son, *itthī mataputtā*, a woman whose son is dead.
(ii) in a karmadhāraya compound expressing a comparison. Although the noun as final element remains nominal in formal terms, it acts as an adjective, as in the common epithet for kings and other heroes *narasīha*, a man-lion, i.e. a lion-like man.

(iii) with the addition of a suffix such as -*(a)ka* / -*ika* or -*ya* / - *īya*: *cetas*, mind, *cetasika*, mental; *thāma*, strength, *thāmaka*, strong; *dhamma*, the Truth, *dhammiya*, in accordance with the Truth; also with the suffixes -*in*, -*vat*, *bala*, strength, *balin*, *balavat*, strong

2.1.1. *vibhatti*, Cases

In declined words the nominative and vocative cases add no meaning to the theme apart from gender and number. The other cases add meanings and connect the word to others in a sentence (*vākya*). The cases are:

vibhatti	PALI NAMES	USES IN PALI
paṭhamā nominative	*kattā*, agent of active verbs *kamma*, object of passive verbs *paccatta*, individual, separate	agent of transitive and intransitive verbs; makes the stem form accord with the agent denoted by the verbal ending, and gives it gender
dutiyā accusative	*kamma*, object of action *upayoga*, application of action	direct object of transitive verbs; secondary object in double accusatives with verbs of speaking, etc.
tatiyā instrumental	*karaṇa*, means, instrument *kattā*, agent of passive verbs	agent of passive verbs; instrument of action; cause or reason (*hetu*) of action; accompaniment of action
catutthī dative	*sampadāna*, giving over (to)	destination of action, indirect object, purpose, suitable object, secondary object of verbs of speaking, etc.
pañcamī ablative	*apādāna*, origin, that from which something is removed *avadhi*, origin *nissakka*, issuing from	that from which action occurs, physically and conceptually; expresses cause, criterion, point of view; object of comparison
chaṭṭhi genitive	*sambandha*, relation *sāmi*, possessor	expresses possessive or partitive relation between two nouns; not related to the verb; used in place of instrumental, dative and ablative

sattamī locative	*adhikaraṇa*, location *okāsa*, place *ādhāra*, basis *bhumma*, ground	point, literal or figurative, at which or when action occurs; end result of motion; used like partitive genitive
aṭṭhamī vocative	*āmantaṇa*, address *sambodhana*, calling *ālapana*, address	regarded as a form or use of the nominative

A. The Nominative is used for;

1. The grammatical subject of sentences or clauses, active or passive:

Bhagavā... dhammaṃ deseti,
the Blessed One teaches the dhamma (D I 62),
Bhagavatā dhammo desīyati,
the dhamma is taught by the Blessed One (D III 264).

2. Any word which qualifies the subject, such as an adjective, predicate, or a term placed in apposition:

sambādho gharāvāso rajāpatho, abbhokāso pabbajjā,
the household life is constricted, full of dust, going forth is the open air (M III 33),
ahaṃ tena samayena rājā Mahāsudassano ahosiṃ,
I was at that time king Mahasudassana (D II 196),
seyyathāpi nāma... ayaṃ Aciravatī nādi pūrā udakassa samatitthikā kākapeyyā,
it is just as if this river Aciravati were full of water, level with the banks, drinkable by crows
(*Aciravatī* might also be in a *ti* clause or followed by the adverb *nāma*, by name) (D I 244).

3. Items referred to in a *ti* clause:

so... evam āha, yaṃ kho idaṃ vuccati cakkhun ti pi sotan ti pi ghānan ti pi jivhā ti pi kāyo ti pi ayaṃ attā anicco... yaṃ kho idaṃ vuccati cittan ti vā mano ti vā viññāṇan ti pi vā ayaṃ vuccati attā nicco...
he says "that which is called 'eye,' 'ear,' 'nose,' 'tongue,' 'body,' this an impermanent self... that which is called 'thinking,' 'mind,' 'consciousness,' this is a permanent self..." (D I 21).

4. The titles of texts: *Dīghanikāyo*, *Sīlakkhandhavaggo*, *Brahmajālo Sutto*.

5. Occasionally, the nominative of an abstract noun is used in an exclamation:

aho acchariyaṃ aho abbhutaṃ aho Buddhānaṃ ānubhāvatā,
O the wonder, O the marvel, O the power of Buddhas! (Ja VI 480).

6. Sometimes a nominative or series of them can introduce another phrase without a usual grammatical connection (the 'Hanging nominative,' *nominativus pendens*):

candanaṃ tagaraṃ vāpi uppalaṃ atha vassikī / etesaṃ gandhajātānaṃ sīlagandho anuttaro,
sandalwood or incense, lotus or jasmine / among these kinds or perfume the perfume of virtue is supreme (Dhp 55).

B. The accusative is used for;

1. The external direct object, including the goal of motion ('external' means external to the action of the verb):

atha kho āyasmā Aṅgulimālo... pattacīvaraṃ ādāya Sāvatthiṃ piṇḍāya pāvisi,
then the Venerable Angulimala took his robe and bowl and entered Savatthi for alms (M II 102)

addasā kho āyasmā Aṅgulimālo... aññataraṃ itthiṃ mūḷhagabbhaṃ,
the Venerable Angulimala saw a woman in difficult labor (ibid.).

2. The internal direct object, including the cognate accusative (so-called because the verb and noun are related):

atha kho bhagavā Gāyasīse... yena Rājagahaṃ tena cārikaṃ pakkāmi mahatā bhikkhusaṅghena saddhiṃ,
then the Blessed One... set out on tour towards Rajagaha, with a large company of monks (Vin I 35).

sattāhajāte bhagavati bhagavato mātā kālaṃ akāsi,
seven days after the Blessed One's birth his mother died (Ud 48).
atha kho Bhagavā... imaṃ udānaṃ udānesi,
then the Blessed One gave voice to this Spirited Utterance (D II 107).

3. With the abstract endings *-ttaṃ* (Sanskrit *-tvam*) and *-tā* as the object of verbs of motion or acquisition to express a change of state

atha kho Jīvako... na cirass' eva viññutaṃ pāpuṇi,
and not long afterwards Jivaka attained maturity (Vin I 269).

4. Double accusatives are common, in a variety of functions

upāsakaṃ maṃ bhavaṃ Gotamo dhāretu,
may the honorable Gotama accept me as a lay disciple (Sn p.25, appositional accusative),
taṃ ahaṃ brūmi brāhmaṇaṃ,
him I call a brahmin (Sn 620, predicative accusative),
te bhikkhū Bhagavantaṃ etad avocuṃ,
those monks said this to the Blessed One (D I 2),
Sakko devānaṃ indo Bhagavantaṃ imaṃ paṭhamaṃ pañhaṃ pucchi,
Sakka, king of the gods, asked the Blessed one this initial question (D II 276).

5. Causatives made from intransitive verbs always take a double accusative

idha bhikkhave bhikkhu... uppannaṃ kāmavitakkaṃ nādhivāseti pajahati... anabhāvaṃ gameti,
here, monks, a monk does not assent to a thought of desire which has arisen, (but) rejects it, makes it non-existent (M I 11).

Other causatives may also take a double accusative
Mahāpajāpatī Gotamī... Bhagavantaṃ janettiyā kālakatāya thaññaṃ pāyesi,
Mahapajapati Gotami made the Blessed One drink at her breast when (his) mother died (M III 253).

Causatives from transitive verbs may also, if rarely, take the accusative (of the object) and instrumental (of the agent)

atha kho chabbaggiyā bhikkhū... tantavāyehi cīvaraṃ vāyapesuṃ,
then the Group of Six Monks... had cloth woven by weavers (Vin III 256)
ekacco passati coraṃ āgucāriṃ rājāno gahetvā... sunakhehi khādāpente,
someone sees kings capture a bandit, a criminal... (and) having him eaten by dogs (A I 47–8).

Aggavaṃsa gives as examples of the two constructions, inter alia
puriso purisaṃ purisena vā pūvaṃ khādeti,
a man has a man eat a cake, or a man has a cake eaten by a man (Sadd 593).

6. It is used with interjections
dhi-r-atthu idha jīvitaṃ,
a curse on life here! (Sn 440).

7. It has various adverbial uses
Time during which
te tattha... ciraṃ dīghaṃ addhānaṃ titthanti,
they stay there long, for a protracted stretch of time (D III 84),
yo kho... aññatitthiyapubbo imasmiṃ dhammavinaye pabbajjaṃ ākaṅkhati so cattāro māse parivasati,
any former member of another sect who wants to go forth in this Dhamma and Discipline must wait for three months (D I 176).

Extent of space
ayaṃ Kusinārā Kusavatī nāma rājadhānī ahosi, puratthimena ca pacchimena ca dvādasa yojanāni āyāmena, uttarena ca dakkhiṇena ca satta yojanāni vitthārena,
this Kusinara was (in the past) a royal city called Kusavati, twelve yojanas long on the eatern and western sides, seven yojanas wide and the north and south (D II 146).

Manner
sādhukaṃ manasikarohi,
pay careful attention (D I 124),
mā kho tvam... atibāḷhaṃ paridevesi,
do not grieve too much (D II 232).

Other examples of the adverbial accusative:

cattāro naṃ devaputtā catuddisaṃ rakkhāya upagacchanti,

four junior gods came to protect him on (all) four sides, lit. with regard to the four directions (D II 12),

dīghaṃ vā assasanto dīgham assasāmī ti pajānāti,

when he is breathing a long in-breath he knows that he is breathing a long in-breath (D II 291),

atha kho Bhagavā Rājagahe yathābhirantaṃ viharitvā āyasmantaṃ Ānandaṃ āmantesi...,

when the Blessed One had stayed at Rajagaha for as long as he wished, he addressed the Venerable Ananda... (D II 81).

8. It is the object of various prepositions and postpositions: *antarā*, between, *pacchā*, after, *yathā*, according to, *vinā*, without, *santike*, in the presence of, and the following, which also occur as prefixes to verbs: *anu*, after, *abhi*, towards, *paṭi*, back to, facing.

C. The Instrumental is used for:

1. The logical subject of passive verbs

svākkhāto Bhagavatā dhammo,

the Dhamma has been well-proclaimed by the Blessed One (D II 9),

sakkā pana etaṃ mayā ñātuṃ,

I can know this (lit. this can be known by me) (D I 187).

2. Cause, or reason

siyā kho pana bhikkhave Satthugāravena pi na puccheyyātha,

it may be monks, that you do not ask questions because of reverence for your Teacher (D II 155),

na akaraṇena Tathāgatā sitaṃ pātukaronti,

Tathagatas do not smile without a reason (M II 45).

3. Accompaniment

atha kho Bhagavā ayasmatā Aṅgulimālena pacchāsamaṇena yena Sāvatthi tena cārikaṃ pakkāmi,

then the Blessed One set out for Savatthi with the Venerable Angulimala as attendant (ascetic) (M II 100).

The words *saha* and *saddhiṃ*, with, are often used as pre- or postpositions in such contexts: *mahatā bhikkhusaṅghena saddhiṃ*, *with a large group of monks*.

4. Means

seyyathāpi Rāhula rañño nāgo... saṅgāmagato purimehi pādehi kammaṃ karoti, pacchimehi pādehi kammaṃ karoti, ... purimena kāyena... pacchimena kāyena... sīsena... kaṇṇehi... dantehi... naṅguṭṭhena... soṇḍāya pi kammaṃ karoti,

It is just as when, Rahula, a royal elephant in battle does his work with front and back legs, with the front and back of his body, with his head, ears, tusks, tail and trunk (M I 414-5),

yattha kho āvuso na jāyati na jīyati na mīyati na cavati na uppajjati, nāhaṃ taṃ gamanena lokassa antaṃ... patteyyan ti vadāmi,

I do not say that one can reach by walking [the commentary Spk II 116 has *padagamanena*] the end of the world where there is no being born, no growing old, no dying, no falling (from one state) and being reborn (in another) (S I 61).

5. Manner

ākāse pallaṅkena kamati,

he travels cross-legged through the sky (D I 78),

rakkhiteneva kāyena rakkhitāya vācāya rakkhitena cittena upaṭṭhitāya satiyā saṃvutehi indriyehi gāmaṃ vā nigamaṃ vā pavisissatī,

he will enter a village or town with body protected, speech protected, mind protected, with mindfulness established and senses controlled (S II 271).

6. Attendant circumstances

kāya nu 'ttha bhikkhave etarahi kathāya sannisinnā,

(engaged in) what kind of talk were you sitting just now? (D II 1)

Abhibhū bhikkhu... dissamānena kāyena dhammaṃ desesi, adissamānena pi... dissamānena heṭṭhimena upaḍḍhakāyena adissamānena uparimena upaḍḍhakāyena... dissamānena uparimena upaḍḍhakāyena adissamānena heṭṭhimena upaḍḍhakāyena dhammaṃ desesi,

then the monk Abhibhu taught the Dhamma with his body visible, (then) with his body invisible, (then) with the lower half of his body visible and the upper half invisible, (and then) with the upper half of his body visible and the lower half invisible S I 156),

Kosinārakā Mallā santhāgāre sannipatitā honti kenacid eva karaṇīyena,
the Mallans of Kusinara were gathered in the meeting-hall on some business (D II 147).

7. In *yena... tena* constructions
atha kho Bhagavā... yena Magadhamahāmattānaṃ āvasatho ten' upasaṃkamati,
the Blessed One approached the dwelling-place of the great ministers of Magadha (D II 88).

With the verb √*ava-śṛ*, the accusative *tad* is found:
atha kho Bhagavā mahatā bhikkhusaṃghena saddhiṃ yena Beluvagāmako tad avasari,
then the Blessed One went with a large group of monks to the village of Beluva (D II 98).

8. Place
dakkhiṇena passena sīhaseyyaṃ kappesi,
he lies down like a lion on his right side (A I 114),
aññen' eva tāni caturāsīti-pabbajjita-sahassāni agamaṃsu, aññena Vipassī bodhisatto,
the 84,000 ascetics went one way, Vipassi the future Buddha another (D II 30).

9. Time
tena kho pana samayena,
at that time (this is a standard means of starting a text or a section of a text),
atha kho āyasmā Ānando etena upāyena paṭhamen' eva yāmena Kosinārake Malle Bhagavantaṃ vandāpesi,
and then, by this means, the Venerable Ananda got (all) the Mallans from Kusinara to pay their respects to the Blessed One in just the first watch (of the night) (D II 148),
kālena dhammasavanaṃ,
hearing the Dhamma at the right time (Sn 265).

10. Phrases with a cognate or semantically related verb and noun
atha kho bhagavā Bāhiyaṃ... iminā saṃkhittena ovādena ovaditvā pakkāmi,
then the Blessed One exhorted Bâhiya briefly (lit.: with this short exhortation) and left (Ud 8),
santena nūn' ajja bhante Bhagavā vihārena vihāsi,
has the Blessed One, sir, passed the time peacefully today? (D II 205)
seyyathā pi... puriso...rukkhaṃ mūle chindeyya... agginā ḍaheyya,
it is just as if a man might uproot a tree and burn it with fire (S II 88).

11. Comparison

na tena seyyo sadiso vā vijjati,

there is no-one better than or the same as he (D III 158).

12. Other adverbial uses

adhivāsesi Bhagavā tuṇhībhāvena,

the Blessed One accepted (the invitation) by remaining silent (D II 84),

addasā kho Selo brāhmaṇo Bhagavato kāye dvattiṃsa mahapurisalakkhaṇāni yebhuyyena ṭhapetvā dve,

the brahmin Sela saw almost all the 32 marks of a Great Man on the Blessed One's body, except for two (Sn p. 107),

ehi tvaṃ brāhmaṇa yena Bhagavā ten' upasaṃkama,... mama vacanena Bhagavato pāde sirasā vandāhi,

go, brahmin, approach the Blessed One and in my name venerate his feet with your head (D II 72),

Vipassī mārisa bhagavā... khattiyo jātiyā ahosi,

sir, the Blessed One Vipassi was a khattiya by birth (D II 50),

dehi je Ambapāli etaṃ bhattaṃ satasahassenā ti,

Ambapali you wretch, give (us the right to offer the Buddha) this meal for a hundred thousand! (D II 96),

idha bhikkhave ekacco puggalo āgāḷhena pi vuccamāno pharusena pi... amanāpena pi... sammodati,

here, monks, a certain person is spoken to severely, harshly, unpleasantly,...(but) rejoices (A I 283-4),

yadā tumhe Kālāmā attanā va jāneyyātha...,

when you know for yourselves, Kalamans... (A I 189).

13. *kiṃ* is used with the instrumental in the senses what is the use of?, away with!, no more of!, and *alaṃ* in that of enough of!, there is no need of!

tena hi, amma, rañño appiyakālato paṭṭhāya kiṃ tumhākaṃ idha vāsena,

so, lady, what is the use of your living here since the king became unkind? (Ja II 205),

tena hi samma sārathi alaṃ dān' ajja uyyānabhūmiyā,

so then good charioteer, that's enough of the pleasure-park for today! (D II 23),

alaṃ Devadatta, mā te rucci saṅghabhedo,

stop, Devadatta! Don't set your mind on a division in the Order! (Vin II 198).

D. The Dative is different in form from the genitive only in the *-a* declension in the singular. In other declensions, therefore, it is often difficult and rarely necessary to decide whether the case is dative or genitive. The examples given here all use the singular of the *-a* declension. It is used for

1. Purpose, result

   bhikkhu paṭisaṅkhā yoniso piṇḍapātaṃ paṭisevati, n' eva davāya na madāya na maṇḍanāya na vibhūsanāya, yāvad eva imassa kāyassa ṭhitiyā yāpanāya,
   the monk (who) seeks alms reflectively (does so) not for sport, nor intoxication (with himself), nor for making (himself) attractive, nor for beautification, but just as much as is necessary for his body to persist, (for him) to keep (it) going (M I 355),
   āciṇṇaṃ kho pan' etaṃ vassaṃ vutthānaṃ bhikkhūnaṃ Bhagavantaṃ dassanāya upasaṃkamituṃ,
   it is the custom for monks who have finished the rains retreat to go to see the Blessed One (Vin I 18),
   siyā kālaññu c' assa garunaṃ dassanāya,
   he should know the right time for seeing teachers (Sn 325),
   n' etaṃ bhikkhave appasannānaṃ vā pasādāya pasannānaṃ vā bhiyyobhāvāya, atha kho taṃ bhikkave appasannanaṃ c' eva appasādāya pasannānaṃ ca ekaccānaṃ aññathattāyā ti,
   'this, monks, (will) not (conduce) to giving confidence to those without confidence, nor to increasing the confidence of those who have it, but to (continued) lack of confidence in those who have none, and to causing some of those who have confidence to become otherwise' (Vin I 45).

2. The dative of *attha* has the sense for the sake of

   yass' atthāya kulaputtā sammad eva agārasmā anagariyaṃ pabbajjenti, tad anuttaraṃ brahmacariyapariyosānaṃ... upasampajja viharissathā ti,
   'you will enter and live in that unsurpassed goal of the celibate life for the sake of which children from good families go forth from home to homelessness' (Vin I 9).

3. Direction

   bhikkhu... manomayaṃ kāyaṃ abhinimmināya cittaṃ abhinīharati abhininnāmeti,
   the monk bends, inclines his mind to the creation of a mind-made body (D I 77),
   sakuṇo jālamutto va appo saggāya gacchati,
   few go to heaven, like a bird released from a net (Dhp 174).

4. Time

adhivāsetu no bhavaṃ Gotamo ajjatanāya bhattaṃ saddhiṃ bhikkhusaṅghena,
may the Blessed One accept a meal from us today, along with the order of monks (D II 88),
aho nūna mahāsamaṇo svātanāya nāgaccheyya,
the great ascetic would certainly not come tomorrow (Vin I 27),
dukkham upenti punapunnaṃ cirāya,
they go to suffering again and again, for a long time (Dhp 342),
karoto cīyati pāpaṃ cirattāya Antaka,
Endmaker (Mara), for (you) who does it evil is heaped up for a long time (M I 338).

5. Some adjectives and indeclinables are used with the dative

appamādarato bhikkhu pamāde bhayadassivā / abhabbo parihānāya nibbānass' eva santike,
the monk who is devoted to carefulness, and sees the danger in carelessness, is incapable of falling away and is near to nirvana (Dhp 32),
evaṃ sante āyasmantānaṃ Nigaṇṭhānaṃ na kallaṃ assa veyyākaraṇāya...,
that being so, it would not be fitting for the Venerable Niganthas to explain... (M II 215),
alaṃ hi te Vaccha aññaṇāya alam sammohāya,
it is enough to cause you bewilderment, Vaccha, enough to confuse you (M I 487),
n' esā bhante kathā Bhagavato dullabhā bhavissati pacchā pi savanāya,
it will not be difficult for the Blessed One to hear this talk afterwards (D I 179).

E. The Ablative, whose endings in the singular can be replaced in some declensions by the suffix *-to*, is used:

1. The point from which, cause, origin, motive, etc.

seyyathā pi mahārāja puriso sakamhā gāmā aññaṃ gāmaṃ gaccheyya, tamhā pi gāmā aññaṃ gāmaṃ gaccheyya, tamhā pi gāmā sakam yeva gāmaṃ pacchāgaccheyya,
it is just as if, great king, a person were to go from his own village to another village, (then) from that village to another village, (then) from that village back to his own village (D I 81).
idha amhākaṃ yo paṭhamaṃ gāmato piṇḍāya paṭikkameyya, so āsanaṃ paññāpeyya...,

whichever of us should return first from the village (after going) for alms, should prepare seats,... (Vin I 157),

āsanne ito Manasākataṃ na-y-ito dūre Manasākataṃ,

Manasakata is near here, not far from here (D I 248),

taṇhāya jāyati soko taṇhāya jāyati bhayaṃ / taṇhāya vippamuttassa n' atthi soko kuto bhayaṃ,

from craving arises grief, from craving arises fear. For the one who is liberated from craving there is no grief, from where (could there arise) fear? (Dhp 216),

so tassa kammassa katattā upacitattā ussannattā vipulattā kāyassa bhedā paraṃ maraṇā sugatiṃ saggaṃ lokaṃ uppajjati,

he, because of doing that karma, accumulating it, because it is plentiful and abundant, after the break-up of the body, after death, is born into a happy destiny, a heavenly world (D III 146),

yā tā honti āpadā aggito vā udakato vā rājato vā corato vā appiyato vā dāyādato vā...,

whatever calmities there are, because of fire, water, kings, bandits, enemies or heirs... (A II 68),

seyyathā pi Citta gavā khīraṃ, khīramhā dadhi, dadhimhā navanītaṃ, navanītamhā sappi, sappimhā sappimaṇḍo,

just as when, Citta, there is milk from a cow, curds from the milk, butter from the curds, ghee from the butter and cream of ghee from the ghee (D I 201),

kodhano Sāriputta Sunakkhatto moghapuriso, kodhā ca pan' assa esā vācā bhāsitā,

Sariputta, this foolish man Sunakkhatta is angry, and what he says is said out of anger (M I 68).

2. In other senses

atth' āvuso dakkhiṇā dāyakato visujjhati no paṭiggāhakato,

there is, friend the (kind of) gift which is purified on the part of the giver but not of the receiver (D III 231),

bhūte bhūtato sañjānāti...deve devato sañjānāti,

he perceives beings as beings,... gods as gods (M I 2),

atha kho āyasmā Vaṅgīso Bhagavantaṃ sammukhā sāruppāhi gāthāhi,

then the Venerable Vangisa praised the Blessed One face to face with some suitable verses (Sn p.79).

3. For comparisons

atth' Ānanda etamhā sukhā aññaṃ sukhaṃ abhikkantataraṃ ca paṇītataraṃ ca,
Ananda, there exists a happiness more excellent and more lofty than this one (M I 398),
ato mahantatarena kho... āvijjakhandhena Jayaseno rājakumāro āvaṭo,
Prince Jayasena is covered with a mass of ignorance greater than this (M III 131).

4. In certain adverbial forms

tasmā or *tato*, therefore, *yasmā* or *yato*, because of which, (time) from which, *ettato*, because of this, *ettavatā* this much, *kittavatā* how much?, *pacchā*, behind, after, *samantato*, on every side, all around, *dakkhiṇato*, to the south, *ubhato*, in both ways, on both sides, *sabbato*, all around, in every respect, *purato*, in front of, *ādito*, from the beginning, initially.

5. Prepositions and nouns used prepositionally with the ablative include

Aḷāra naññatra manussalokā / suddhī ca saṃvijjati saññamo ca,
Alara, there is no purity or restraint apart from (in) the human world (Ja V 173),
idha bhikkhave imaṃ eva kāyaṃ uddhaṃ pādatalā adho kesamatthakā... paccavekkhati,
here, monks, a monks reviews this very body upwards from the soles of the feet and downwards from the tips of his hair... (S V 278),
iti ha tena khaṇena tena muhuttena yāva Brahmalokā saddo abbhugacchati,
and so in that moment, in that instant the sound went up as far as the Brahma world (Vin III 19),
Vipassissa bhikkhave bhagavato... pubbeva sambodhā anabhisambuddhassa bodhisattassa sato etad ahosi,
this thought, monks, came to the Blessed One Vipassi before his awakening, when he was a future Buddha, not a fully awakened Buddha (S II 5),
samaṇaṃ khalu bho Gotamaṃ tiro raṭṭhā tiro janapadā sampucchituṃ āgacchanti,
(people) come across the kingdom, across the countryside to question the ascetic Gotama (D I 116),
atho ārā pamādamhā,
is he far from negligence? (Sn 156).

F. The Genitive is a case whose relation to the rest of the sentence is for the most part adnominal rather than adverbal. That is to say, in the same way as is an adjective, it is connected to a noun rather than directly to the verb, as are the other cases except the vocative. The adjective phrase *rājā Māgadho*, the Magadhan king (D 72) is formally equivalent to *rājā Magadhānaṃ*, the king of the Magadhans (cp *Magadhānaṃ Giribbajaṃ*, (the town) Giribbaja [Rājagaha] of the Magadhans, Vin I 43). It is used in:

1. The possessive genitive
   tass' imāni satta ratanāni ahesuṃ,
   he had these seven jewels (D III 58),
   kim ahaṃ sīlasampannā satthu sāsanakārikā / nibbānaṃ nādhigacchāmi,
   why do I, who am virtuous and who follow the Teacher's instructions, not attain nirvana? (Thī 113),
   ajja kho pan' Ānanda rattiṃ pacchimayāme... Tathāgatassa parinibbānaṃ bhavissati,
   today, Ananda, in the last watch of the night the Tathagata's final nirvana will take place (D II 134).

2. The partitive genitive has the sense, like the partitive locative, 'from among'
   tesaṃ ñeva kho Vāseṭṭha sattānaṃ ekacce sattā araññāyatane paṇṇakuṭīsu taṃ jhānaṃ anabhisambhuṇamānā,
   some of these beings, Vasettha, being unable to maintain the life of meditation in forest leaf-huts (D III 94),
   Sambuddho dvipadaṃ seṭṭho,
   the Fully Awakened One is the best of the two-footed (S I 6)
   imesaṃ pana brāhmaṇa catunnaṃ aṅgānaṃ sakkā ekaṃ aṅgaṃ ṭhapayitvā tīhi aṅgehi samannāgataṃ brāhmaṇaṃ paññāpetuṃ,
   it is possible, brahmin, to leave one factor out from the four factors and declare that he who has the (other) three is a brahmin (D I 121).

3. The subjective genitive (i.e., the genitive would be the subject if the word qualifying it were converted to a verb)
   idaṃ pacchimakaṃ Ānanda tathāgatassa Vesālidassanaṃ bhavissati,
   this will be the Tathagata's last sight of Vesali (D II 122) (a verbal equivalent would be *tathāgato Vesāliṃ dakkhati*),

evaṃ etassa kevalassa dukkhakkhandassa samudayo hoti,
such is the arising of this whole mass of suffering (D I 33)
(a verbal equivalent would be *evaṃ eso kevalo dukkhakkhando samudayati*),

4. The objective genitive (i.e., the genitive would be the direct object if the word qualifying it were converted to a verb)
tapo ca brahmacariyā ca ariyasaccāna dassanaṃ,
asceticism, the life of celibacy, seeing the Truths of the Noble Ones, (Sn 267)
(a verbal equivalent would be *yo ariyasaccāni passati*)
catunnaṃ bhikkhave dhammānaṃ ananubodhā appaṭivedhā evaṃ idam addhānaṃ sandhāvitaṃ saṃsaritaṃ mamañc' eva tuṃkhākaṃ,
it is because of the failure to understand and to penetrate four things that this long road of samsara has been traveled, by me and by you (D II 122)
(the verbal equivalent would be *yasmā cattāro dhamme na anubujjhāma*)

5. Time
atha kho Bhaggava acelo Kandaramasuko na cirass' eva... kālaṃ akasi,
and not long afterwards, Bhaggava, the naked ascetic Kandaramasuko died (D III 11)
tena kho pana samayena Rājagahako seṭṭhi kālass' eva uyyānaṃ agamāsi,
at that time a merchant from Rajagaha went out early to the park (Vin II 146).

6. Other uses
sammādiṭṭhissa bho sammāsaṃkappo pahoti,
from Right View arises Right Intention (D II 217),
Kusāvatiyā Ānanda rājadhāniyā catunnaṃ vaṇṇānaṃ dvārāni ahesuṃ,
in the royal town of Kusavati, Ananda, there were doors of four colors (D II 170),
amataṃ tesaṃ bhikkhave aparibhuttaṃ yesaṃ kāyagatāsati aparibhuttā,
the deathless has not been enjoyed by those who have not enjoyed (the practice of) mindfulness of the body (A I 45),
idha bhikkhave asappuriso yo hoti parassa avaṇṇo taṃ puṭṭho pi pātukaroti. ko pana vādo puṭṭhassa?
here, monks a bad man is one who reveals what is unpraiseworthy in another even when he is not asked. What to say of him when he is asked? (A II 77),
kacci maṃ samma Jīvaka na paccatthikānaṃ desi?
good Jivaka, you are not giving me over to my enemies? (D I 50)
te rañño cakkavattissa anuyuttā ahesuṃ,
they became client(-king)s of the wheel-turning king (D III 62),

atha kho rañño Māgadhassa Ajātasattussa... ahud eva bhayaṃ ahu chambhitattaṃ ahu lomahaṃso,
then the Magadhan king Ajatasattu was afraid, stupefied, his hair stood on end (lit. there was fear, stupefaction, horripilation of him) (D I 4).

With adjectives

kusalo kho ahaṃ diṭṭhadhammikānaṃ atthānaṃ,
I am expert in matters of the here-and-now (D II 241),
sutavā ca kho bhikkhave ariyasāvako ariyānaṃ dassavī ariyadhammassa kovido...,
monks, a well-taught noble follower who looks to the Noble Ones and is skilled in the noble Dhamma... (M I 137),
sādhu no bhavaṃ Gotamo... bhāsatu, sace bhoto Gotamassa agarū ti,
'please may the honorable Gotama speak to us..., if it is not troubling to the honorable Gotama' (Sn p.50),
na kho etaṃ Phagguna paṭirūpaṃ kulaputtassa... pabbajitassa,
Phagguna this is not appropriate for a son of good family who has been ordained (M I 123),
rūpasaddagandharasaphoṭṭhabbāni yāni na pabbajitassa sāruppāni,
sights, sounds, smells, tastes and things to touch which are not suitable for one who is ordained (Vin IV 160).

With verbs

baddho kabalaṃ na bhuñjati / sumarati nāgavanassa kuñjaro,
the elephant when bound eats no food, but remembers the elephant-forest (Dhp 324),
na tvaṃ tāta Raṭṭhapāla kassaci dukkhassa jānāsi,
Ratthapala, dear, you have no knowledge of any suffering (M II 56),
devā pi tesaṃ pihayanti sambuddhānaṃ satīmataṃ,
even the gods envy those mindful, fully awakened ones (Dhp 181),
āyasmato Sāriputtassa sutvā bhikkhū dhāressanti,
if they hear the Venerable Sariputta the monks will remember (M I 14).

With adverbs and prepositions:

dakkhiṇena dvārena nikkhamitvā dakkhiṇato nagarassa... sīsaṃ assa chindiṃsu,
they went out of the south gate, and to the south of the city they cut off his head (D III 67),

Ānando... antarena yamakasalānaṃ uttarasīsakaṃ mañcakaṃ paññāpesi,
Ananda... prepared a bed for the Blessed One between the twin Sal trees, with its head to the north (D II 137),
seyyathā pi nāma pavaso tattassa nibbāyamānassa upari santānakaṃ hoti,
just as there is the spreading out of skin on top of boiled milk-rice as it cools down (D III 85),
bhagavato purato aṭṭhāsi,
he stood in front of the Blessed One (Vin I 3),
bhagavato avidūre atikkamanti,
they passed by not far from the Blessed One (Sn p.48).

G. The Locative is used for:

1. place (literal or non-literal) at which, in which, on which, into which, from which

ekaṃ samayaṃ Bhagavā Sāvatthiyaṃ viharati Pubbārāme Mīgara-mātu pāsāde,
at one time the Blessed One was living in the palace (built by) Migara's mother in the Eastern Park at Savatthi (D III 80),
yo kho Devadatta samaggaṃ saṃghaṃ bhindati... kappaṃ nirayamhi pacati,
Devadatta, whoever breaks up a united monastic group... cooks for an eon in hell (Vin II 198),
so anekavihitaṃ iddhividhaṃ paccanubhoti,... tirokuḍḍaṃ tiropākāraṃ tiropabbataṃ asajjamāno gacchati seyyathā pi ākāse, paṭhaviyā pi ummujjananimmujjanaṃ karoti seyyathā pi udake, udake pi abhijjamāne gacchati seyyathā pi paṃhaviyā, ākāse pi pallaṅkena kamati seyyathā pi pakkhī sakuṇo,
he realizes various forms of magical power: he goes unhindered through walls, ramparts and mountains as if he were in the sky, he dives into the earth and emerges from it as if into and out of water, he walks on water without its (surface being) being broken, as if on the earth, he travels cross-legged in the sky as if he were a bird with wings (M II 18),
atha kho Bhagavā... paññatte āsane nisīdi,
and then the Blessed One... sat down on the appointed seat (D I 109)
atha kho āyasmā Mahākassapo maggā okkamma aññatarasmin rukkhamūle nisīdi,
and then the Venerable Mahakassapa went down from the road and sat at the foot of a tree (D II 162),

sādhukaṃ manasi-karotha,
keep it in mind, pay attention (D I 124),
mettāvihārī yo bhikkhu / pasanno Buddhasāsane,
the monk who lives in loving-kindness, with serene confidence in the Buddha's Teaching (Dhp 368),
pañhan taṃ samaṇa pucchissāmi, sace me na vyākarissasi... pādesu gahetvā paragaṅgāya khipissāmi,
I will ask you a question, ascetic, and if you do not answer... I will grab you by the feet and throw you across the Ganges (Sn p.32),
vuttaṃ kho pan' etaṃ Bhagavatā, yaṃ kiñci vedayitaṃ taṃ dukkhasmin ti,
this has been said by the Blessed One: 'whatever is experienced is in (the category of) suffering' (S IV 216),
kim pan' Ānanda bhikkhusaṅgho mayi paccāsiṃsati?
what, then Ananda, does the order of monks expect from me? (D II 100),
atha kho Raṭṭhapālo kulaputto mātāpitūsu pabbajjaṃ alabhamāno,
then, Ratthapala, the son of good family, not obtaining from his mother and father (permission) to become a monk (M II 57),
yaṃ nūnāhaṃ samaṇesu Sakyaputtesu pabbajjeyan ti,
'what now if I were to ordain among (these) ascetics, sons of the Sakyans?' (Vin I 57).

2. comparison
anamatagge saṃsārato mahiṃ Jambudīpaṃ upanītaṃ / kolaṭṭhimattaṅguḷikā mātāmātūsu eva nappahonti,
(remember) the great earth (of) Jambudipa compared to that which is without beginning or end for one who is in samsara; little balls (of earth) the size of jujube kernels are not equal to the mothers (one has had) (Thī 498),
aññataro bhikkhu Bhagavantaṃ etad avoca, kīvadīghaṃ nu kho bhante Padume niraye āyuppamāṇan ti... (avoca Satthā)... te gaṇitā vidūhī tilavāhā / ye padume niraye upanītā / nahutāni hi koṭiyo pañca bhavanti / dvādasa koṭisatani pun' aññā,
a monk said to the Blessed One, 'How long is the length of life in the Paduma hell?'... (the Teacher said) wise men have counted the (number of) sesame seeds which (can be) compared to (life in) the Paduma hell; they are fifty million myriads and another 120 million (Sn pp. 125–6, verse 677).

3. 'with regard to,' 'in respect of,' 'in re':
ariyasāvako rūpasmiṃ nibbindati,

the noble follower becomes dissatisfied with body (M I 139),

kiñ ca bhikkhave bkikkhuno sukhasmiṃ?

monks, what (meaning) is there for a monk in happiness? (D III 78),

so bhāgineyyaṃ sayam anukampamāno / samādāpesī asamadhurassa dhamme,

feeling spontaneous compassion for his nephew he encouraged him in the Dhamma of the one who has no equal (Sn 695),

api nu so puriso evaṃkārī tasmiṃ kulle kiccakārī assā ti,

would that man in so doing be doing what should be done in relation to that raft? (M I 135).

4. Adverbial senses of space and time

sace hi mayaṃ bho Kaccāna suneyyāma tam Bhagavantaṃ dasasu yojanesu, dasa pi mayaṃ yojanāni gaccheyyāma tam Bhagavantaṃ dassanāya... vīsatiyā yojanesu... tiṃsatiyā yojanesu...,

if we heard, Kaccana sir, that the Blessed One was within ten leagues we would go ten leagues to see the Blessed One,... twenty leagues,... thirty leagues (M II 90)

yasmiṃ samaye (attā) upeti saññī tasmiṃ samaye hoti, yasmiṃ samaye apeti asaññī tasmiṃ samaye hoti,

at the time when (the self) comes, then (a person) is conscious, when it goes then he is unconscious (D II 180),

upāsake no bhagavā dhāretu ajjatagge pāṇupete saranaṃ gate,

may the Blessed One accept us as lay-followers, taken refuge (in him), from this day onwards for as long as we live (Vin I 4),

5. The partitive locative has the sense, like the partitive genitive, 'from among'

atthi nu kho me imesu pañcasu kāmaguṇesu aññatarasmiṃ va aññatarasmiṃ vā āyatane uppajjati cetaso samudācāro ti,

'Does any (improper) activity of mind arise for me in one or another area from among these five classes of sense-pleasure?' (M III 114),

tena kho pana samayena catasso bhāginiyo bhikkhunīsu pabbajitā honto Nandā Nandavatī Sundarīnandā Thullanandā ti tāsu Sundarīnandā taruṇapabbajitā abhirūpā hoti dassanīyā...,

at that time four sisters had been ordained among the nuns, Nanda, Nandavati, Sundarinanda, and Thullananda. Among them Sundarinanda had been ordained while young, and she was (the most) beautiful, good to look at... (Vin IV 211).

G. The Vocative case is used solely for addressing a listener:

ambho purisa kiṃ tuyh' iminā dujjīvitena... ti,

hey, man, what's the use of this wretched life to you? (Vin III 73).

etu kho bhante bhagavā, sāgataṃ bhante bhagavato,

Sir, may the Blessed One come, Sir, welcome to the Blessed One (D I 179).

Frequent vocatives are: *bhikkhave*, monks, *āvuso*, friend, *ayya (= ariya)*, noble one, *tāta*, dear, *ammā*, mother (used as a respectful address to any woman), etc.

Absolute constructions

An absolute construction, which usually contains a noun and a participle, both in the same case, is syntactically separate from the main clause. It functions as an adverbial phrase in relation to the main clause, typically though not only to indicate time, manner or circumstance. The word 'absolute' was not used in this way by classical Latin writers, and seems to have been a development of later grammar in Europe. In order of frequency, absolutes are in the locative, genitive, accusative, and, rarely if at all, instrumental and nominative cases.

1. Locative absolute

Pali grammarians cite the Pāṇinian rule (II 3, 37):

yassa bhāvena bhāvalakkhaṇaṃ bhavati, tasmiṃ sattamī vibhatti bhavati,

the seventh case-ending is (used) for that by the action of which there is the characterisation of a (different) action (or state) (Saddanīti 728, Moggallāna #37, Payogasiddhi 35), and cite Pāṇinian examples such as

gosu duyhamānesu gato duddhāsu āgato,

he went when the cows were being milked and came back when they had been milked.

Other examples cited in grammars are

atha kho Māro pāpimā acirapakkhante āyasmante Ānande yena Bhagavā ten' upasamakami,

Then the evil Mara, soon after the Venerable Ananda had left, approached the Blessed One (D II 104, cited Saddanīti 728),

maccu gacchati ādāya pekkhamāne mahājane,
death goes, taking (him, them) as the people look on (unknown, cited Saddanīti 725, Moggallāna #37, Payogasiddhi #35) [on this phrase see further under Genitive Absolutes]

Some more examples

atha kho sā nādikā... āyasmante upasaṃkamante acchā vippasannā anāvilā sandittha,
and while the Venerable Ananda was approaching (it) that stream became clear, pellucid, no (longer) muddy (D II 129),
sattāhapabbajite kho pana bhikkhave rājisimhi dibbaṃ cakkaratanaṃ antaradhāyi,
seven days, monks, after the royal sage had gone forth, the divine Wheel-jewel disappeared (D III 60),
adhanānaṃ dhane ananuppādiyamāne, daliddiyaṃ vepullaṃ agamāsi; daliddiye vepullagate, aññataro puriso paresaṃ adinnaṃ theyyasaṃkhātaṃ ādiyi.
When money was not given those without it, poverty increased; poverty having increased, a certain man took from others what they had not given, that is, (committed) theft (D III 65),

Phrases without a noun, such as *evaṃ sante*, this being so, *evaṃ vutte*, when this was said, are common.

2. Genitive absolute

Pali grammarians cite the Pāṇinian rule (II 3, 38) *chaṭṭhi cānādare*, the sixth also (can be used like the locative) when there is the sense of disregard (Saddanīti 725, Moggallāna #37, Payogasiddhi #35). It is often, though not always the case that the sense of a genitive absolute is despite. The most common example given is

ākoṭayanto te neti Sivirājassa pekkhato,
he took them (the children) away beating them although (their father) the king of the Sivis was looking on (Ja VI 548).

Grammarians give as a example of *anādara* the sentence cited above under the locative beginning with *maccu*. Aggavaṃsa (ibid.) gives as alternative examples *rudato dārakassa pabbaji* and *rudantasmiṃ dārake pabbaji*, he left although the child was crying.

Some more examples

so kho ahaṃ... akāmakānaṃ mātāpitunnaṃ assumukkhānaṃ rudantaṃ... agarasmā anagāriyaṃ pabbajiṃ,

and I... although my parents were unwilling and were crying with tears on their faces,... went forth from home to homelessness (D I 163).

tatra ca me brāhmaṇa viharato mago vā āgacchati moro vā kaṭṭhaṃ pateti vāto vā paṇṇasaṃaṃ ereti,

and as I lived there, brahmin, an animal came or a peacock caused a twig to fall, or the wind rustled a pile of leaves (M I 20–21),

tatra kho āyasmā Sāriputto acirapakkhantassa Bhagavato bhikkhū āmantesi,

then the Venerable Sariputta addressed the monks, not long after the Blessed One had left (M III 249).

3. Instrumental and Accusative absolutes

No premodern Pali grammarian classified any usages of the instrumental and accusative with locative and genitive as *bhāvalakkhaṇa* or *anādara*. Modern scholars have spoken of instrumental examples as semi-absolute, and of an accusative absolute.

Instrumental

so bhante kakkaṃako sabbehi aḷehi saṃchinnehi sambhaggehi sampalibhaggehi abhabbo taṃ pokkharaṇiṃ puna otarituṃ,

that crab, sir, with claws cut off, broken, smashed, is not able to return to the pond (S I 123),

so 'mhi etarahi rūḷhena vaṇena saṃchavinā arogo sukhī,

now that the wound has healed and is covered with skin I am well and happy (M II 217),

atha kho... āyasmā Vidhuro bhinnena sīsena lohitena gaḷantena Kakusandhaṃ yeva bhagavantaṃ... anubandhi,

then the Venerable Vidhura, his head split and blood running, followed the Blessed One Kakusandha (M I 336–7),

aññena bhesajjena karaṇīyena, aññaṃ bhesajjaṃ viññāpeti, āpatti pācittiyassa,

(if) although one medicine is necessary he asks for another, there is a fault of expiation (Vin IV 103)

These uses could also be seen as instrumentals of attendant circumstance.

Accusative

atha kho Ambapāligaṇikā Bhagavantaṃ bhuttaviṃ onītapattapāṇiṃ aññataraṃ nīcaṃ āsanaṃ gahetvā ekamantaṃ nisīdi,

then Ambapali the courtesan, when the Blessed One had washed his bowl and hands, sat down to one side on a low seat (D II 97–8),

nīte dārake adassanaṃ gamite na phali hadayaṃ satadhā vā sahassadhā vā,

when his children were led away and had gone out of sight, his heart did not break into a hundred or a thousand (pieces) (Mil 275),

kumariyo yā c' imā gottarakkhitā / jiṇṇā ca yā yā ca sabhattu-itthiyo / tā chandarāgaṃ purisesu uggataṃ / hiriyā nivārenti sacittam attano,

young women and those who are are (still) guarded by their family, women who are old and those who (still) have husbands, when desire has arisen in men (for them) out of modesty control their own hearts ((Ja V 410).

Phrases without a noun, such as *evaṃ santaṃ*, this being so, are also found.

These usages can be regarded as extensions of the adverbial and referential uses of the accusative. The following sentence has been cited as containing an accusative absolute:

jānāhi yadi vā taṃ bhavantaṃ Gotamaṃ tathā santaṃ yeva saddo abbhuggato yadi vā no tathā,

find out whether, the honorable Gotama being indeed so, the report has arisen [i.e. is correct] or whether (he is) not so D I 88, M II 134).

A version without the participle is cited by grammarians (Kaccāyana Be 157, Saddanīti 716) to illustrate *kammapavacanīya*, a class of prepositions or prefixes governing nouns in the accusative case, here *abhi*

taṃ kho pana bhavantaṃ gotamaṃ evaṃ kalyāṇo kittisaddo abbhuggato,

a report has arisen as follows about the Honorable Gotama (Vin III 1),

and it seems possible to analyze the previous phrase containing the participle *santaṃ* in the same way.

4. Nominative Absolute

It is sometimes claimed that there exists a nominative absolute in Pali, but the evidence is not clear-cut. English absolute phrases are sometimes said to be nominative:

the job finished, I went home

No-one seeming interested, she let the matter drop. Likewise French:

le cas écheant, *nous irons vendredi*, if necessary we will go on Friday.

Nominative absolutes have been seen in Aśokan edicts. In Pali there is:

ayaṃ hi dhammo nipuṇo sukho ca / yo 'yaṃ tayā Bhagavā suppavutto / tam eva sabbe sussūsamānā / tvan no vada pucchito buddhaseṭṭha,

the subtle dhamma which brings happiness has been well-set out by you, Blessed One; (we are) all wanting to hear it, tell us when asked, excellent Buddha (Sn 383).

In prose one might expect genitives in line 3, to agree with *no* in line 4. If one understands a verb such as *homa* or *bhavāma* in line 3 it can be taken as a sentence in itself.

The grammatical text *Niruttidīpanī* (but no other) cites, along with other examples of the Pāṇinian *bhāvalakkhaṇa*:

gacchanto so Bhāradvājo addasā accutaṃ isiṃ,

going, Bharadvaja saw the sage Accuta (Ja VI 532),

yāyamāno maharājā addā sīdantare nage,

as he traveled (in a chariot), the great king saw mountains in the Sidantara ocean (Ja VI 125).

In both cases, modern grammar would see the participles simply as adjectives qualifying the subject of the main clause. Saddanīti cites both sentences, the first several times, but not to illustrate *bhāvalakkhaṇa*.

In some cases some manuscripts contain nominative absolutes where others have locatives:

saṃvaṭṭamāno loko [or *saṭvaṭṭamāne loke*] *yebhuyyena sattā Ābhassarāsaṃvaṭṭanikā honti*,

when the world evolves, beings for the most part become Abhassara gods (D I 17, cp. D III 84),

Govindo brāhmaṇo kālakato [or *Govinde brāhmaṇe kālakate*] *rājā Disampatī paridevesi*,

when Govinda the brahmin died king Disampati grieved (D II 231).

It is not certain if these instances are evidence of a nominative absolute, the 'Hanging nominative' (*nominativus pendens*), or neither.

2.1.2 *kāraka*, Factors of Action

Although like the other cases, the sixth/genitive and eighth/vocative are marked by their distinctive endings, neither is regarded in Pali grammar as being a *kāraka*, a factor of action. Aggavaṃsa's account of the cases and factors of action is as follows:

> *kiriyānimittaṃ kārakaṃ. yaṃ sādhanasabhāvattā mukhyavasena vā upacāravāsena vā kiriyābhipphattiyā nimittaṃ, taṃ vatthukārakaṃ nāma bhavati; mukhyopacāravasena hi kiriyaṃ karoti kārakaṃ... taṃ chabbidaṃ: kattu-kamma-karaṇa-sampadān'-āpādān'-okāsavasena. kiriyābhisambandhalakkhaṇaṃ kārakaṃ.*
>
> A factor of action is an element of the action. A thing which, being by nature a means of realization, is an element in the accomplishment of an action, directly or indirectly, is called a factor of action. It is sixfold: agent [nominative], object [accusative], means [instrumental], beneficiary* [dative], point of departure [ablative], place [locative]. A factor of action is characterized by connection to the action.
>
> * beneficiary, like other translations suggested for *sampadāna* (recipient, dation) is not fully satisfactory.

AGENT / NOMINATIVE

> *yo kurute yo vā jāyati, so kattā. yo attappadhāno hutvā gamanapacanādikaṃ kiriyaṃ kurute yo vā jāyati, so kārako kattā bhavati... so tividho, suddhakattā hetukattā kammakattā. tattha*
>
> Whoever does (something), or is born*, is an agent. When someone, himself being predominant (in the action), performs an action such as going or cooking, or when he is born, he is (called) the factor of action consisting in the agent. This is threefold: an agent pure and simple, a causal agent, an object-agent.
>
> * This refers to a topos of Sanskrit grammar: whether someone who does not yet exist can be said to do something, i.e. be born. Aggavaṃsa gives the usual explanation, that grammatical forms refer directly not to things but to words or ideas in the mind: *yam asantaṃ santaṃ viya buddhiyā parikappīyati tañ ca kattusaññaṃ bhavati*, what does not exist is conceived in the mind in the same way as what does exist, and this also comes to receive the designation 'agent.'

[1] *yo sayam eva kiriyaṃ karoti, so suddhakattā nāma, taṃ yathā: puriso maggaṃ gacchati, sūdo bhattaṃ pacati, putto jāyati, buddhena jito Māro, Upaguttena baddho Māro.*

A person who performs an action by himself is an agent pure and simple, that's to say: a person goes [intransitive] on the road, a cook cooks [transitive] a meal, a child is born [intransitive], Mara was conquered by the Buddha [passive, agent is the Buddha], Mara was bound by Upagutta [passive, agent is Upagutta].

[2] *yo aññaṃ kammāni yojeti, so hetukattā nāma. so hi parassa kiriyāya kāraṇabhāvena hinoti gacchati pavattatī ti hetu, hetu ca so kattā cā ti atthena hetukattā: Yaññadatto Devadattaṃ gamayati.*

A person who incites another to (perform) actions is called a causal agent. A person who is the reason for the action of another is the cause (for saying of the other person or thing) 'He sends, he goes, it occurs,' and so is a causal agent in the sense that he is both cause and agent: 'Yaññadatta gets Devadatta to go.'

[3] *yo parassa kiriyaṃ paṭicca kammabhūto pi sukarattā sayam eva sijjhanto viya hoti, so kammakattā nāma, kammañ ca taṃ kattā cā ti atthena: sayam eva kaṃo karīyati, sayam eva pacīyati odāno ti evaṃ tividhā bhavanti kattāro.*

Whatever, although an object because of (something or) someone else's action, seems to accomplish (the action) easily by itself, is an object-agent: the mat is made by itself, the rice cooks itself. Thus agents are threefold.

api ca [4] abhihitakattā [5] anabhihitakattā cā ti ime dve te ca tayo ti kattūnaṃ pañcavidhattam api icchanti garū. tattha

But (some) authorities want there to be a fivefold division of agents: as well as those three (they say) there are also these two: [4] the expressed agent and [5] the unexpressed agent. In this regard [they say]

[4] *puriso maggaṃ gacchati, ayam abhihitakattā ākhyātena kathitattā*

In 'a person goes on the road' there is an expressed agent because (the agent) is referred to by the verb [i.e. its ending *ti*];

[5] *sūdena pacīyati odāno, ahinā daṭṭho naro, ayam anabhihitakattā ākhyātena kitena vā akathitattā.*

In 'the rice is cooked by the cook' and 'the man has been bitten by a snake,' there is is an unexpressed agent because (the agent) is not referred to either by the verb or by a *kit* suffix [see 3.3].

abhinipphādanalakkhaṇaṃ kattukārakaṃ.

The factor of action consisting in the agent has the characteristic of bringing (something) about.

DIRECT OBJECT / ACCUSATIVE

yaṃ kurute yaṃ vā passati taṃ kammaṃ. karīyate taṃ kirīyāya papuṇīyate ti kammaṃ.

What (someone) does or what (someone) sees is an object. It is done, realized through action, so it is an object.

kiriyāpattilakkhaṇaṃ kammakārakaṃ taṃ tividhaṃ nibbattanīyādivasena, sattavidhaṃ api keci icchanti icchitādivasena. tattha

The factor of action consisting in the object has the characteristic of realizing the action, (and) it is threefold in terms of what is to be produced, etc.; but some want it to be sevenfold, in terms of what is wanted, etc. In this regard

[1] *rathaṃ karoti, sukhaṃ janayati, puttaṃ vijāyati, aladdhaṃ patthetī ti idaṃ nibbattanīyaṃ nāma.*

He makes a cart, he gives rise to happiness, she bears a child, he wishes for what he does not have: this is called something to be produced.

[2] *kaṭṭham aṅgāraṃ karoti, suvaṇṇaṃ keyuraṃ kaṃakaṃ vā karoti, vīhayo lunāti, idaṃ vikaraṇīyaṃ nāma. taṃ duvidhaṃ, paricattakāraṇaṃ aparicattakāraṇaṃ. tattha*

He makes wood into charcoal, he makes gold into a bracelet or ring, he harvests rice, this is called something to be changed and this (itself) is twofold: where the (material) cause does not remain, and where it does remain. In this regard

[2A] *paricattakāraṇaṃ nāma yaṃ kāraṇassa vināsena sambhūtaṃ.*

Something is called a material cause which does not remain when something comes into being by the destruction of its (material) cause [e.g. wood → charcoal].

[2B] *aparicattakāraṇaṃ nāma yattha kāraṇabhūte vatthumhi vijjamāne yeva guṇantaruppattiyā vohārabhedo dissati.*

Something is called a material cause which does remain because (merely) a change in expression is seen when a different quality arises, and the thing which was the (material) cause still exists [e.g. gold → bracelet].

[3] *nivesanam pavisati, ādiccaṃ namassati, rūpaṃ passati, dhammaṃ suṇāti, pandite payirupāsati, manasā Pāṭaliputtaṃ gacchati, idaṃ pāpanīyaṃ nāma. tathā hi nivesanaṃ pavisatīti ādisu nivesanādinaṃ kiriyāya na koci viseso karīyati aññatra sampattimattā.*

He enters the house, he worships the sun, he sees a form, he hears dhamma, he reveres (his) teachers, he goes to Pataliputta mentally, this is called something to be attained. In (sentences) such as ' he enters the house', nothing specific is done by the action of the house, etc., other than just accomplishing (the action).

[3A] *bhattaṃ bhuñjati icc ādisu bhattādi icchitakammaṃ nāma.*

In (sentences) such as 'He eats food', the food etc. is called a desired object.

[3B] *visaṃ gilati icc ādisu visaṃ anicchitakammaṃ nāma.*

In (sentences) such as 'He swallows the poison' the poison is called an undesired object.

[3C] *gāmaṃ gacchanto rukkhamūlaṃ upasaṃkamati icc ādisu rukkhamūlādi nevicchitanānicchitakammaṃ nāma.*

In (sentences) such as 'going to the village he approaches the root of a tree', the root of a tree etc. consitute an object neither desired nor undesired.

[4] *ajaṃ gāmaṃ nayati, Yaññadattaṃ kambalaṃ yācati brāhmaṇo, samiddhaṃ dhanaṃ bhikkhati, rājānaṃ etad abravi icc ādisu ajādayo kathitakammaṃ nāma, gāmādayo akathitakammaṃ. tathā hi ajaṃ gāmaṃ nayatī ti ettha ajo kathitakammaṃ dvikammikāya nayanakiriyāya pattum icchitatarattā, gāmo pana appaddhānattā akathitakammaṃ esa nayo itaresu pi.*

In (sentences) such as 'He leads a goat to the village,' 'a brahmin asks Yaññadatta for a blanket,' 'He asks a rich man for money, he says this to the king' the goat etc., is called the expressed object, the village etc. the unexpressed object. For in 'He leads a goat to the village,' the goat is the expressed object because (the agent) desires to complete (the action) more (with regard to the goat) by the action of leading which has (these) two objects, while the village is unexpressed because it is less important. The same analysis holds also in the other cases.

[5] *puriso purisaṃ kammaṃ kāreti icc ādisu pana āṇattapurisādayo kattukammaṃ nāma, kattā ca so kammaṃ cā ti atthena.*

In (sentences) such as '(one) man makes another perfom an action,' the man who is ordered etc. is called an agent-object, because he is both an agent and an object.

[6] *mayā ijjate buddho, Yaññadatto kambalaṃ yācīyate brāhmaṇena, nāgo maṇiṃ yācito brāhmaṇena icc evamādisu buddhādayo abhihitakammaṃ nāma, ākhyātena paccayena vā kathitattā.*

In (sentences) such as 'the Buddha receives an offering from me,' 'Yaññadatta is asked for a blanket by the brahmin,' 'the naga was asked for a gem by the brahmin,' the Buddha' etc. is called an expressed object, because they are referred to by the verb and/or the suffix.

[7] *chattaṃ karoti, ghaṭaṃ karoti icc ādisu chattādayo anabhihitakammaṃ nāma, akhyātena akathitattā.*

In (sentences) such as 'He makes an umbrella,' 'he makes a pot,' the umbrella etc. is called an unexpressed object, because it is not referred to by the verb.

MEANS / INSTRUMENTAL

yena kurute yena vā passati, taṃ pi karaṇaṃ. kariyati kiriyaṃ jāneti anena kattuno upakaraṇabhūtena vatthunā ti karaṇaṃ. ettha ca sati pi sabbakārakānaṃ kiriyāsādhatte yena kurute ti ādi visesetvā-vacanaṃ kattūpakaraṇabhūtesu sādhanesu sādhakatamass' eva gahaṇatthaṃ. kiriyāsambhāralakkhaṇaṃ karaṇakārakaṃ. taṃ duvidhaṃ ajjhattikabahīravasena: cakkhunā rūpaṃ passati, sotena saddaṃ suṇāti... manasā dhammaṃ vijānāti; hatthena kammaṃ karoti, pharasunā rukkhaṃ chindati.

That by which (someone) does (something), or that by which (someone) sees (something), is the means. An action is performed (by an agent), (an agent) instigates an action, with this thing which is the agent's instrument: this is the means. In this regard although all factors of (an) action bring it to fruition, the phrase which specifies (the instrumental) as 'that by which/whom (someone) does (something) is for the sake of grasping that it is the most important among the means of realization which are the agent's instruments. The factor of action consisting in the means has the characteristic of implementing the action. This is twofold, internal and external: he sees an form with his eye, he cognizes a mental object with his ear, he understands the dhamma with his mind; he performs an action with his hand, he cuts a tree with an axe.

BENEFICIARY / DATIVE

yassa dātukamo yassa vā ruccati, taṃ sampadānaṃ. yassa vā dātukāmo yassa vā ruccati, yassa vā khamati yassa vā dhārayate, taṃ kārakaṃ sampadānasaññaṃ: sāmaṇassa dānaṃ dātukāmo, sāmaṇassa cīvaraṃ dadāti, tassa purisassa bhattaṃ ruccati, gamanaṃ mayhaṃ ruccati, mā āyasmantānaṃ saṅghabhedo ruccittha, Devadattassa suvaṇṇacchattaṃ dhārayate Yaññadatto.

The person to whom (one) wants to give (something), or the person to whom (something) is pleasing, this is the beneficiary. The person to whom (someone) wants to give (something), or the person to whom (something) is pleasing, or the person to whom (something) seems fit, the person to whom (someone) owes (something), this is the factor of action designated the beneficiary: he wants to give a gift to the ascetic, he gives a robe to the ascetic, a meal pleases the man, going pleases me, may splitting the Monastic Order not please the venerable ones, Yaññadatta owes Devadatta a golden umbrella.

sammā pakārena assa dadātī ti sampadānaṃ paṭiggāhako. paṭiggahaṇalakkhaṇaṃ sampadānakarakaṃ. taṃ pi etaṃ sampadānaṃ tividhaṃ hoti: anirākaraṇajjhesanānumativasena. tathā [1] kiñci dīyamānassa anirākaraṇena sampadānasaññaṃ labhati, yathā Buddhassa pupphaṃ dadāti, rukkhassa jalaṃ dadātī ti [2] kiñci ajjhesanena yācakānaṃ bhojalaṃ dadatī ti, [3] kiñci anumatiyā Nārāyanassa baliṃ dadāti, bhikkhussa bhattaṃ dadātī ti

'He gives (something) to him in the right manner', (so) the receiver is the beneficiary. The factor of action consisting in the beneficiary is characterized by receiving. This beneficiary is threefold, in terms of whether (the beneficiary) does not refuse, is keen (to receive the gift), or (simply) consents to it. In some cases [1] (someone) acquires the designation 'beneficiary' by not refusing what is given, such as in 'He gives a flower to the Buddha,' (or) 'He gives water to a tree'; in some cases [2] by wanting (what is given), 'He gives food to beggars', in some cases [3] by consenting (to what is given), 'He makes an offering to Narayana,' he gives the monk a meal.'

POINT OF DEPARTURE / ABLATIVE

yato vā apeti yato vā āgacchati taṃ karakaṃ apādanasaññaṃ hoti. apecca ito ādadātī ti apādānaṃ, ito vatthuto kāyavasena cittavasena vā apagantvā aññaṃ gaṇhātī ti attho.

That from which (someone) goes away or that from which (someone) comes is the factor of action designated the point of departure. Leaving here he takes (it) away' is the point of departure, which means that he goes away from this place, bodily or mentally, and chooses another.

taṃ pana apādanaṃ duvidhaṃ [1] kāyasaṃyogapubbaka-[2]cittasaṃyogapubb akāpagamanavasena, tathā [3]calāvadhi-[4]niccalāvadhivasena. atha vā pana tividhaṃ: calāvadhiniccalāvadhi-[5]nevacalāvadhi-naniccalāvadhivasena, tathā [6]niddiṭṭhavisaya [7]uppattavisaya[8]anumeyyavisayavasena.

This point of departure is twofold: if there is the going away from a previous [1] bodily or [2] mental connection, and likewise if there is a [3] movable or [4] immovable limit (terminus a quo). Alternatively it is threefold: if there is a [3] movable, [4] immovable or [5] a neither-movable-nor-immovable limit, and likewise if its sphere (of operation) is [6] indicated (by the verb), [7] implied, or [8] inferred.

gāmā apenti munayo ti ādisu hi [1] kāyasaṃyogapubbakassa apagamanassa vijjamānattā gāmādi apādānaṃ kāyasaṃyogapubbakaṃ nāma, [2] pānātipātā viramatī ti ādisu pana cittasaṃyogapubbakassa apagamanassa vijjamānattā pānātipātādi apādānaṃ cittasaṃyogapubbakaṃ nāma. tathā dhāvatā hatthimhā patito aṃkusaggaho ti ādisu hatthiādi apadānaṃ calamariyādabhūtattā [3] calāvadhi nāma… pabbatā otaranti vanacarā ti ādisu pabbatādi apādānaṃ niccalamariyādabhūtattā [4] niccalāvadhi nāma, … imehi dvīhi pakārehi vinimuttaṃ buddhasmā pati Sāriputto, kāmato jāyate bhayan ti ca ādisu buddhādi apādānaṃ [5] n' eva calāvadhi n' eva niccalāvadhi nāma, avadhibhāvena agahetabbattā evaṃ apadānaṃ duvidhaṃ tividhañ ca bhavati.

[1] In (sentences) such as 'the sages leave the village,' because there is a departure which has a previous bodily connection, a departure from the village is called one which has a previous bodily connection; [2] in (sentences) such as 'He refrains from killing living beings,' because there is a departure which has a previous mental connection, a departure from killing living beings etc. is called one which has a previous mental connection. Likewise in (sentences) such as 'the mahout fell from the stampeding elephant,' departure from the elephant etc. is called [3] one with a movable limit, because a movable terminus exists; in (sentences) such as 'the forest-dwellers come down from the mountain,' departure from the mountain etc. is called [4] one with an immovable limit, because an immovable terminus exists; separate from both these modes, in (sentences) such as 'Sariputta [preached] in place of the Buddha,' and 'fear is born from desire,' departure from the Buddha etc. is [5] not said to have a movable or immovable limit, because he cannot be apprehended as a limit. In this way the point of departure is twofold and threefold.

puna taṃ tividhañ ca nidiṭṭhavisayādivasena. tattha gāmā apagacchatī ti ādi niddiṭṭhavisayaṃ hoti apādānavisayassa [6] kiriyāvisesassa nidiṭṭhattā; kusūlato pacati, abhidhammā kathayati, valāhakā vijjotatī ti [7] upattavisayaṃ nāma, valāhakā niggamma vijjotatī ti ādinā upādeyyo ettha kiriyāviseso; Mādhurā Pāṭaliputtakehi abhirūpatarā ti [8] anumeyyavisayaṃ nāma, Mādhurā Pāṭaliputtakehi ukkaṃsīyati kenaci guṇenā ti anumeyyo ettha kiriyāviseso.

But again it is threefold, as to whether its sphere (of operation) is indicated (by the verb), etc. In this regard in (sentences) such as 'He went away from the village,' [6] the sphere of operation is indicated because to indicate the specific form of the verb is also to indicate the sphere of operation of the point of departure [i.e. given *apagacchati* one knows it must govern an ablative]; [7] 'He prepares food from the granary,' 'He preaches from the Abhidhamma,' 'lightning flashes from a cloud,' the sphere of operation is implied, (since) here specification (of the ablative) by a verb is to be assumed, by means of (sentences) such as 'lightning comes out from a cloud'; [8] in 'the Madhurans are better-looking than the Pataliputtans' the sphere of operation is to be inferred, (since) here specification (of the ablative) by a verb is to be inferred, by means of (a sentence) such as 'the Madhurans are above the Pâtaliputtans in some respect.'

PLACE / LOCATIVE

yo ādhāro tam okāsaṃ. yo kattukammasamavetānaṃ nisajjapacanādikiriyānaṃ ādhārakaṭṭhena ādhāro, taṃ kārakaṃ okāsasaññaṃ hoti. bhuso kiriyaṃ dharetī ti ādhāro, so eva tāsaṃ kiriyānaṃ patiṭṭhānatthena okasattā okāsaṃ nāmā ti vuccati. tathā hi kaṭe nisīdati Devadatto ti ettha kaṭo Devadattaṃ dhārento taṃsamavetaṃ āsanakiriyaṃ dhāreti, thāliyaṃ odānaṃ pacatī ti ettha thālī taṇḍulaṃ dharentī taṃsamavetaṃ pi pacanakiriyaṃ dhāreti.

That which is the support is the place. That which is the support in the sense of sustaining the actions of sitting, cooking, etc. which inhere in the agent and object, is the factor of action which is designated 'location.' It strongly supports the action, so it is a support. It is also called 'location' because it provides a site for these actions in the sense of a foundation. Thus in 'Devadatta sits on the mat' the mat, supporting Devadatta, supports the action of sitting which inheres in him; in 'He cooks the rice in a pot,' here too the pot, holding the rice, sustains the action of cooking which inheres in it.

so 'yam okāso catubbidho: vyāpiko opasilesiko sāmīpiko vesayiko ti tattha [1] vyāpiko nāma sakalo ādhārabhūto attho ādheyyena patthaṭo hoti, taṃ yathā: tilesu telaṃ, ucchusu raso, dadhimhi sappī ti. [2] opasilesiko nāma paccekasiddhānaṃ bhāvānaṃ yattha upasileso upagamo hoti, tam yathā: kaṃe nisīdatī ti. [3] sāmīpiko nāma yattha samīpe sāmīpikavohāraṃ katvā ādhārabhāvo vikappīyati, taṃ yathā: Sāvatthiyaṃ viharati, Gaṅgāyaṃ vajo ti.... [4] vesayiko nama yattha aññatthabhāvavasena desantarāvacchedavasena vā ādhāraparikappo, taṃ yathā bhūmisu manussā, jalesu macchā, ākāse sakuṇā ti... ādhāraṇalakkhaṇaṃ okāsakāraṃ.

This location is fourfold: pervading, with close contact, neighboring, indicating the domain. In this regard, [1] the pervading is when the whole thing which is the support is permeated by what is supported, such as 'oil in sesame seeds,' 'juice in sugarcanes,' 'ghee in curds.' [2] 'with close contact' is when there is close contact, proximity between two things which are established separately, as in 'He sits on the mat.' [3] The neighboring is when the existence of a support in (some) neighborhood is discerned by an expression for the neighborhood, as in 'He is living in Savatthi,' 'a cowpen on the Ganges.'... [4] Indicating the domain is when a support is determined by means of a difference in place or dissimilar states of being, as in 'Human beings live on the earth, fish in the seas and birds in the sky.' The factor of action consisting in location is characterized by (the act of) supporting.

GENITIVE AND VOCATIVE

na chaṭṭhivibhitattho kārakaṃ, yathāmantaṇaṃ.

The meaning expressed by the sixth case is not a factor of action, likewise the vocative.

The genitive is usually known, by synecdoche, by one relation it expresses, ownership, *sāmi*. Others are:

relation		example	
bhacca [= bhṛtya]	maintained by	*rañño puriso*	the king's man
santaka	belonging to	*rañño raṭṭhaṃ*	the king's realm
samīpa	in the vicinity of	*ambavanassa*	not far from the
		avidūre	mango-grove
samūha	accumulation of	*dhaññānaṃ rasi*	heap of grains
avayava	part of	*rukkhassa sākhā*	branch of a tree
vikāra	alteration of	*suvaṇṇassa vikati*	alteration of gold

kiriyāsambandhābhāvā n' esā kārakatā sambhavati; sāmibhāvo hi kiriyā-kārakabhāvassa phalabhāvena gahito. tathā hi rañño puriso ti vutte, yasmā rājā dadāti puriso ca paṭigaṇhati, tasmā rājapuriso ti viññayati.

There is no factor of action here [in the uses of the genitive] because there is no (immediate) connection with the action (of the verb). For the existence of a possessor is apprehended as a result of the existence of the verb and the factor(s) of action, as when it is said that 'He is the king's man,' it is because the king provides and the man receives that he is known as 'the king's man.'

Aggavaṃsa explains cases which may seem to be genitives which have a direct connection to the action of the verb, such as *pitussa sarati*, he remembers his father, or *rañño sammato*, appointed by the king, as not being true genitives (*chaṭṭhī suddhā*) since they occur with the sense of other cases, so that the sentences are equivalent to *pitaraṃ sarati*, *raññā sammato*.

THE VOCATIVE

katābhimukho tu pacchā kiriyāya yojīyati, gaccha, bhuñjā ti. tasmā āmantaṇasamaye kiriyāyogābhāvato n' etaṃ kārakavohāraṃ labhati

But it is (only after a person has been) made to face (the speaker) that he/she be connected to an action, (in words such as) go, eat!' Therefore because at the time of the address there is no connection to action, it cannot receive the name 'factor of action.'

2.1.3 Nominal Paradigms

According to Pali grammar, the declension of nouns, adjectives, participles, pronouns, pronominal adjectives and numerals consists in

(i) a theme, (*pātipadika*), stem (*liṅga*) or word (*sadda*), and
(ii) an inflectional suffix (*vibhatti*, division).

There are two basic kinds of stem:

(i) those which are unchangeable
(ii) those which are changeable, of which there are two kinds
 (iia) those with two stems
 (iib) those with three stems.

(i) Unchangeable stem paradigms

Masculine, feminine and neuter stems in *-a*, *-ā*: *kanta*, lovely, pleasant

singular	MASCULINE	alternatives	FEMININE	alternatives	NEUTER	alternatives
nominative	*kanto*		*kantā*		*kantaṃ*	
accusative	*kantaṃ*		*kantaṃ*		*kantaṃ*	
instrumental	*kantena*		*kantāya*		*kantena*	
dative	*kantāya*	*kantassa*	*kantāya*		*kantāya*	*kantassa*
ablative	*kantā*	*kantasmā* *kantamhā*	*kantāya*		*kantā*	*kantasmā* *kantamhā*
genitive	*kantassa*		*kantāya*		*kantassa*	
locative	*kante*	*kantasmiṃ* *kantamhi*	*kantāya*	*kantāyaṃ*	*kante*	*kantasmiṃ* *kantamhi*
vocative	*kanta*		*kante*		*kanta*	
plural	MASCULINE	alternatives	FEMININE	alternatives	NEUTER	alternatives
nominative	*kantā*		*kantā*	*kantāyo*	*kantāni*	*kantā*
accusative	*kante*		*kantā*	*kantāyo*	*kantāni*	*kante*
instrumental	*kantehi*		*kantāhi*		*kantehi*	
dative	*kantānaṃ*		*kantānaṃ*		*kantānaṃ*	
ablative	*kantehi*		*kantāhi*		*kantehi*	
genitive	*kantānaṃ*		*kantānaṃ*		*kantānaṃ*	
locative	*kantesu*		*kantāsu*		*kantesu*	
vocative	*kantā*		*kantā*	*kantāyo*	*kantāni*	*kantā*

Neuter plural nominative and accusative can also take masculine endings, and very rarely masculines can take those of the neuter.

It has been claimed that there is an instrumental singular ending in masculine and neuter *-ā*, which would be a Vedic form. The evidence for this is disputed, however, and the form, if genuine, seems to be restricted to certain adverbial uses.

The ablative singular endings *-asmā*, *-amhā*, and accusative plural *-e*, are from the pronominal declension.

There are some rarer forms: instrumental singular in *-asā*, masculine nominative plural in *-āse*, masculine accusative plural in *-aṃ* (= *ān*).

This is the only declension to distinguish between dative and genitive, in the masculine and neuter singular.

There is a very common ablative singular in *-to*, possible in all declensions, and often used adverbially.

There are some rare instances of masculine and neuter nominative singular in *-e*, which are regarded as Māgadha dialect forms.

The feminine of some adjectives in *-a* can follow the *-ī* declension.

Masculine, feminine and neuter stems in *-i*: *muni* (m) sage, *jāti* (f) birth, *aṭṭhi* (n) bone,

SINGULAR	MASCULINE	alternatives	FEMININE	alternatives	NEUTER	alternatives
NOMINATIVE	*muni*		*jāti*		*aṭṭhi*	*aṭṭhiṃ*
ACCUSATIVE	*muniṃ*		*jātiṃ*		*aṭṭhi*	*aṭṭhiṃ*
INSTRUMENTAL	*muninā*		*jātiyā*	*jaccā*	*aṭṭhinā*	
DATIVE	*munino*	*munissa*	*jātiyā*	*jaccā*	*aṭṭhino*	*aṭṭhissa*
ABLATIVE	*muninā*	*munismā* *munimhā*	*jātiyā*	*jaccā*	*aṭṭhinā*	*aṭṭhismā* *aṭṭhimhi*
GENITIVE	*munino*	*munissa*	*jātiyā*	*jaccā*	*aṭṭhino*	*aṭṭhissa*
LOCATIVE	*munini*	*munismiṃ* *munimhi*	*jātiyā*	*jātiyaṃ*	*aṭṭhini*	*aṭṭhismiṃ* *aṭṭhimhi*
VOCATIVE	*muni*		*jāti*			*aṭṭhi*
PLURAL	MASCULINE	alternatives	FEMININE	alternatives	NEUTER	alternatives
NOMINATIVE	*munayo*	*munī*	*jātiyo*	*jātī*	*aṭṭhīni*	*aṭṭhī*
ACCUSATIVE	*munayo*	*munī*	*jātiyo*	*jātī*	*aṭṭhīni*	*aṭṭhī*
INSTRUMENTAL	*munīhi*		*jātīhi*		*aṭṭīhi*	
DATIVE	*munīnaṃ*		*jātīnaṃ*		*aṭṭhīnaṃ*	
ABLATIVE	*munīhi*		*jātīhi*		*aṭṭhīhi*	
GENITIVE	*munīnaṃ*		*jātīnaṃ*		*aṭṭhīnaṃ*	
LOCATIVE	*munīsu*		*jātīsu*		*aṭṭhīsu*	
VOCATIVE	*munayo*	*munī*	*jātiyo*		*aṭṭhīni*	*aṭṭhī*

Feminine stems in *-ī*: *nadī*, river

	SINGULAR	alternatives	PLURAL	alternatives
NOMINATIVE	*nadī*		*nadiyo*	*nadī*
ACCUSATIVE	*nadiṃ*		*nadiyo*	*nadī*
INSTRUMENTAL	*nadiyā*	*najjā*	*nadīhi*	
DATIVE	*nadiyā*	*najjā*	*nadīnaṃ*	
ABLATIVE	*nadiyā*	*najjā*	*nadīhi*	
GENITIVE	*nadiyā*	*najjā*	*nadīnaṃ*	
LOCATIVE	*nadiyā*	*nadiyaṃ*	*nadīsu*	
VOCATIVE	*nadī̆*		*nadiyo*	*nadī*

The nominative singular of certain words can be *-i*, *siri*, fortune, *hiri*, modesty, *itthi* (*thi*), woman.

Masculine, feminine and neuter stems in *-u*: *bandhu* (m) relative, *dhenu* (f) cow, *cakkhu* (n) eye

SINGULAR	MASCULINE	alternatives	FEMININE	alternatives	NEUTER	alternatives
NOMINATIVE	*bandhu*		*dhenu*		*cakkhu*	*cakkhuṃ*
ACCUSATIVE	*bandhuṃ*		*dhenuṃ*		*cakkhu*	*cakkhuṃ*
INSTRUMENTAL	*bandhunā*		*dhenuyā*		*cakkhunā*	
DATIVE	*bandhuno*	*bandhussa*	*dhenuyā*		*cakkhuno*	*cakkhussa*
ABLATIVE	*bandhunā*	*bandhusmā*, *bandhumhā*	*dhenuyā*		*cakkhunā*	*cakkhusmā*, *cakkhumhā*
GENITIVE	*bandhuno*	*bandhussa*	*dhenuyā*		*cakkhuno*	*cakkhussa*
LOCATIVE	*bandhusmiṃ*	*bandhumhi*	*dhenuyā*	*dhenuyam*	*cakkhusmiṃ*	*cakkhumhi*
VOCATIVE	*bandhu*		*dhenu*		*cakkhu*	*cakkhuṃ*
PLURAL	MASCULINE	alternatives	FEMININE	alternatives	NEUTER	alternatives
NOMINATIVE	*bandhavo*	*bandhū*	*dhenuyo*	*dhenū*	*cakkhūni*	*cakkhū*
ACCUSATIVE	*bandhavo*	*bandhū*	*dhenuyo*	*dhenū*	*cakkhūni*	*cakkhū*
INSTRUMENTAL	*bandhūhi*		*dhenūhi*		*cakkhūhi*	
DATIVE	*bandhūnaṃ*		*dhenūnaṃ*		*cakkhūnaṃ*	
ABLATIVE	*bandhūhi*		*dhenūhi*		*cakkhūhi*	
GENITIVE	*bandhūnaṃ*		*dhenūnaṃ*		*cakkhūnaṃ*	
LOCATIVE	*bandhūsu*		*dhenūsu*		*cakkhūsu*	
VOCATIVE	*bandhavo*	*bandhū*	*dhenuyo*	*dhenū*	*cakkhūni*	*cakkhū*

bhikkhu, monk, has a vocative plural *bhikkhave*

Masculine and feminine stems in *-ū*: *viññū* (m) wise (man), *sassū* (f) mother-in-law

SINGULAR	MASCULINE	alternatives	FEMININE	alternatives
NOMINATIVE	*viññū*		*sassū*	
ACCUSATIVE	*viññuṃ*		*sassuṃ*	
INSTRUMENTAL	*viññunā*		*sassuyā*	
DATIVE	*viññuno*	*viññussa*	*sassuyā*	
ABLATIVE	*viññunā*	*viññusmā* *viññumhā*	*sassuyā*	
GENITIVE	*viññuno*	*viññussa*	*sassuyā*	
LOCATIVE	*viññusmiṃ*	*viññumhi*	*sassuyā*	*sassuyaṃ*
VOCATIVE	*viññū*		*sassū*	
PLURAL	MASCULINE	alternatives	FEMININE	alternatives
NOMINATIVE	*viññuno*	*viññū*	*sassuyo*	*sassū*
ACCUSATIVE	*viññuno*	*viññū*	*sassuyo*	*sassū*
INSTRUMENTAL	*viññūhi*		*sassūhi*	
DATIVE	*viññūnaṃ*		*sassūnaṃ*	
ABLATIVE	*viññūhi*		*sassūhi*	
GENITIVE	*viññūnaṃ*		*sassūnaṃ*	
LOCATIVE	*viññūsu*		*sassūsu*	
VOCATIVE	*viññuno*		*sassuyo*	*sassū*

Neuter stems in *-as*: *sotas*, stream

	SINGULAR	alternatives	PLURAL
NOMINATIVE	*soto*	*sotaṃ*	*sotāni*
ACCUSATIVE	*soto*	*sotaṃ*	*sotāni*
INSTRUMENTAL	*sotasā*	*sotena*	*sotehi*
DATIVE	*sotaso*	*sotassa*	*sotānaṃ*
ABLATIVE	*sotasā*	*sotā*	*sotehi*
GENITIVE	*sotaso*	*sotassa*	*sotānaṃ*
LOCATIVE	*sotasi*	*sote*	*sotesu*
VOCATIVE	*soto*	*sota*	*sotāni*

There are not many nouns in *-as*; *yasas*, fame, *cetas*, mind, intention, *manas*, mind, *saras*, lake, *vayas*, age, *rajas*, dust, *tapas*, asceticism, *siras*, head, and some others. The word *candimas*, moon, has nominative singular *candimā*, but otherwise declines as an *-a* stem. Words in *-is* and *-us* mostly convert to *-i* and *-u* stems.

(ii) Changeable stems

Changeable stems have either two stems, the strong and the weak, or three, the strong, middle, and weak. The distribution of these stems in the various cases, which is slightly different from Sanskrit, is:

strong: nominative (vocative) and accusative singular, nominative (vocative) plural
middle: before endings beginning with a consonant
weak: before endings beginning with a vowel

With two stems:

Agent nouns and relational nouns in *-ar*, *satthar* (m) teacher, *pitar* (m) father, *mātar* (f) mother

Agent nouns have a strong stem in *-ār*, relational nouns in *-ar*, but there is considerable variation in stem forms

SINGULAR	AGENT NOUN	alternatives	MASCULINE RELATIONAL	alternatives	FEMININE RELATIONAL	alternatives
NOMINATIVE	*satthā*		*pitā*		*mātā*	
ACCUSATIVE	*satthāraṃ*		*pitaraṃ*		*mātaraṃ*	
INSTRUMENTAL	*sattharā*	*satthārā* *satthunā*	*pitarā*		*mātarā*	
DATIVE	*satthu*	*satthuno* *satthussa*	*pitu*	*pituno* *pitussa*	*mātu*	*mātuyā* *mātāya*
ABLATIVE	*sattharā*	*satthārā*	*pitarā*		*mātarā*	*mātuyā*
GENITIVE	*satthu*	*satthuno* *satthussa*	*pitu*	*pituno* *pitussa*	*mātu*	*mātuyā* *mātuya*
LOCATIVE	*satthari*		*pitari*		*mātari*	*mātuyā* *mātuyaṃ*
VOCATIVE	*satthā*	*sattha* *satthe*				

PLURAL	AGENT NOUN	alternatives	MASCULINE RELATIONAL	alternatives	FEMININE RELATIONAL	alternatives
NOMINATIVE	*satthāro*		*pitaro*		*mātaro*	
ACCUSATIVE	*satthāro*		*pitaro*	*pitare*	*mātaro*	
INSTRUMENTAL	*satthārehi*	*satthūhi*	*pitarehi*	*pitūhi*	*mātūhi*	
DATIVE	*satthārānaṃ*	*satthūnaṃ*	*pitarānaṃ*	*pitūnaṃ*	*mātūnaṃ*	
ABLATIVE	*satthārehi*	*satthūhi*	*pitarehi*	*pitūhi*	*mātūhi*	
GENITIVE	*satthārānaṃ*	*satthūnaṃ*	*pitarānaṃ*	*pitūnaṃ*	*mātūnaṃ*	
LOCATIVE	*satthāresu*	*satthūsu*	*pitaresu*	*pitūsu*	*mātūsu*	
VOCATIVE	*satthāro*					

Possessive adjectives in *-in*, e.g. *balin*, possessing strength, strong, have a strong stem *balin-*, and a weak stem *bali-*. Masculine singular is in *-ī*. The feminine is formed as an *-ī* stem on the stem *-inī*.

SINGULAR	MASCULINE	alternatives	FEMININE	alternatives	NEUTER	alternatives
NOMINATIVE	*balī*	*bali*	*balinī*	*balini*	*bali*	*baliṃ*
ACCUSATIVE	*balinaṃ*	*baliṃ*	*baliniṃ*		*bali*	*baliṃ*
INSTRUMENTAL	*balinā*		*baliniyā*		*balinā*	
DATIVE	*balino*	*balissa*	*baliniyā*		*balino*	*balissa*
ABLATIVE	*balinā*	*balismā* *balimhā*	*baliniyā*		*balinā*	*balismā* *balimhā*
GENITIVE	*balino*	*balissa*	*baliniyā*		*balino*	*balissa*
LOCATIVE	*balini*	*balismiṃ* *balimhi*	*baliniyā*	*baliniyaṃ*	*balini*	*balismiṃ* *balimhi*
VOCATIVE	*bali*		*balinī*	*balini*	*bali*	
PLURAL	**MASCULINE**	**alternatives**	**FEMININE**	**alternatives**	**NEUTER**	**alternatives**
NOMINATIVE	*balino*	*balī*	*baliniyo*	*balinī*	*balīni*	*balī*
ACCUSATIVE	*balino*	*balī*	*baliniyo*	*balinī*	*balīni*	*balī*
INSTRUMENTAL	*balīhi*		*balinīhi*		*balīhi*	
DATIVE	*balīnaṃ*		*balinīnaṃ*		*balīnaṃ*	
ABLATIVE	*balīhi*		*balinīhi*		*balīhi*	
GENITIVE	*balīnaṃ*		*balinīnaṃ*		*balīnaṃ*	
LOCATIVE	*balīsu*		*balinīsu*		*balīsu*	
VOCATIVE	*balino*	*balī*	*baliniyo*	*balinī*	*balīni*	*balī*

Possessive adjectives in *-vant*, *-mant*, e.g. *guṇavant*, having virtue, virtuous have a strong stem in *-ant*, and a weak in *-at*. They can decline in two ways: first, as in Sanskrit, alternating between these two stems, and second, using the strong stem alone and following the paradigm of *-a* stems. The feminine of adjectives in *-vant*, *-mant* is usually formed from the weak stem, as given here, but it sometimes uses the strong stem.

SINGULAR	MASCULINE	alternatives	FEMININE	alternatives	NEUTER	alternatives
NOMINATIVE	*guṇavā*	*guṇavanto*	*guṇavatī*		*guṇavaṃ*	*guṇavantaṃ*
ACCUSATIVE	*guṇavantaṃ*		*guṇavatiṃ*		*guṇavaṃ*	*guṇavantaṃ*
INSTRUMENTAL	*guṇavatā*	*guṇavantena*	*guṇavatiyā*		*guṇavatā*	*guṇavantena*
DATIVE	*guṇavato*	*guṇavantāya*	*guṇavatiyā*		*guṇavato*	*guṇavantāya*
ABLATIVE	*guṇavatā*	*guṇavantā*	*guṇavatiyā*		*guṇavatā*	*guṇavantā*
GENITIVE	*guṇavato*	*guṇavantassa*	*guṇavatiyā*		*guṇavato*	*guṇavantassa*
LOCATIVE	*guṇavati*	*guṇavante*	*guṇavatiyā*	*guṇavatiyaṃ*	*guṇavati*	*guṇavante*
VOCATIVE	*guṇavā̆*	*guṇavanta*	*guṇavati*		*guṇavaṃ*	*guṇavanta*
PLURAL	**MASCULINE**	**alternatives**	**FEMININE**	**alternatives**	**NEUTER**	**alternatives**
NOMINATIVE	*guṇavanto*	*guṇavantā*	*guṇavatiyo*	*guṇavatī*	*guṇavanti*	*guṇavantāni*
ACCUSATIVE	*guṇavanto*	*guṇavante*	*guṇavatiyo*	*guṇavatī*	*guṇavanti*	*guṇavantāni*
INSTRUMENTAL	*guṇavantehi*		*guṇavatībhi*		*guṇavantehi*	
DATIVE	*guṇavataṃ*	*guṇavantānaṃ*	*guṇavatīnaṃ*		*guṇavataṃ*	*guṇavantānaṃ*
ABLATIVE	*guṇavantehi*		*guṇavatībhi*		*guṇavantehi*	
GENITIVE	*guṇavataṃ*	*guṇavantānaṃ*	*guṇavatīnaṃ*		*guṇavataṃ*	*guṇavantānaṃ*
LOCATIVE	*guṇavantesu*		*guṇavatīsu*		*guṇavantesu*	
VOCATIVE	*guṇavanto*	*guṇavantā*	*guṇavatiyo*	*guṇavatī*	*guṇavanti*	*guṇavantāni*

(Alternative forms here which follow the *-a* paradigm also have their own alternatives, given under that paradigm above.)

arahant, a standard word for an enlightened person, which is a present participle of √*arh* → *arahati*, to be worthy, has masculine singular nominative *arahā* or *arahaṃ* or *arahanto*.

mahant, big, great, has *mahā* or *mahanto* in masculine nominative and vocative, which follow the strong/weak *-ant/-at* and *-a* paradigms respectively. The feminine is usually *mahatī* etc., though *mahantī* is also found.

The participle from √*bhū*, *bhavant-*, is declined like other participles when used as such; used as a word of polite address it declines differently, changing *-ava-* → *-o-*. There is a Māgadha dialect form of the vocative, *bhante*.

SINGULAR	MASCULINE	FEMININE	PLURAL	MASCULINE	FEMININE
NOMINATIVE	*bhavaṃ*	*bhotī*	NOMINATIVE	*bhavanto or bhonto*	*bhotiyo*
ACCUSATIVE	*bhavantaṃ*	*bhotiṃ*	ACCUSATIVE	*bhavante*	*bhotiyo*
INSTRUMENTAL	*bhotā*	*bhotiyā*	INSTRUMENTAL	*bhavantehi*	*bhotīhi*
DATIVE	*bhoto*	*bhotiyā*	DATIVE	*bhavataṃ*	*bhotīnaṃ*
ABLATIVE	*bhotā*	*bhotiyā*	ABLATIVE	*bhavantehi*	*bhotīhi*
GENITIVE	*bhoto*	*bhotiyā*	GENITIVE	*bhavataṃ*	*bhotīnaṃ*
LOCATIVE	*bhoti*	*bhotiyā or bhotiyaṃ*	LOCATIVE	*bhavantesu*	*bhotīsu*
VOCATIVE	*bho or*	*bhoti*	VOCATIVE	*bhavanto or bhonto*	*bhotiyo*

With three stems:

	SANSKRIT	PALI
STRONG	*rājān*	*rājān*
MIDDLE	*rājan*	*rāju*
WEAK	*rājñ*	*raññ or rājin*

n.b. the Sanskrit middle stems drop the final *-n* before consonant endings

	SINGULAR				PLURAL			
	Sanskrit		Pali		Sanskrit		Pali	
NOMINATIVE	strong	*rājā*	*rājā*	strong	strong	*rājānaḥ*	*rājāno*	strong
ACCUSATIVE	strong	*rājānaṃ*	*rājānaṃ*	strong	weak	*rājñaḥ*	*rājāno*	strong
INSTRUMENTAL	weak	*rājñā*	*raññā or rājinā*	weak	middle	*rājabhiḥ*	*rājūhi*	middle
DATIVE	weak	*rājñe*	*rañño*	weak	middle	*rājabhyaḥ*	*raññaṃ*	weak
ABLATIVE	weak	*rājñaḥ*	*raññā or rājinā*	weak	middle	*rājabhyaḥ*	*rājūhi*	middle
GENITIVE	weak	*rājñaḥ*	*rañño*	weak	weak	*rājñāṃ*	*raññaṃ*	weak
LOCATIVE	weak or middle	*rājñi or rājani*	*rājini*	weak	middle	*rājasu*	*rājūsu*	middle
VOCATIVE	middle	*rajān*	*rājā*	strong	strong	*rājānaḥ*	*rājāno*	strong

The weak stem of neuter *karman/kamma*, action, inserts *a* in Sanskrit, *a* or *u* in Pali. In Sanskrit this is because a weak stem **karmn* would be difficult to pronounce, and in Pali both for that reason and because **kammn* would violate the Law of Mora. In Sanskrit neuter *nāman*, name, has a weak stem *nāmn*, but in Pali *nāma* declines entirely as an -*a* stem, apart from an adverbial use of accusative *nāma*. The three stems are:

karma	Sanskrit	Pali
strong	*karmān*	*kammān*
middle	*karma*	*kamma(n)*
weak	**karmn* → *karmaṇ*	**kammn* → *kamman* or *kammun*

nāma	Sanskrit	Pali
strong	*nāmān*	*nām*
middle	*nāman*	*nām*
weak	*nāmn*	*nām*

SINGULAR	Sanskrit	Pali		Sanskrit	Pali
NOMINATIVE	*karma*	*kamma*	middle	*nāma*	*nāmaṃ*
ACCUSATIVE	*karma*	*kamma*	middle	*nāma*	*nāmaṃ* or *nāma*
INSTRUMENTAL	*karmaṇā*	*kammanā* or *kammunā*	weak	*nāmnā*	*nāmena*
DATIVE	*karmaṇe*	*kammano* or *kammuno*	weak	*nāmne*	*nāmāya*
ABLATIVE	*karmanaḥ*	*kammanā* or *kammunā*	weak	*nāmnaḥ*	*namā*
GENITIVE	*karmaṇaḥ*	*kammano* or *kammuno*	weak	*nāmnaḥ*	*nāmassa*
LOCATIVE	*karmani*	*kammani*	weak	*nāmni* or *nāmani*	*nāme*
VOCATIVE	*karma*	*kamma*	middle	*nāma*	*nāmaṃ*
PLURAL	Sanskrit	Pali		Sanskrit	Pali
NOMINATIVE	*karmāṇi*	*kammāni*	strong	*nāmāni*	*nāmāni*
ACCUSATIVE	*karmāṇi*	*kammāni*	strong	*namāni*	*nāmāni*
INSTRUMENTAL	*karmabhiḥ*	*kammehi*	middle	*nāmabhiḥ*	*nāmehi*
DATIVE	*karmabhyaḥ*	*kammānaṃ* or *kammunaṃ*	middle	*nāmabhyaḥ*	*nāmānaṃ*
ABLATIVE	*karmabhyaḥ*	*kammehi*	middle	*nāmabhyaḥ*	*nāmehi*
GENITIVE	*karmṇām*	*kammānaṃ* or *kammunaṃ*	weak	*nāmnām*	*nāmānaṃ*
LOCATIVE	*karmasu*	*kammesu*	middle	*nāmasu*	*nāmesu*
VOCATIVE	*karmāṇi*	*kammāni*	strong	*nāmāni*	*nāmāni*

2.2. *sabbanāma*, Pronouns and Pronominal Adjectives

Aggavaṃsa lists these twenty-seven *sabbanāmāni*, names for everything, in this order:

sabba	all, every
katara	which (of two)
katama	which (of many)
ubhaya	both
itara	other (of two)
añña	other (of many)
aññatara	a certain (of many)
aññatama	a certain (of two)
pubba	former
para	(an)other
apara	(an)other
dakkhiṇa	right, south
uttara	upper, north, more than
adhara	lower

ya	who/what
ta	he/this
eta	this
ima	this
amu	that
kim	what?
*eka**	one
ubha	both
dvi	two
ti	three
catu	four
tumha	you
amha	I/we

* Aggavaṃsa discusses *ekacca*, one/some, under *eka*. It is unclear why he includes numbers 1–4. Apart from *dvi*, which is historically dual, these are the only numbers which have three genders.

In western terms, Pali has personal, demonstrative, relative, interrogative, and indefinite pronouns:

category	English	Pali (nominative case)	
personal	I, you, he, she, it	*ahaṃ, tvaṃ, so, sā, taṃ*	
demonstrative	this, that, these, those	*so, sā, taṃ eso, esā, etaṃ*	*ayaṃ, ayaṃ, idaṃ amu, asu, aduṃ*
relative	who, whom, whose, which, that	*yo, yā, yaṃ*	
interrogative	who, whom, whose, which, what	*ko, kā, kiṃ*	
indefinite	anyone, anything, who/whatever	*koci, kāci, kiñci*	

Words which sound and may seem similar in English are in fact in different categories: pronouns, pronominal adjectives and adverbs. In Pali, pronouns and pronominal adjectives decline, but adverbs do not:

	Interrogative		Relative		Demonstrative			
	Pali	English	Pali	English	Pali		English	
pronouns, pronominal adjectives	*ko*	who, what, which?	*yo*	who, that, which	*so, sā, taṃ ayaṃ, idaṃ amu, asu, aduṃ*		this, that [or he, she, it]	
					Pali	English	Pali	English
adjectives	*kīdisa*	of what kind?	*yādisa*	of which kind	*tādisa*	of that kind?	*īdisa*	of this kind
	kittaka	how much?	*yattaka*	as many as however much	*tattaka*	so much	*ettaka*	this much
adverbs	*kva(ṃ) kuhim*	where?	*yattha, yahiṃ*	where	*tattha, tahiṃ amutra*	there	*idha, ittha, ettha, atra*	here
	kadā	when	*yadā*	when	*tadā*	then	*idāni etarahi*	now
	kuto	whence?	*yato*	whence, from where	*tato*	from there	*ito, ato*	from here
	kasmā	why, from what?	*yasmā*	because	*tasmā*	therefore		
	kathaṃ	how	*yathā*	(just) as	*iti, evam tathā*	so, thus	*itthaṃ*	thus

Nouns and most adjectives describe their referent, pronouns and pronominal adjectives simply point to it. The first and second person personal pronouns, I/we, you/you, do not have gender. They always act as pronouns and as noun-substitutes. Third person pronouns, when used both as personal and demonstrative pronouns, take the number and gender of that to which they refer. In practice the difference between calling a word a pronoun or a pronominal adjective can be minimal, given that the noun qualified by a pronominal adjective can be implicit.

(i) *sā bhuñjati*, she eats, *te bhuñjanti*, they eat, *na taṃ passanti*, they do not see him

(ii) *sā itthī bhuñjati*, that woman eats, *te bhikkhuno bhuñjanti*, those monks eat, *na imaṃ purisaṃ passanti*, they do not see this man

In (i) *sā*, *te* and *taṃ* are pronouns, she, they, and him, and their case is determined only by their role in the sentence (*sā*, *te* are nominative, *taṃ* accusative). In (ii) *sā*, *te* and *imaṃ* are pronominal adjectives, their gender and case being determined by the nouns *itthī*, *bhikkhuno*, and *purisaṃ*, which they qualify.

(iii) *sā taṃ rajjati* $=_1$ she loves him [pronoun]; and/or $=_2$ she loves this (man) [pronominal adjective qualifying the implicit noun *purisaṃ*]

Personal Pronouns:

I	you (singular)	he	she	it	we	you (plural)	they masculine	they feminine	they neuter
ahaṃ	*tvaṃ*	*so*	*sā*	*taṃ*	*amhe*	*tumhe*	*te*	*tā*	*tāni*
		eso	*esā*	*etaṃ*			*ete*	*etā*	*etāni*
		ayaṃ	*ayaṃ*	*idaṃ*			*ime*	*imā*	*idāni*
		amu	*asu*	*adu(ṃ)*			*amū*	*amū*	*amū(ni)*

The first persons *ahaṃ/amhe* are *attani vattabba*, to be spoken with regard to oneself.

The second persons *tvaṃ/tumhe* are *yena katheti tasmiṃ vattabba*, to be spoken with regard to the person with whom one is speaking.

Third person personal and demonstrative pronouns are described as follows, but as in English they are by no means always used in exactly this way:

PRONOUN	DESCRIPTION	REFERS TO SOMEONE OR SOMETHINGWHO/ WHICH IS:	
ta	*param-mukha*	not present	that
eta	*samīpa*	close by	this
ima	*accantasamīpa*	very close by	this (here)
amu	*dūra*	far away	[yonder]

Declension of *ahaṃ/amhe*, I/we, *tvaṃ/tumhe*, you.

SINGULAR	I	alternatives	you	alternatives
NOMINATIVE	*ahaṃ*		*tvaṃ*	*tuvaṃ*
ACCUSATIVE	*maṃ*	*mamaṃ*	*tvaṃ*	*taṃ, tuvaṃ*
INSTRUMENTAL	*mayā*		*tvayā*	*tayā*
DATIVE	*mama*	*mayhaṃ, mamaṃ, amhaṃ*	*tava*	*tuyhaṃ, tavaṃ, tumhaṃ*
ABLATIVE	*mayā*		*tvayā*	
GENITIVE	*mama*	*mayhaṃ, mamaṃ, amhaṃ*	*tava*	*tuyhaṃ, tavaṃ, tumhaṃ*
LOCATIVE	*mayi*		*tvayi*	*tayi*
PLURAL	we	alternatives	you	alternatives
NOMINATIVE	*mayaṃ*	*amhe*	*tumhe*	
ACCUSATIVE	*amhe*	*asme, asmākaṃ, amhākaṃ, amhaṃ*	*tumhe*	*tumhākaṃ*
INSTRUMENTAL	*amhehi*		*tumhehi*	*tumhebhi*
DATIVE	*amhākaṃ*	*asmākaṃ, amhaṃ*	*tumhākaṃ*	*tumhaṃ*
ABLATIVE	*amhehi*		*tumhehi*	*tumhebhi*
GENITIVE	*amhākaṃ*	*asmākaṃ, amhaṃ*	*tumhākaṃ*	*tumhaṃ*
LOCATIVE	*amhesu*		*tumhesu*	

These pronouns also have very common enclitic forms, which means that they never come first in a phrase or clause, and almost always refer to what immediately precedes them. [The word 'enclitic' comes from Greek 'to lean', referring to certain words without an accent which 'leant back' on the preceding word to give its last syllable a secondary accent.] They are:

	aham	*amhe*	*tvam*	*tumhe*
accusative		*no*		*vo*
instrumental	*me*	*no*	*te*	*vo*
dative	*me*	*no*	*te*	*vo*
genitive	*me*	*no*	*te*	*vo*

The use of first and second person pronouns, like imperatives, is affected by social hierarchy. The first person plural is likely to replace the first person singular, for reasons of politeness, especially but not only when speaking to someone in a superior position. The second singular is used for intimates and inferiors, as with French *tu* and German *du*.

Declension of the third person personal/demonstrative pronouns or pronominal adjectives *sa/esa*:

	MASCULINE	alternatives	FEMININE	alternatives	NEUTER	alternatives
SINGULAR	he		she		it	
NOMINATIVE	*so*	*sa*	*sā*		*taṃ*	
ACCUSATIVE	*taṃ*		*taṃ*		*taṃ*	
INSTRUMENTAL	*tena*		*tāya*		*tena*	
DATIVE	*tassa*		*tāya*	*tassā, tissā(ya)*	*tassa*	
ABLATIVE	*tasmā*	*tamhā*	*tāya*		*tasmā*	*tamhā*
GENITIVE	*tassa*		*tāya*	*tassā, tissā(ya)*	*tassa*	
LOCATIVE	*tasmiṃ*	*tamhi*	*tāya*	*tayaṃ, tissaṃ*	*tasmiṃ*	*tamhi*
PLURAL	they		they		they	
NOMINATIVE	*te*		*tā*		*tāni*	
ACCUSATIVE	*te*		*tā*		*tāni*	
INSTRUMENTAL	*tehi*	*tebhi*	*tāhi*		*tehi*	*tebhi*
DATIVE	*tesaṃ*	*tesānaṃ*	*tāsaṃ*	*tāsānaṃ*	*tesaṃ*	*tesānaṃ*
ABLATIVE	*tehi*	*tebhi*	*tāhi*		*tehi*	*tebhi*
GENITIVE	*tesaṃ*	*tesānaṃ*	*tāsaṃ*	*tāsānaṃ*	*tesaṃ*	*tesānaṃ*
LOCATIVE	*tesu*		*tāsu*		*tesu*	

There is a defective pronoun—defective because it only appears in some cases—based on the stem *-na*, which has the same range of meaning as *sa/esa*:

naṃ and *enaṃ* occur as accusative singular masculine, feminine, and neuter
nassa occurs as dative and genitive singular, masculine and neuter
ne occurs as accusative plural masculine
nesaṃ occurs as dative and genitive plural masculine

Declension of the third person personal/demonstrative pronouns or pronominal adjectives *ayaṃ*, *idaṃ*:

SINGULAR	MASCULINE	alternatives	FEMININE	alternatives	NEUTER	alternatives
NOMINATIVE	*ayaṃ*		*ayaṃ*		*idaṃ*	
ACCUSATIVE	*imaṃ*		*imaṃ*		*idaṃ*	*imaṃ*
INSTRUMENTAL	*iminā*	*anena*	*imāya*		*iminā*	*anena*
DATIVE	*imassa*	*assa*	*imāya*	*imissā(ya)* *assā(ya)*	*imassa*	*assa*
ABLATIVE	*imasmā*	*imambhā*, *asmā*	*imāya*		*imasmā*	*imambhā*, *asmā*
GENITIVE	*imassa*	*assa*	*imāya*	*imassā(ya) assāya*	*imassa*	*assa*
LOCATIVE	*imasmiṃ*	*asmiṃ*	*imāya*	*imissā*, *imissaṃ* *imāyaṃ*, *assaṃ*	*imasmiṃ*	*asmiṃ*
PLURAL	MASCULINE	alternatives	FEMININE	alternatives	NEUTER	alternatives
NOMINATIVE	*ime*		*imā*	*imāyo*	*imāni*	
ACCUSATIVE	*ime*		*imā*	*imāyo*	*imāni*	
INSTRUMENTAL	*imehi*	*ehi*	*imāhi*		*imehi*	*ehi*
DATIVE	*imesaṃ*	*esaṃ*, *esānaṃ* *imesānaṃ*	*imāsaṃ*	*imāsānaṃ*, *āsaṃ*	*imesaṃ*	*esaṃ*, *esānaṃ* *imesānaṃ*
ABLATIVE	*imehi*	*ehi*	*imāhi*		*imehi*	*ehi*
GENITIVE	*imesaṃ*	*esaṃ*, *esānaṃ* *imesānaṃ*	*imāsaṃ*	*imāsānaṃ*, *āsaṃ*	*imesaṃ*	*esaṃ*, *esānaṃ* *imesānaṃ*
LOCATIVE	*imesu*	*esu*	*imāsu*		*imesu*	*esu*

Declension of the third person personal/demonstrative pronouns or pronominal adjectives *asu/amu*, *aduṃ*:

SINGULAR	MASCULINE	alternatives	FEMININE	alternatives	NEUTER	alternatives
NOMINATIVE	*asu*	*amu*	*asu*		*aduṃ*	
ACCUSATIVE	*amuṃ*		*amuṃ*		*aduṃ*	*amuṃ*
INSTRUMENTAL	*amunā*		*amuyā*		*amunā*	
DATIVE	*amussa*		*amuyā*	*amussā*	*amussa*	
ABLATIVE	*amusmā*	*amumhā*	*amuyā*		*amusmā*	*amumhā*
GENITIVE	*amussa*		*amuyā*	*amussā*	*amussa*	
LOCATIVE	*amusmiṃ*	*amumhi*	*amuyaṃ*	*amussaṃ*	*amusmiṃ*	*amumhi*

PLURAL	MASCULINE	alternatives	FEMININE	alternatives	NEUTER	alternatives
NOMINATIVE	*amū*		*amū*	*amuyo*	*amū*	*amūni*
ACCUSATIVE	*amū*		*amū*	*amuyo*	*amū*	*amūni*
INSTRUMENTAL	*amūhi*		*amūhi*		*amūhi*	
DATIVE	*amūsaṃ*	*amūsānaṃ*	*amūsaṃ*	*amūsānaṃ*	*amūsaṃ*	*amūsānaṃ*
ABLATIVE	*amūhi*		*amūhi*		*amūhi*	
GENITIVE	*amūsaṃ*	*amūsanaṃ*	*amūsaṃ*	*amūsanaṃ*	*amūsaṃ*	*amūsanaṃ*
LOCATIVE	*amūsu*		*amūsu*		*amūsu*	

amu is rare in itself, being found more often in the adverb *amutra*, there, and the adjectives *asuka* or *amuka*, which mean a certain, usually in a narrative where they indicate that the name of the person, thing or place concerned is of no importance.

The following pronominal and related forms in English have no direct correlate in Pali:

possessive pronouns: mine, yours, his, hers, its, ours, theirs
possessive adjectives: my, your, his, her, its, our, their, ones
reflexive pronouns: myself, yourself, himself, herself, itself, ourselves, yourselves, oneself

Interrogative pronouns and pronominal adjectives are used in *pucchanā*, questioning

SINGULAR	MASCULINE	alternatives	FEMININE	alternatives	NEUTER	alternatives
NOMINATIVE	*ko*		*kā*		*kiṃ*	
ACCUSATIVE	*kaṃ*		*kaṃ*		*kiṃ*	
INSTRUMENTAL	*kena*		*kāya*		*kena*	
DATIVE	*kassa*		*kāya*	*kassā, kissā*	*kassa*	
ABLATIVE	*kasmā*	*kismā*	*kāya*		*kasmā*	*kismā*
GENITIVE	*kassa*	*kissa*	*kāya*	*kassā, kissā*	*kassa*	*kissa*
LOCATIVE	*kasmiṃ*	*kamhi, kismiṃ, kamhi*	*kāya*	*kayaṃ kissaṃ,*	*kasmiṃ*	*kamhi, kismiṃ, kamhi*
PLURAL	MASCULINE	alternatives	FEMININE	alternatives	NEUTER	alternatives
NOMINATIVE	*ke*		*kā*	*kāyo*	*ke*	
ACCUSATIVE	*ke*		*kā*		*ke*	
INSTRUMENTAL	*kehi*	*kebhi*	*kāhi*		*kehi*	*kebhi*
DATIVE	*kesaṃ*	*kesānaṃ*	*kāsaṃ*	*kāsānaṃ*	*kesaṃ*	*kesānaṃ*
ABLATIVE	*kehi*	*kebhi*	*kāhi*		*kehi*	*kebhi*
GENITIVE	*kesaṃ*	*kesānaṃ*	*kāsaṃ*	*kāsānaṃ*	*kesaṃ*	*kesānaṃ*
LOCATIVE	*kesu*		*kāsu*		*kesu*	

kiṃ is the form taken in compounds.

Relative pronouns and pronominal adjectives are *aniyamattha*, of undetermined meaning (undetermined, that is, until they are determined by their correlative).

SINGULAR	MASCULINE	alternatives	FEMININE	alternatives	NEUTER	alternatives
NOMINATIVE	*yo*		*yā*		*yaṃ*	
ACCUSATIVE	*yaṃ*		*yaṃ*		*yaṃ*	
INSTRUMENTAL	*yena*		*yāya*		*yena*	
DATIVE	*yassa*		*yāya*	*yassā*	*yassa*	
ABLATIVE	*yasmā*	*yamhā*	*yāya*		*yasmā*	*yamhā*
GENITIVE	*yassa*		*yāya*	*yassā*	*yassa*	
LOCATIVE	*yasmiṃ*	*yamhi*	*yāya*	*yāyaṃ*	*yasmiṃ*	*yamhi*
PLURAL	MASCULINE	alternatives	FEMININE	alternatives	NEUTER	alternatives
NOMINATIVE	*ye*		*yā*		*yāni*	
ACCUSATIVE	*ye*		*yā*		*yāni*	
INSTRUMENTAL	*yehi*	*yebhi*	*yāhi*		*yehi*	*yebhi*
DATIVE	*yesaṃ*	*yesānaṃ*	*yāsaṃ*	*yāsānaṃ*	*yesaṃ*	*yesānaṃ*
ABLATIVE	*yehi*	*yebhi*	*yāhi*		*yehi*	*yebhi*
GENITIVE	*yesaṃ*	*yesānaṃ*	*yāsaṃ*	*yāsānaṃ*	*yesaṃ*	*yesānaṃ*
LOCATIVE	*yesu*		*yāsu*		*yesu*	

Relative clauses in Pali often cause trouble to students who have not studied an inflected language before. These are are some basic principles to remember:

> They can be introduced by a relative pronoun (e.g. who, which), a relative adverb (e.g. when, where), or a relative adjective (e.g. of which kind, as many... [as]), which usually has a correlative in the main clause: *tādisa... yādisa*, *tattaka... yattaka*

Relative clauses occur less in Pali than in English because Pali, like Sanskrit and to a lesser extent German, has the ability to make up compounds ad hoc which replace relative clauses. To understand the grammatical form of relative pronouns the vital principle to remember is this:

Relative pronouns take their number and gender from the antecedent, but their case from their function in the relative clause.

The generalizing who/whatever... is expressed either by repeating both relative and antecedent, or by adding *koci*, *kāci*, *kiñci*, etc. to the relative clause, with a single antecedent

sace kho ahaṃ yo yo paresaṃ adinnaṃ theyyasaṅkhātaṃ ādiyissati, tassa tassa dhanam anuppadassāmi, evamidaṃ adinnādānaṃ pavaḍḍhissati,
if I give money to whomever steals from others, then his stealing will increase (D III 67).
tesaṃ tucchaṃ musā vilāpo ye keci atthikavādaṃ vadanti,
whoever professes the doctrine that there is reality (to merit, another world, etc.) is (characterized by) vanity, falsehood, mendacity (D I 55, said by a non-Buddhist)

Various uses of relatives cannot be translated literally in English:
anacchariyaṃ kho pan' etaṃ Ānanda, yaṃ manussabhūto kālaṃ kareyya,
it is not surprising, Ananda, that a human being should die (D II 93).
n' esa dhammo, mahārāja, yaṃ tvaṃ gaccheyya ekako,
it is not right, great king, that you should go alone (Ja VI 495).

The form *yadidaṃ* is used in various ways:
akaraṇīyā va bho Gotama Vajjī raññā Ajātasattunā, yadidam yuddhassa aññatra upalāpanāya aññatra mithu-bhedā,
Gotama sir, king Ajatasattu cannot beat the Vajjis, that is to say, simply by means of war, without deceit and causing dissension (D II 75).
cirassaṃ kho, bhante, bhagavā imaṃ pariyāyam akāsi yadidaṃ idhāgamanāya,
it is a long time (since) the Blessed One made the resolution to come here (D III 2).

yadagge or yadaggena is used in the sense of beginning with, from that time on:
mānusakaṃ vassasataṃ atītaṃ yadagge kāyamhi idhūpapanno,
A thousand human years have passed since I arose here in a [divine] body (Vv 129).

2.3 *saṃkhyā*, Numerals

Both cardinal and ordinal numbers can take many different forms. Those given here are a selection.

Cardinal numbers can be:

adjectives, *saṃkhyeyya-padhāna*, where the superordinate is to be enumerated (*cattāro purisā*, four people) or

nouns, *saṃkhyā-padhāna*, where the enumeration is the superordinate (*devānaṃ koṭisataṃ*, hundreds of millions of gods [lit. a hundred ten-millions]).

Ordinal numbers are *saṃkhyā-pūraṇa*, that which completes a count

1. *eka*, one (some)

SINGULAR	MASCULINE	alternatives	FEMININE	alternatives	NEUTER	alternatives
NOMINATIVE	*eko*		*ekā*		*ekaṃ*	
ACCUSATIVE	*ekaṃ*		*ekaṃ*		*ekaṃ*	
INSTRUMENTAL	*ekena*		*ekāya*		*ekena*	
DATIVE	*ekassa*		*ekāya*	*ekassā, ekissā(ya)*	*ekassa*	
ABLATIVE	*ekasmā*	*ekamhā*	*ekāya*		*ekasmā*	*ekamhā*
GENITIVE	*ekassa*		*ekāya*	*ekassā, ekissā(ya)*	*ekassa*	
LOCATIVE	*ekasmiṃ*	*ekamhi*	*ekāya(ṃ)*	*ekissā, ekissaṃ*	*ekasmiṃ*	*ekamhi*
PLURAL	MASCULINE	alternatives	FEMININE	alternatives	NEUTER	alternatives
NOMINATIVE	*eke*		*ekā*		*ekāni*	
ACCUSATIVE	*eke*		*ekā*		*ekāni*	
INSTRUMENTAL	*ekehi*	*ekebhi*	*ekāhi*		*ekehi*	*ekebhi*
DATIVE	*ekesaṃ*	*ekesānaṃ*	*ekāsaṃ*	*ekāsānaṃ*	*ekesaṃ*	*ekesānaṃ*
ABLATIVE	*ekehi*	*ekebhi*	*ekāhi*		*ekehi*	*ekebhi*
GENITIVE	*ekesaṃ*	*ekesānaṃ*	*ekāsaṃ*	*ekāsānaṃ*	*ekesaṃ*	*ekesānaṃ*
LOCATIVE	*ekesu*		*ekāsu*		*ekesu*	

In the plural *eka* means some. It can be used like the English indefinite article, a, or a certain; as an adjective it can have other meanings, e.g. alone.

2, 3, *dvi*, *ti*

2. *dvi*		3. *ti*		
ALL GENDERS		MASCULINE	FEMININE	NEUTER
NOMINATIVE	*dve, duve*	*tayo*	*tisso*	*tīṇi*
ACCUSATIVE	*dve, duve*	*tayo*	*tisso*	*tīṇi*
INSTRUMENTAL	*dvībhi*	*tībhi*	*tībhi*	*tībhi*
DATIVE	*dvinnaṃ*	*tiṇṇaṃ tiṇṇannaṃ*	*tissannaṃ*	*tinnaṃ tinnannaṃ*
ABLATIVE	*dvībhi*	*tībhi*	*tībhi*	*tībhi*
GENITIVE	*dvinnaṃ*	*tiṇṇaṃ tinnannaṃ*	*tissannaṃ*	*tinnaṃ tiṇṇannaṃ*
LOCATIVE	*dvīsu*	*tīsu*	*tīsu*	*tīsu*
in compounds *di-*, *du-*, *dvā-*, *dve-*		in compounds *ti-*		

4, 5, *catu*, *pañca*

4. *catu*	MASCULINE	FEMININE	NEUTER
NOMINATIVE	*cattāro, caturo*	*catasso*	*cattāri*
ACCUSATIVE	*cattāro, caturo*	*catasso*	*cattāri*
INSTRUMENTAL	*catū̆hi*	*catū̆hi*	*catū̆hi*
DATIVE	*catunnaṃ*	*catassannaṃ*	*catunnaṃ*
ABLATIVE	*catū̆hi*	*catū̆hi*	*catū̆hi*
GENITIVE	*catunnaṃ*	*catassannaṃ*	*catunnaṃ*
LOCATIVE	*catū̆su*	*catū̆su*	*catū̆su*
in compounds *catu-*			

5. *pañca*
pañca
pañca
pañcahi
pañcannaṃ
pañcahi
pañcannaṃ
pañcasu
in compounds *pañca*

6 to 18 are either used undeclined or are declined like *pañca*.

6. *cha(ḷ)*	11. *ekādasa, ekārasa*	16. *soḷasa, sorasa*
7. *satta*	12. *dvādasa, bārasa*	17. *sattadasa, sattarasa*
8. *aṭṭha*	13. *terasa, teḷasa*	18. *aṭṭhadasa, aṭṭharasa*
9. *nava*	14. *catuddasa, cuddasa*	
10. *dasa*	15. *pañcadasa, pannarasa, paṇṇarasa*	

19 and following:

numbers ending in *-i* are declined like *jāti* (singular)
numbers ending in *-ā* are declined like *kaññā* (singular)
numbers ending in *-aṃ* are declined like *rūpaṃ* (singular and plural)

19. *ekūnavisati (20 minus one)*	30. *tiṃsati, tiṃsā, tiṃsaṃ, tiṃsa*
20. *vīsati, vīsā, vīsaṃ, vīsa*	40. *cattālisa, cattārisa*
21. *ekavīsati*	50. *paññāsa, paññāsaṃ, paññāsā*
22. *dvāvīsati, bavisa*	60. *saṭṭhi*
23. *tevīsati*	70. *sattati, sattari*
24. *catuvīsati*	80. *asīti*
25. *pañcavīsati*	90. *navuti*
26. *chabbīsati*	100. *sataṃ*
27. *sattavīsati*	1000. *sahassaṃ*
28. *aṭṭhavīsati*	100,000. *satasahassaṃ, lakkhaṃ*
29. *ekūnatiṃsati*	10,000,000. *koṭi*

Numbers are used with other words in various ways:

ekūnatiṃso vayasā... / yaṃ pabbajiṃ,
I was twenty-nine (years) of age when I went forth (D II 151),

seyyathāpi brāhmaṇa kukkuṭiyā aṇḍāni aṭṭha vā dasa vā dvadasa vā tān' assu,
just as, brahmin, a hen might have eight or ten or twelve eggs (Vin I 3),

aṭṭha cat tarīsaṃ vassāni / komārabrahmacariyaṃ cariṃsu te,
for forty-eight years they led the celibate life of youth (Sn 289),

saddhaṃ viriyaṃ samādhiñ ca satipaññañ ca bhāvayaṃ / pañca pañcahi hantvāna...,
developing confidence, energy, concentration, mindfulnes and wisdom, striking the five [senses] with the[se] five,... (Th 745),

tesaṃ kho pana bhikkhu caturāsītiyā nagarasahassānam ekañ ñeva taṃ nagaraṃ hoti yaṃ aham tena samayena ajjhāvasami Kusāvātī rājadhānī,
monk, of the eighty-four thousand cities there was but one city in which I lived at that time, the royal city of Kusavati (S III 145),

tīhi ākārehi tisso vijjā samāpajjiṃ... tissannaṃ vijjānaṃ lābhi 'mhi,
in three ways I will attain the three knowledges... I have acquired the three knowledges (Vin III 94),

taṇhādhanusamuṭṭhānaṃ dve ca pannarasāyutaṃ / passa...,
see (the arrow) which comes from the bow of craving, connected with the twice fifteen (wrong views) (Th 753),

asītiko me vayo vattati,
I am eighty years old (D II 100).

Numbers, especially high ones, are used in compounds: *dvisataṃ*, two hundred; *satasahassaṃ*, one hundred thousand.

Ordinal numbers are used in the same way as other adjectives:

first	*paṭhama*
second	*dutiya*
third	*tatiya*
fourth	*catuttha*
fifth	*pañcama*
sixth	*chaṭṭhama, chaṭṭha*
seventh	*sattama*
eighth	*aṭṭhama*
ninth	*navama*
tenth	*dasama*

eleventh	*ekādasama, ekādasa, ekārasa*
twelfth	*dvādasama, dvādasa, bārasa*
thirteenth	*terasama, terasa*
fourteenth	*catuddasama, cātuddasa, cuddasa*
fifteenth	*pañcadasama, pannarasama, paṇṇarasa*
sixteenth	*soḷasama, soḷasa*
seventeenth	*sattadasama, sattadasa*
eighteenth	*aṭṭhādasama, aṭṭhadasa*
nineteenth	*ekūnavisatima*
twentieth	*vīsatima, vīsa*
twenty-first	*ekavīsatima*
thirtieth	*tiṃsatima, tiṃsa*
fortieth	*cattaḷīsatima, cattaḷīsa*
fiftieth	*paññasatima, paññasa*
sixtieth	*saṭṭhima*
seventieth	*sattatima*
eightieth	*asītitama, asīta*
ninetieth	*navutima, navuta*
one hundredth	*satama. satatama*
one thousandth	*sahassama. sahassatama*

Ordinals above one thousandth are the same as cardinals, declined in *-a*. Sometimes cardinal numbers are used as ordinals, especially in compounds:

ito so... ekanavutikappo yaṃ aham anussarāmi,
I can remember (as far as) the ninety-first eon (ago) from now (S IV 324),
tiṃsativassamhi mato,
I died in my thirtieth year (Thī 443).

There are various numeral suffixes, such as:
- *ka*: *ekaka*, consisting of one; *duka*, dyad, pair; *tika*, triad, *pañcaka*, group of five,
- *iṃ*: *sakiṃ*, once,
- *dhā*: *ekadhā*, in one way, *sattadhā*. sevenfold, *sahassadhā*, thousandfold,
- *kkhattuṃ*: *dvittikkhattuṃ*, two or three times, *dasakkhattuṃ*, ten times.

3 *ākhyāta*
Verbs

3.1. Introduction

The conjugation of verbs consists in:

(i) a root (*dhātu*)
(ii) a personal ending (*paccaya*, *vibhatti*),

and sometimes

(iii) suffixes added to the root before an ending (*no*) *vikaraṇa* (*-paccaya*)
(iv) an augment (prefix) *a-* (*akārāgama*)
(v) reduplication (*abbhāsa)* of the root vowel.

Sanskrit grammarians divided verbs into ten classes, referring to them by one of the roots each class contained: *bhū-ādi gaṇā*, (verb) categories such as (that beginning with) *bhū*. Pali grammarians used more than one scheme of classification, similar to but never the same as the Sanskrit. These are the classes used in Sanskrit, by Aggavaṃsa and Kaccāyana (followed here), by Moggallāna, the *Bālāvatāra*, *Dhātumañjusā*, and by the *Dhātupāṭha*:

gaṇa	Sanskrit	Kaccāyana, Aggavaṃsa	Moggallāna, *Bālāvatāra, Dhātumañjusā*	*Dhātupāṭha*
1	*bhū*	*bhū*	*bhū*	*bhū*
2	*ad*	*rudh*	*rudh*	*rudh*
3	*hū*	*div*	*div*	*div*
4	*div*	*su*	*su*	*tud*
5	*su*	*kī*	*kī* (includes √ *gah*)	*ji*
6	*tud*	*gah*	*tan*	*kī*
7	*rudh*	*tan*	*cur*	*su*
8	*tan*	*cur*		*tan*
9	*krī*			*cur*
10	*cur*			

Learning the enumeration of these classes is not so important in Pali as in Sanskrit: it is more important to know the sound and orthographic changes, and what suffix each verb takes. This is the scheme used by Kaccāyana and Aggavaṃsa:

gaṇa	*dhātu*		*paccaya*	examples
	Sanskrit	Pali		
1[1]	*bhū*	*bhū*	*a*	√*bhū* → *bhavati* (be), √*nī* → *nayati* (lead), √*hṛ* → *harati* (carry), √*sru* → *savati* (flow)
2	*rudh*	*rudh*	*majjhaṭṭhāne niggahītāgamo* (with *ṃ* infixed)	√*rudh* → *rundhati* (obstruct), √*chid* → *chindati* (cut), √*bhuj* → *bhuñjati* (eat), √*lip* → *limpati* (smear)
3	*div*	*div*	*ya*	√*div* → *dibbati* (play), √*yudh* → *yujjhati* (fight), √*mlā* → *milāyati* (fade), √*man* → *maññati* (think)
4	*śru*	*su*	*nu, no, nā. unā*	√*su* → *suṇāti or suṇoti* (hear), √*śak* → *sakkoti* (be able), √*pra-āp* → *pāpuṇoti or pāpuṇāti* (obtain)
5	*kṝ*	*kī*	*nā or no*	√*kṝ* → *kiṇāti or kiṇoti* (buy), √ *jñā* → *jānāti* (know)
6	*gṛh*	*gah*	*ppa ṇhā*	√*gah* → *gheppati* or gaṇhāti*
7[1]	*tan*	*tan*	*o*	√*tan* → *tanoti* (stretch), √*kṛ* → *karoti* (do, *weak stem kuru-*), √*pra-āp* → *pappoti* (obtain)
8[2]	*cur*	*cur*	*e, aya*	√*cur* → *corayati or coreti* (steal), √*pūj* → *pūjeti* (worship), √*dis* → *deseti* (teach)

[1] Root vowel can take *guṇa*.

[2] Root vowel can take *guṇa* or *vṛddhi*.

* This form is standardly given by grammarians, although it has not yet been cited in use.

Verbs express agency is various ways:

there are the four agents mentioned in the accounts of the nominative and accusative cases (p. 42ff. above)

the agent pure and simple (*suddhakattā*), expressed by the nominative or, with passive verbs, the instrumental case

the causal agent (*hetukattā*), the subject of a causative verb

the object-agent (*kammakattā*), the subject of passive verbs used reflexively,

the agent-object (*kattukamma*), the secondary agent caused to act by a causative verb.

There are also two forms of passive verb (Sadd 6ff.):

the *kammakiriyāpada*, verb which expresses the action of the object

the *bhāvakiriyāpada*, verb which expresses a state-of-being.

Verbs can be *sakammaka* or *akammaka*, with an object or without an object. These terms are often translated as transitive and intransitive, but more precisely they refer to the presence or absence of an object, a *kamma*. An intransitive verb, such as a verb of motion, need have no *kamma*, transitive verbs have one, causative verbs usually have at least two. Aggavaṃsa gives as examples of *tikammaka* verbs, verbs with three objects (Sadd 12),

suvaṇṇaṃ kaṭakaṃ poso kāreti purisaṃ,

a man has a man make a gold bracelet, and

puriso purisaṃ gāmaṃ rathaṃ vāheti,

a man has a man drive a cart to a village.

It is possible, though by no means necessary, that the addition of a prefix changes a verb from *akammaka* to *sakammaka*: *vadati*, speak; *upavadati*, criticize; *patati*, fall; *adhipatati*, fall on, attack.

The following is an analysis of two sentences with *sakammaka* verbs, in Western terms Active and Passive, *itthī pacati odānaṃ*, the woman cooks rice, and *odāno pacīyati itthiyā*, rice is cooked by the woman.

In the first, *itthī* is an agent expressed by the nominative case (*abhihitakattā*, *pathamā vibhatti*), while *odānaṃ* is a direct object not expressed by the verb, but by the accusative case (*anabhihitakamma*, *dutiyā vibhatti*). In it:

the root √*pac* expresses the action (*kiriyā*) of cooking

the ending *-ti* expresses the idea of an agent (*kattā*)

the nominative *itthī* is in apposition to *-ti* and refers to the same agent
the accusative *odānaṃ* expresses an object of action not already expressed in the verb.
Thus there is an action, *pac*, qualified by an agent, *itthī*, and by an object, *odānaṃ*.
In the second, *odāno* is an object expressed by the nominative case (*abhihitakamma*, *pathamā vibhatti)*, while *itthiyā* is an agent unexpressed by the verb, but by the instrumental (*anabhihitakattā*, *tatiyā vibhatti*). In it:
the root √*pac* expresses the action of cooking, and it has an object, the rice
the ending *-ti* on a passive stem expresses the idea of an object
the nominative *odāno* is in apposition to *-ti* and refers to the same object
the instrumental *itthiyā* expresses the idea of an agent not already present in the verb.
Thus there is an action, *pac*, qualified by an object, *odāno*, and by an agent, *itthiyā*.

parassapada, *attanopada*, word for another, word for oneself, usually translated Active and Middle Voice, are terms which only rarely indicate differences in meaning. They refer to alternative sets of endings, which can be used for *sakammaka* and *akammaka* verbs. When there is difference in sense, it is this:

parassapadāni parassa atthabhūtāni padāni, words for someone else are words whose aim (goal, benefit, etc.) is for someone other (than the subject) (Sadd 16): e.g. *itthī odānaṃ pacati*, the woman cooks rice

attanopadāni attano atthabhūtāni padāni, words for oneself are words whose aim (goal, benefit, etc.) is oneself (= the subject) (ibid.): e.g. *itthī odānaṃ pacate*, the woman cooks herself rice

3.2. *tyādayo vibhattiyo*, endings such as ti (i.e Conjugations)

ākhyātassa kiriyālakkhaṇattasucikā tyādayo vibhattiyo.
Endings such as *ti*, etc. indicate the character of the action (performed by) a verb (Sadd 13). They are also called *purisasaññā*, designations for person.
vibhattī ti ken' atthena... kālādivasena dhātvattham vibhajatī ti vibhatti,
(When people say, in relation to verbs) 'Division,' what does division mean? Division is when one divides the meaning of a root, in terms of time, etc. (Sadd 15).

These forms of the verb are what Western grammar would see as Conjugations, divided into tenses, moods, and systems: Pali has

a) three tenses, Past (aorist), Present and Future
b) four moods, Indicative, Imperative, Optative and Conditional. (Unlike English, the Pali optative can have differing tenses.)
c) four systems, i.e. groups of conjugations, the Causative, Desiderative, Intensive and Denominative. These systems are neither tenses nor moods: in principle they can have all the tenses, moods and voices available to the simple form of the verb, but in practice, while the causative is very frequent in all tenses and moods, the Desiderative, Intensive, and Denominative are rarely used in other than the indicative present active.

Pali follows the Sanskrit norm in that, as a general rule:

a) it derives the Present Indicative, the Imperative, and the Optative from the present stem
b) it derives everything else from the root.

However, very much more frequently than Sanskrit, other conjugations are also derived from the present stem. For example
√*gam*, go, has the present stem *gacch-*, from which are derived:
present indicative *gacchati*, imperative *gacchatu*, optative *gaccheyya*.
Other forms can be derived directly from √*gam*, and also from *gacch*.

	ROOT	PRESENT STEM		ROOT	PRESENT STEM
FUTURE	*gamissati*	*gacchissati*	INFINITIVE	*gantuṃ*	*gacchituṃ*
AORIST	*agami*	*agacchi*	FUTURE PASSIVE PARTICIPLE	*gantabba*	*gacchitabba*
CAUSATIVE	*gamāpeti*	*gacchāpeti*	ABSOLUTIVE	*gantvā*	*gacchitvā*
PAST PASSIVE PARTICIPLE	*gata**	*gacchita*	PASSIVE	*gamīyati*	*gacchīyati*

* this is from an original root √*gṃ → *gṃta → gata, not from √gam. It is inaccurate to say that the m from √gam is dropped.

Of the nine Pāṇinian verbal classes given in 1.3 above Pali grammarians ignored the periphrastic future (3. *śvastanī*), and provided rules and definitions for the other eight, although the perfect (2. *parokkhā*) and imperfect (6. *hiyyatanī*) were almost wholly absent from the Pali texts which preceded them. In what follows the definitions and examples of the six conjugations actually used are taken from Aggavaṃsa (Sadd 812ff.), in the order that he, like Kaccāyana, deals with them. Endings are:

		paṭhama ekavacana	*paṭhama bahuvacana*	*majjhima ekavacana*	*majjhima bahuvacana*	*uttama ekavacana*	*uttama bahuvacana*
vattamānā	*parassapada*	*ti*	*anti*	*si*	*ttha*	*mi*	*ma*
present	*attanopada*	*te*	*ante*	*se*	*vhe*	*e*	*mhe*
pañcamī	*parassapada*	*tu*	*antu*	*hi*	*tha*	*mi*	*ma*
imperative	*attanopada*	*taṃ*	*antaṃ*	*su*	*vho*	*e*	*āmase*
sattamī	*parassapada*	*eyya*	*eyyuṃ*	*eyyāsi*	*eyyātha*	*eyyāmi*	*eyyāma*
optative	*attanopada*	*etha*	*eraṃ*	*etho*	*eyyavho*	*eyyaṃ*	*eyyāmhe*
ajjattanī	*parassapada*	*a*	*u*	*e*	*ttha*	*a*	*mhă*
aorist	*attanopada*	*ttha*	*re*	*ttho*	*vho*	*i*	*mhe*
bhavissantī	*parassapada*	*ssati*	*ssanti*	*ssasi*	*ssatha*	*ssāmi*	*ssāma*
future	*attanopada*	*ssate*	*ssante*	*ssase*	*ssavhe*	*ssaṃ*	*ssāmhe*
kālatipatti	*parassapada*	*ssā*	*ssaṃsu*	*sse*	*ssatha*	*ssaṃ*	*ssamha*
conditional	*attanopada*	*ssatha*	*ssiṃsu*	*ssase*	*ssavhe*	*ssaṃ*	*ssamhāse*

Conjugation of the *vattamānā* (present): Present Indicative verbs in *-a*, *-e* and *-o*:

	ACTIVE			MIDDLE		
	√*gam*	√*kṛ*	√*dis*	√*gam*	√*kṛ*	√*dis*
SINGULAR 1	*gacchāmi**	*karomi*	*desemi*	*gacche*	*[kubbe**]*	*desaye****
2	*gacchasi*	*karosi*	*desesi*	*gacchase*	*kuruse*	*desayase*
3	*gacchati*	*karoti*	*deseti*	*gacchate*	*kurute*	*desayate*
PLURAL 1	*gacchāma*	*karoma*	*desema*	*gacchamhe*	*kurumhe*	*desayamhe*
2	*gacchatha*	*karotha*	*desetha*	*gacchavhe*	*kuruvhe*	*desayavhe*
3	*gacchanti*	*karonti*	*desenti*	*gacchante or gacchare*	*kurunte*	*desayante or desayare*

* in the present tense, and anywhere else it occurs, the first person singular. ending *-āmi* can drop the final *i*, thus *gacchāmi* → **gacchāṃ* → *gacchaṃ* by the Law of Mora.

** root √*kṛ* in Sanskrit has a strong form *kar-* and a weak *kurv-*. In Pali the latter can become *kubb-* or *kuru-*. There is a present middle *kubbe*, *kubbase*, *kubbate*, etc., of which the first person singular is given here since the form in *kuru-* does not have one.

*** verbs in *–aya-* or *–e-* always use *–aya-* in their middle forms

paccuppanne kāle vattamānā, the present is for contemporary time (Sadd 812–3)

(i) *kāle ti c'ettha kiriyā adhippetā. Bhagavā Sāvatthiyaṃ viharati Jetavane.*
The action/verb is intended here (for) '(this) time.' The Blessed One is living in the Jeta grove at Savatthi.

(ii) *taṃsamīpe 'tīte* , (and) for the recent past
tassa paccuppannassa kālassa samīpe tabbohārūpacārato atīte kāle vattamānā vibhatti hoti: kuto nu tvaṃ bhikkhu āgacchasi, ettha ca āgantvā nisinno so bhikkhū ti daṭṭhabbaṃ.
The present conjugation is (used) for past time as an idiomatic, secondary meaning when it is close to the current time. It is to be understood (from sentences such as) 'where have you come from, monk?' and 'this monk has come here and sat down.'

(iii) *yāva pure purāyoge 'nāgate*, (and) to the future with *(the nipāta-s) yāva pure, purā*
yāva pure purā icc etesaṃ nipātānaṃ yoge anāgate kāle vattamānā vibhatti hoti: yāvad eva anatthāya ñattaṃ bālassa jayati, pure adhammo dippati, dante ime chinda purā marāmi, purā vassati devo.

The present conjugation is (used) for future time in connection with these *nipāta*-s: *yāva*, *pure*, *purā*. 'a reputation for skill arises for a fool only to his disadvantage,' 'before non-Dhamma gains luster,' 'cut these tusks before I die,' ' before it rains.'

(iv) *ekaṃsāvassambhāviyāniyāmatthesu*, (and to the future) in the sense of what is certain, inevitable or uncertain

ekaṃsatthe avassambhāviyatthe aniyamatthe ca icc etesu atthesu anāgate kale vattamānā vibhatti hoti. ekaṃsatthe tāva: nirayaṃ nanu gacchāmi n' atthi me ettha saṃsayo, avassambhaviyatthe: dhuvaṃ buddho bhavām' ahaṃ; aniyamatthe: manasā ce paduṭṭhena bhāsati vā karoti vā ettha hi kālaniyamo na kato.

The present conjugation is (used) for future time in these meanings: inevitability, certainty, undeterminedness. Inevitability: 'I will go to hell, I've no doubt about that.' Certainty: 'I will certainly become a Buddha.' Undeterminedness: in this (sentence) 'If one speaks or acts with evil mind,' no determination as to time is made.

(v) *matantare kadā-karahīnaṃ yoge vā*, or, in (the Teachers') opinion, with *kadā*, *karahi*

garūnaṃ matantare kadā karahi icc etesaṃ yoge anāgate kale vattamānā vibhatti hoti vā kadā gacchati, karahi gacchati vā ti kiṃ kadā bhante gamissati, karahi gamissati.

Or, in the Teachers' opinion, the present conjugation is (used) for future time with the (words) *kada*, *karahi* (when, at what time), (such that) 'when is he going? at what time is he going?' (have the sense) 'when, sir, will he go, at what time will he go?'

(vi) *nanumhi puṭṭhapaṭivacane 'tīte ca*, and for the past (using) *nanu* (certainly) in a reply to a question

garūnaṃ matantare nanusaddūpapade pañhapubbake puṭṭhapaṭivacane atīte ca vattamānā vibhatti hoti. akāsi kaṭaṃ Devadatta? nanu karomi bho puṭṭhapaṭivacane ti akāsi kaṭaṃ Devadatto.

Or, in the Teachers' opinion, the present conjugation is also (used) for past time in a reply to a previously-posed question in the accessory word *nanu*: 'Did you make a mat Devadatta? Certainly I have made (one), sir. In a reply to the question [one could say] 'Devadatta made a mat.'

(vii) *nanusu ca vā*, or (using the words) *na* (not) and *nu* (indeed)
garūnaṃ matantare nasadde nusadde copapade puṭṭhapaṭivacane atīte vattamānā vibhatti hoti vā: akāsi kaṭaṃ Devadatta, na karomi bho nākāsiṃ vā, ahaṃ nu karomi ahaṃ nv akāsiṃ.

Or, in the Teachers' opinion, the present conjugation is also (used) for past time in a reply to a question (using) the accessory words *na* and *nu*: 'Did you make a mat Devadatta? No, I have not, sir' or 'I did not make (one).' 'Indeed I have made (one)' or 'Indeed I did make (one).'

(viii) *atthappakāsanasamatthe ca*, and when it is capable of expressing the (right) meaning.
atthappakāsanasamatthe atite kāle ca vattamānā vibhatti hoti: bhayaṃ tadā na bhavati, bhayaṃ tadā nāhosī ti attho.

And the present conjugation is also (used) for past time when it is capable of expressing the (right) meaning: 'then there is no fear' in the sense of 'then there was no fear.'

This sense is called by western grammar the historic present, and it is extremely common in all kinds of text.

Conjugation of the *pañcamī* (fifth, imperative)

		ACTIVE			
singular 1	*gacchāmi*		*desemi*		*karomi*
2	*gaccha or gacchāhi**		*desehi*		*karohi*
3	*gacchatu*		*desetu*		*karotu*
plural 1	*gacchāma*		*desema*		*karoma*
2	*gacchatha*		*desetha*		*karotha*
3	*gacchantu*		*desentu*		*karontu*
		MIDDLE			
singular 1	*gacche*		*desaye*		*kare*
2	*gacchassu*		*desayassu*		*karassu*
3	*gacchataṃ*		*desetaṃ*		*kurutaṃ*
plural 1	*gacchāmase*		*desayāmase*		*karomase*
2	*gacchavho*		*desayavho*		*karuvho*
3	*gacchantaṃ*		*desayantaṃ*		*karontaṃ*

* The ending *-hi* (with *ā*) is optional in *-a* conjugations but obligatory for those in *-ā*, *-e* and *-o*.

The imperative has these meanings (Sadd 813-4):

āṇatti	command	*Vaṅke vasatu pabbate*	let him (go) live on Mt. Vanka
akkosa	bad wish	*corā taṃ khaṇḍhākhaṇḍikaṃ chindantu*	may thieves cut him into little pieces
āsiṭṭha	good wish	*arogā sukhitā hotha*	may you be well and happy
sapatha	curse	*akkhayaṃ hotu te bhayaṃ*	may your fear(s) never cease
yācana	request	*dadāhi pavaraṃ nāgaṃ*	give (me) the excellent elephant
vidhi	instruction	*puññaṃ karotu*	he/she should make merit
nimantaṇa	request	*adhivāsetu me Bhagavā bhattaṃ*	may the Blessed One accept a meal from me
āmantaṇa	invitation	*Siviraṭṭhe pasāsatu*	let him rule in the Sivi kingdom
ajjhiṭṭha	request	*desetu Bhagavā dhammaṃ*	may the Blessed One teach the Dhamma
sampucchana	reflection	*kin nu kho bho Abhidhammaṃ suṇāmi udāhu Vinayaṃ*	Shall I listen to Abhidhamma or to Vinaya?
paṭṭhanā	hope	*imaṃ jivitā voropetuṃ samattho homi*	May I be able to kill this man!

Conjugation of the *sattamī* (seventh, optative)

ACTIVE			
SINGULAR	*gaccheyyāmi, gaccheyyaṃ, gacche*	*deseyyāmi (etc.)*	*kareyyāmi (etc.)*
2	*gaccheyyāsi, gaccheyya, gacche*	*deseyyāsi*	*kareyyāsi*
3	*gaccheyyāti, gaccheyya, gacche*	*deseyyāti*	*kareyyāti*
PLURAL	*gaccheyyāma, gacchema, gacchemu*	*deseyyāma*	*kareyyāma*
2	*gaccheyyātha, gacchetha*		*kareyyatha*
3	*gaccheyyuṃ, gaccheyyu*		*kareyyuṃ*
MIDDLE			
SINGULAR	*gaccheyya(ṃ)*	*deseyya*	*kareyya, kayirami*
2	*gacchetho*	*desetho*	*karetho, kayirāsi*
3	*gacchetha*	*desetha*	*karetha, kayira*
PLURAL	*gacchemase*	*desemase*	*karemase, kayirāma*
	gaccheyyavho	*deseyyavho*	*kareyyavho, kayirātha*
	gaccheraṃ	*deseraṃ*	*kareraṃ, kayiruṃ*

Some verbs form an optative in *-yā* (as in Sanskrit *-yāt*), added to the present stem without a final vowel and sometimes with the insertion of a svarabhakti vowel:

√*jñā* → *jānāti* → *jān+yā* → *jaññā*
√*vad* → *vadati* → *vad+yā* → *vajjā*
√*kṛ* → *karoti* → *kar+i+yā* → (metathesis) *kayirā*
√*dā* → *dadāti* → *dad+yā* → *dajjā*

Double optative formations are sometimes found. They add the *-eyy* affix to a stem already formed with *-yā*: *dajjeyyāti*, he should give.

The optative has these meanings particular to it (Sadd 815):

term	meaning	example	translation
anumati	permission	*tvaṃ gaccheyyāsi*	you may go
parikappa	supposition	*sace pi vāto giriṃ vaheyya*	even if the wind were to carry a mountain away
vidhi	instruction	*gāmaṃ gaccheyya*	you should go to the village
nimantaṇa	request	*idha bhavaṃ bhuñjeyya*	would you eat here, Sir (please)?
āmantaṇa	invitation	*idha bhavaṃ nisīdeyya*	you may sit here, Sir
ajjhiṭṭha	request	*ajjhāpeyya maṇavakaṃ*	would you teach the young man?
sampucchana	reflection	*kiṃ nu khalu bho Dhammaṃ ajjheyyaṃ udāhu Vinayaṃ*	Should I study the Dhamma or the Vinaya?
paṭṭhanā	hope	*dadeyyaṃ na vikampeyyaṃ*	may I give and not quake

and three more which it shares with the imperative:

term	meaning	example	translation
pesa	exhortation	*imperative: bhavaṃ khalu kaṭaṃ karotu*	(Come), sir, make a mat
		optative: bhavaṃ khalu kaṭaṃ kareyya	Sir, you should make a mat
atisagga	authorization	*imperative: bhavaṃ khalu puññaṃ karotu*	Sir, make merit
		optative: bhavaṃ khalu puññaṃ kareyya	Sir, you may make merit
pattakāla	opportunity	*imperative: ayaṃ te saccakālo, saccaṃ vadatu*	this is a time for truth for you; tell the truth
		optative: ayaṃ te saccakālo, saccaṃ vadeyyāsi	this is a time for truth for you; you should tell the truth

Then Aggavaṃsa appends more uses:

> *kāla-samaya-velasu yaṃhi sattamī,*
> the seventh (is used) with *yaṃ* for time, moment, point
> *yaṃsaddūpapadavisaye kāla-samaya-velāsu sattamī vibhatti hoti: kālo yaṃ bhuñjeyya bhavaṃ, samayo yaṃ bhuñjeyya bhavaṃ, velā yaṃ bhuñjeyya bhavaṃ. ettha yaṃsaddo nipāto.*
> The seventh conjugation (is used) for time, moment, point when in the sphere of influence of the accessory word *yaṃ*: it is the time when you [lit. 'your honor'] should eat, it is the moment for you to eat, (this) is the point at which you should eat. Here *yaṃ* is a *nipāta.*

araha-sattisu ca, and in regard to desert and capacity

> *arahe sattiyañ ca sattamī vibhatti hoti. tesv ārahe: bhavaṃ khalu kaññaṃ gaheyya, bhavaṃ etaṃ arahati. sattiyaṃ: bhavaṃ khalu bharaṃ vaheyya, iha bhavaṃ vattuṃ sakkuṇeyya, ko imaṃ vijataye jaṭaṃ, ettha ca ko vijataye ti ko vijateṭuṃ samattho ti attho.*
> The seventh conjugation (is used) in regard to desert and capacity. Of these (first) desert: you, sir, should get the girl, you, sir, deserve her; (second) capacity: sir, you can carry the burden, here he (or: you) should be able to speak. In 'who could disentangle this tangle?' the meaning of 'who could disentangle' is 'who has the capacity to disentangle?'

The Present Indicative, Imperative and Optative of √*as*, and √(*b*)*hū*, to be, are:

		√*as*		
SINGULAR	present	imperative	optative 1	optative 2
1	*asmi* or *amhi*	*asmi* or *amhi*	*assaṃ*	*siyaṃ*
2	*asi*	*āhi*	*assa*	*siyā*
3	*atthi*	*atthu*	*assa*	*siyā*
PLURAL				
1	*asmā* or *amhā̆*	*asmā* or *amhā̆*	*assāma*	[-]
2	*attha*	*attha*	*assatha*	[-]
3	*santi*	*santu*	*assu*	*siyuṃ* or *siyaṃsu*

	√(*b*)*hū*	
present	imperative	optative
homi	*homi*	*huveyyaṃ*
hosi	*hohi*	*huveyyāsi*
hoti	*hotu*	*huveyyāti*
homa	*homa*	*huveyyāma*
hotha	*hotha*	*huveyyātha*
honti	*hontu*	*huveyyuṃ*

Conjugation of the *ajjattanī* (aorist)

The aorist can seem confusing because of its many different paradigms. If one wanted to write Pali, this would be a problem; but modern students wish only to read it, and aorist forms are usually easy to recognize. The aorist is formed in four ways, as in Sanskrit, but in Pali changes caused by the meeting of consonants, etc., sometimes make the formal derivation of aorists difficult to discern. Each has the augment (prefix) *a*-, and is formed

(i) from the root directly
(ii) with thematic -*a*-
(iii) with -*s*
(iv) with -*iṣ*

(i) root aorist:

SINGULAR	√*dā*	√*kṛ*	√*bhū*
1	*adaṃ*	*akaṃ*	*ahuṃ*
2	*adā ado*	*akā*	*ahŭ*
3	*adā*	*akā*	*ahŭ*
PLURAL			
1	*adamhă*	*akamhă*	*ahumhă*
2	*adattha*	*akattha*	
3	*aduṃ adū*		*ahuṃ, ahū*

(ii) thematic *a*- aorist:

SINGULAR	√*gam*		√*vac*		√*dṛś* *	
1	*agamaṃ*		*avacaṃ*	*avocaṃ*	*addasaṃ*	*addasāsi(ṃ)*
2	*agamā*		*avaca*	*avoca*	*addasa*	
3	*agamā*		*avaca*	*avoca*	*addasā*	*addasasi*
PLURAL						
1	*agamāma*	*agamamha*	*avacumha*	*avocumha*	*addasāma*	
2	*agamatha*	*agamattha*	*avacuttha*	*avocuttha*	*addasatha*	
3	*agamuṃ*		*avacuṃ*	*avocuṃ*	*addasuṃ*	*addasāsuṃ addasaṃsu*

* these forms of *dṛś* are based on an expanded root √*draś*; the alternative forms add endings of the -*s* type.

(iii) *-s* aorist, added either to root in *guṇa* or to verbs with *-e-* / *-aya-*; from √*śru*, √*kṛ*, √*diś*, √*jñā* there are (forms preceded by a hyphen only occur with prefixes):

SINGULAR	√*sru*	√*grah*	√*kṛ*	√*diś*	√*jñā*
1	*assosiṃ*	*aggahesiṃ*	*akāsiṃ*	*desesiṃ*	*-aññāsiṃ*
2	*assosi*	*aggahesi*	*akāsi*	*desesi*	*aññāsi*
3	*assosi*	*aggahesi*	*akāsi*	*desesi*	*aññāsi*
PLURAL					
1	*assumha*	*aggahesimha*	*akamha*	*desimha*	*aññāsimha*
2	*assuttha*	*aggahesittha*	*akattha*	*desittha*	*[-]*
3	*assosuṃ*	*aggahesuṃ*	*akāsuṃ* or *akaṃsu*	*desesuṃ*	*-aññāsuṃ, aññaṃsu*

(iv) the *i(s)*- aorist is added either to the root in *guṇa* or to the present stem. Because of the rules for word formation in Pali, the Sanskrit *s* is mostly lost.

√*gam*	(i) from root	(ii) from present stem		*pra-viś*	√*anu-mud*
agamiṃ	*agamisaṃ* *agamissaṃ*	*gacchiṃ*	*gacchisaṃ* *gacchissaṃ*	*pāvisiṃ**	*anumodiṃ*
agami		*gacchi*	*gañchi*	*pāvisi*	*anumodi*
agami	*agamī*	*gacchi*	*gañchi*	*pāvisi*	*anumodi*
agamimha		*gacchimha*		*pāvisimha*	*anumodimha*
agamittha		*gacchittha*		*pāvisittha*	*anumodittha*
agamisuṃ *agamuṃ*	*agamiṃsu*	*gacchisuṃ* *gañchuṃ*	*gacchiṃsu*	*pāvisiṃsu* *pāvisuṃ*	*anumodisuṃ* *anumodiṃsu*

* the long *ā* here is *pa* + *a* (augment) → *pā*.

The following are common aorists of √*gam*, √*bhū* → *hū*, √*dṛś*:

√*gam*		√*(b)hū*		√*dṛś*	
agamāsiṃ	*agamamha*	*ahosiṃ*	*ahumha*	*addasaṃ*	*addasāma*
agamāsi	*agamattha*	*ahosi*	*(ahuvattha)*	*addasā*	*addasatha*
agamāsi	*agamaṃsu*	*ahosi*	*ahesuṃ*	*addasā*	*addasaṃsu*

There are various examples of the Middle voice in the aorist, though it is not possible to give a full paradigm. Here are some of the more common forms:

	ROOT AORIST	THEMATIC *a*- AORIST	*s*- AORIST	*is*- AORIST
SINGULAR 1				
2		*akarase* (√*kṛ*)		
3	*adattha* (√*dā*)	*akarattha* (√*kṛ*) *abhāsatha* (√*bhās*)	*udapattha* (√*ud-pat*)	*pucchittha* (√*puch*)
PLURAL 1		*akaramhase* (√*kṛ*)		
2				
3		*amaññaruṃ* (√*man*) *abajjhare* (√*bandh*)		

ajjatanī samīpamhi, the past-of-today (aorist) is (used for) what is close (Sadd 816)

ajja pabhuti atīte kāle paccakkhe apaccakkhe vā samīpe ajjatanī vibhatti hoti: so maggaṃ agami, te maggaṃ agamuṃ.

The aorist conjugation is (used) for what is close in the past, whether it has been witnessed or not witnessed, beginning from (the start of) today: he went on the road, they went on the road.

The meaning of the aorist in practice is that of a simple past tense:

adhivāsesi Bhagavā tuṇhībhāvena,

the Blessed One assented by remaining silent (D II 84),

idam avoca bhagavā. idaṃ vatvā Sugato uṭṭhay' āsanā vihāraṃ pāvisi,

the Blessed One said this, and having said it got up from his seat and went into the monastery (D II 7),

evaṃ bhante ti kho āyasmā Ānando Bhagavato paṭissutvā pattaṃ gahetvā yena sā nādikā ten' upasamkami. atha kho sā nādika cakkachinnā parittā luḷitā āvilā sandamāna āyasmante Ānande upasaṃkamante acchā vippasannā anāvilā sandittha,

'Yes, sir' Ananda replied, and taking the bowl he went to the stream. That stream, flowing disturbed, turbid, with little (water because it had been) churned up by the wheels (of carts), at Ananda's approach flowed pellucid, clear, transparent. (D II 129).

Conjugation of the *bhavissantī* (future).

The Future tense uses the same endings as the present, almost always active.
It is formed:
(i) by adding the affix *-ss-* to the root, with or without the connecting vowel *-i-* and with or without strengthening to guṇa strength.
(ii) by adding *-iss-* to the present stem minus its final vowel, if any
(iii) in *-e* verbs by adding *-ess*.

From √*gam*

ACTIVE		
gamissāmi		*gamissāma*
gamissasi		*gamissatha*
gamissati		*gamissanti*

MIDDLE		
gamissaṃ		*gamissāmhe*
gamissase		*gamissavhe*
gamissate		*gamissante*

ROOTS ENDING:	ROOT	FUTURE FROM ROOT	PRESENT STEM	FUTURE FROM PRESENT STEM
IN SHORT VOWEL	*śru*	*sussati, sossati*	*suṇoti, suṇāti*	*suṇissati*
	hṛ	*hassati, hissati*	*harati*	*-harissati*
	hu	*[-]*	*juhoti*	*juhossati, juhissati*
	kṛ	*kassati, kāhati*	*karoti*	*karissati*
IN LONG VOWEL	*dā*	*dassati*	*dadāti, deti*	*dadissati*
	nī	*nessati, nayissati*	*nayati*	*[nayissati]*
	jñā	*ñassati*	*jānāti*	*jānissati*
	(b)hū	*hossati, hessati, hohiti, bhavissati*	*hoti, bhavati*	*[bhavissati]*
	sthā	*-ṭhassati*	*tiṭṭhati*	*tiṭṭhissati,-ṭhahissati*
IN CONSONANT, WITH SHORT MEDIAL VOWEL	*labh*	*lacchati labhissati*	*labhati*	*[labhissati]*
	dṛś	*dakkhati, dakkhiti, dakkhissati*	*[passati]*	
	chid	*checchati*	*chindati*	*chindissati*
	bhuj	*bhokkhati*	*bhuñjati*	*bhuñjissati*
	gṛh	*gahessati*	*gaṇhāti*	*gaṇhissati*
IN CONSONANT, WITH LONG MEDIAL VOWEL	*bhās*	*[-]*	*bhāsati*	*bhāsissati*
	pūj	*[-]*	*pūjeti*	*pūjessati*
	yāc		*yācati*	*yācissati*

anāgate bhavissantī, so gacchissati, the future is for what has not (yet) come, he will come (Sadd 818)

The simple future:

sabbadhammamūlapariyāyaṃ vo bhikkhave desessāmi. taṃ suṇātha, sādhukaṃ manasi karotha, bhāsissāmī ti,

Monks, I will teach you a discourse on the root of all dhammas. Pay attention and I will speak (M I 1).

The future can be used for generalizing statements

sabbe 'va nikkhipissanti bhūtā loke samussayaṃ,

all beings in (this) world will throw the body aside (D II 157),

and for the conclusion of an inference:

addasā kho Doṇo brāhmaṇo Bhagavato padesu cakkāni..., disvān' etad ahosi: acchariyaṃ vata bho abbhūtaṃ vata bho na vat' imāni manussabhūtassa padani bhavissantīti,

the brahmin Dona saw the wheels on the footprints of the Blessed One and thought: 'amazing, marvelous, these cannot be the footprints of a human being' (A II 37),

kathañ hi nāma yogenātīte 'nāgatassêva payogo,.... kathañ hi nāma tvaṃ moghapurisa evaṃ svākkhāte dhammavinaye udarassa kāraṇā pabbajjissasi? Vinaye Mahāvagge pāḷī esā. kathañhināmayogena ti kimatthaṃ: kathaṃ nu tvaṃ mārisa oghaṃ atarī ti ādisu kathañhināmassa abhāvato atīte anāgatassa viya payogo na hotī ti dassanatthaṃ.

With (the phrase) *kathaṃ hi nāma* it is as if there were the application of the future to the past... This text is in the Mahavagga of the Vinaya: 'monk, how can you have gone forth in the Dhamma and Vinaya, which have been clearly explained, for the sake of your stomach?' What is the sense of 'with (the phrase) *kathaṃ hi nāma*?' It is to show that it is not as if there were the application of the future to the past in (sentences) such as 'sir, how did you cross the ocean?', because (the phrase) *kathaṃ hi nāma* is absent.

Conjugation of the *kālātipatti* or *kāratipatti* (conditional)

kiriyātipanne 'tīte 'nāgate ca kalatipatti,

the conditional is used for past and future when there is no accomplishing of an action (Sadd 821)

kālatipattī ti ken' aṭṭhena kālātipatti? kālassātipatanavacanaṭṭhena; tathā hi kālassa atipatanaṃ accayo atikkamitvā pavatti kālātipatti, labhitabbassa atthassa nipphattirahitaṃ kiriyātikkamanaṃ – kālo ti c' ettha kiriyā adhippetā, karaṇaṃ kāro, kāro eva kālo. rakārassa lakāraṃ katvā uccāraṇavasena - ayaṃ pana vibhatti tabbācakattā kālātipattī ti.

What does 'non-accomplishment of an act' mean? It means that (the conditional) expresses the non-accomplishment of an act; for thus there is the passing by, the leaving aside, the continuing on after passing over an act. It is a passing over of an action, which fails to succeed in an aim to be achieved. By *kālo* an action is referred to, the doing of an action; the syllable *la* is put in place of *ra* for the sake of (easier) pronunciation. This conjugation is called '*kālatipatti*' because it expresses that (Sadd 59).

The conditional, which is used for hypothetical or counterfactual assertions, is formed by adding the past augment to the future stem, with aorist endings.

ACTIVE			MIDDLE		
agamissaṃ or *-āmi*		*agamissāma*	*agamissaṃ*		*agamissāmhase*
agamissa or *-i*		*agamissatha*	*agamisse*		*agamissavhe*
agamissā̆		*agamissaṃsu*	*agamissatha*		*agamissiṃsu*

In the Vessantara Jātaka Maddī falls to the ground, and Vessantara, thinking her dead, says:

aṭṭhāne videse matā Maddī, sace hi 'ssā Jetuttaranagare kālakiriyā abhavissa mahanto parihāro abhavissa, dve raṭṭhā caleyyuṃ, ahaṃ pana araññe ekako, kin nu kho karissāmi,

It's not right for Maddi to die in a foreign place. If her death had been in the city of Jetuttara there would have been great honor (shown to her) (and) two kingdoms would have shuddered. But I am alone in the forest—what will I do? (Ja VI 566),

and later:

sace hi mayā putte datvā cittaṃ pasādetuṃ nâbhavissa imāni me acchariyāni na pavatteyyuṃ,

if I had not been able to calm my mind when I gave away the children, these miracles would not have happened (Ja VI 567),

Here the conditional and optative verbs seem to express much the same kind of counterfactual.

Passive voice.

Passives are more often conjugated with Active endings than with Middle. Their stems are made in three ways:

(i) by adding *-ya* to the root

(ii) by adding *ĭ̄ya* to the root

(iii) by adding *ĭ̄ya* to the present stem.

There are also some special rules:

final *-ā* often → *-ī*

final *i/u* usually → *ī/ū* (*-īy* can appear as *-iyy* and *-ūy* as *-uyy*)

ṛ/ṝ usually → *īr/ūr*

verbs in *-e/-aya* drop *-e/-aya* before adding *ĭ̄ya*.

√jña → ñāyati	*√ha* →$_1$ *hāyati*	*√dā → dīyati*
√pra-jñā → paññāyati	→$_2$ *hīyati*	*√vac → vuccati*
√śru → sūyati/suyyati	*√hṛ → hīrati*	*√pūj → pūjiyati*
√labh → labbhati	*√kṛ* →$_1$ *kīryati* (→ **kīrrati* →) *kīrati*	*√diś → desiyati*
√vah → vuhyati → vuyhati	→$_2$ *kayyati, kayyate*	*√bandh → bajjhati*
√chid →$_1$ *chijjati*	→$_3$ *kariyati, kayirati*	*√yaj* →$_1$ *yajīyati*
→$_2$ *chindiyati*	*√lip → lippati*	→$_2$ *ijjati*
√pā → pīyati	*√kṝ → kirĭ̄yati*	*√pṝ → pūriyati*

Once the passive stem has been formed, it is in theory possible to form any other tense and mood with it, simply by adding the appropriate endings from the Active voice. In practice, however, only the Aorist occurs with any frequency, almost always in the 3rd person.

The passive in the western sense is the *kammakiriyāpada*, verb which expresses the action of the object

yaṃ kammam eva padhānato gahetvā niddisīyati [kiriyā]padaṃ, taṃ kammatthadīpakaṃ,

a verb which when expressed refers in essence only to the object is one which has the object as its denotation.

It is the object which determines the form of the verb, as singular or plural, etc.: in *bhikkhunā dhammo bhavīyate, bhikkhunā dhammā bhavīyante, bhikkhūhi dhammo bhavīyate, bhikkhūhi dhammā bhaviyante,* dhamma[s] is/are developed by the monk[s], the form of the verb is determined by *dhammā* and not *bhikkhu,* although the latter is the logical subject (Sadd 7).

Pūraṇo Kassapo maṃ etad avoca… paradāraṃ gacchato, musā bhaṇato, karoto na karīyati pāpaṃ,
Purana Kassapa said to me…'for one who goes to another's wife, who tells lies, for someone who acts (thus) no evil is done (D I 53)

na candimasūriyā paññāyanti,
(at that time) the sun and moon were not perceived (D III 85),

yassa kho pana, bhante, evaṃ aṭṭhaṅgasamannāgato saro hoti, so vuccati brahmassaro ti,
sir, the person whose voice has these eight qualities is called 'one of excellent voice' (D II 211).

Passive endings are also used for:
verbs used reflexively, i.e. which have an object-agent (*kammakattā*), and verbs which expresses a state-of-being (*bhāvakiriyāpada)*
yaṃ kammuno kiriyāpadena samānagatikaṃ katvā vinā kammena niddisīyati kiriyāpadaṃ... taṃ tattha bhavatthadīpakaṃa,
when a verb is expressed which is morphologically the same as a passive verb but has no object, it is one which has a state-of-being as its denotation. The more commo n examples of this use a future passive participle: *tvaṃ avuso Pāṭikaputta... Sammasambuddhe āsādetabbaṃ maññasi,* do you, friend Patikaputta, think it is possible to vie against Fully Awakened Buddhas? (D III 24),
dassane Bhagavā sati kathaṃ paṭipajjitabbaṃ,
and if there is sight (of women), Blessed One, what behavior is appropriate? (D II 141).

Examples of finite forms given by grammarians, which are presented as the equivalent of action nouns are: *ṭhīyate* = *ṭhānaṃ* or *ṭhiti*, (there is a) standing, *bhūyate* = *bhavanaṃ* (there is an) existing, (Sadd 7), *nandīyate* = *nandanaṃ* (there is) joy (Kacc Be 261)

The four 'Systems': Causatives, Desideratives, Intensives, Denominatives

hetukattukiriyāpada (causative)

The Causative and Double Causative, which can be used in any of the tenses, moods or other forms of the simple verb, are formed by adding affixes:
(i) to the root, often strengthened
(ii) to the present stem.

The affixes are:
(i) causative: *-aya-* or *-e-*, often prefixed by *ăp-* when formed from the present stem
(ii) double causative: *-ăpaya-* or *-ăpe-*, added to the causative stem formed according to (i).

Both Causatives decline as verbs in *-a-* with affix *-aya-*, or as verbs in *–e-*. Examples are given here in *-e-*.

ROOT	CHANGE (IF ANY)	EXAMPLES
WITH FINAL *ā*	→ insert *-p-*	√*jhā* → *jhāpeti*, √*mā* → *māpeti* √*sthā* → *ṭhapeti*
WITH FINAL VOWEL OTHER THAN *ā*	→ *vṛddhi* strength	√*kṛ* → *kāreti*, √*bhū* → *bhāveti* √*śru* → *sāveti*
WITH MEDIAL VOWEL a followed by a single consonant	→ *vṛddhi* strength	√*pat* → *pāteti*, √*car* → *cāreti*
WITH MEDIAL VOWEL OTHER THAN a	→ *guṇa* strength	√*bhid* → *bhedeti*, √*muc* → *moceti*, √*ruh* → *ropeti*

Causative endings added to the present stem:

ROOT	PRESENT	CAUSATIVE
chid	*chindati*	*chindayati* or *chindeti*
ni-sad	*nisīdati*	*nisīdayati* or *nisīdeti*
gṛh	*gaṇhāti*	*gaṇhāpayati* or *gaṇhāpeti*
vyadh	*vijjhati*	*vijjhayati* or *vijjheti*

Causative stems with *-ăp-*, from either the root or present stem, give rise to double causatives with *–ăpāp-*, as in some of these examples:

ROOT	PRESENT	CAUSATIVE	DOUBLE CAUSATIVE
sthā	*tiṭṭhati*	*ṭhapayati, ṭhapeti*	*ṭhapāpayati, ṭhapāpeti*
kṛ	*karoti*	*kārayati, kāreti*	*kārāpayati, kārāpeti*
gam	*gacchati*	*gāmayati, gāmeti*	*gāmāpayati, gāmāpeti*
śru	*{suṇoti}{suṇāti}*	*sāvayati, sāveti*	*sāvāpayati, sāvāpeti*
khip	*khipati*	*khepayati, khepeti*	*khepāpayati, khepāpeti*
bhuj	*bhuñjati*	*bhojayati, bhojeti*	*bhojāpayati, bhojāpeti*
vac	*vacati*	*vācayati, vāceti*	*vācāpayati, vācāpeti*
dṛś	*passati*	*dassayati, dasseti*	*dassāpayati, dassāpeti*
jñā	*jānāti*	*jānāpayati, jānāpeti*	*jānāpāpayati, jānāpāpeti*
chid	*chindati*	*chedayati, chedeti*	*chedāpayati, chedāpeti*

It will be clear from the above that some verbs can form causatives in various ways. These morphological differences do not always correspond to analogously different kinds of meaning.

Causatives are very frequent, sometimes acting as intransitive verbs, but usually as transitive verbs with one or more objects:

seyyathāpi, Ānanda, jajjarasakaṭaṃ vedhamissakena yāpeti, evameva kho, Ānanda, vedhamissakena maññe tathāgatassa kāyo yāpeti,
Ananda, just as an old cart keeps going trembling in all manner of ways, so too, Ananda, the Tathagata's body, indeed, keeps going trembling in all manner of ways (D II 100),

naṃ migagaṇaṃ uyyānaṃ pavesetvā...,
having made that herd of deer enter the park,... (Ja I 150),

atha kho rājā Māgadho Seniyo Bimbisāro... paṇītaṃ khādanīyaṃ bhojanīyaṃ paṭiyādāpetvā Bhagavato kalaṃ ārocāpesi,
then Seniya Bimbisara, the king of Magadha, had excellent food, both hard and soft, prepared, and then had (someone) tell the Blessed One that it was time (to eat) (Vin I 38),

atha kho bhikkhave Dīghāvukumāro Barāṇasiṃ pavisitvā suraṃ nīharitvā gumbiye pāyesi,
then, monks, Prince Dighavu went into Banaras, brought back liquor and gave it to the troops to drink (Vin I 345),

asubhāya cittaṃ bhāvehi ekaggaṃ susamāhitaṃ,
develop a mind which is one-pointed and well-concentrated on the unpleasant (Sn 341).

Aggavaṃsa exemplifies causatives (Sadd 597–8):

so antakammani. arahattamaggo mānaṃ siyati, kammaṃ pariyosiyati imāni tāva suddhakattupadāni. ettha mānaṃ siyati ti mānaṃ samucchindati; kammaṃ pariyosiyatī ti kammaṃ nipphajjati, pari-ava-upasaggavasena hi idaṃ padaṃ akammakaṃ bhavati, attho pana pariyosanaṃ gacchatī ti sakammakavasena gahetabbo.
The verb root *so* has the sense of making an end. (In) 'the path to Arahantship ends pride,' or 'an action comes to an end,' the verbs have agents pure and simple. Here 'ends pride' (means) cuts off pride, 'an action comes to an end' (means) 'the action comes to a conclusion.' (In the latter) the verb is intransitive, with the prefixes *pari* and *ava*, but the meaning is to be taken transitively, '(the action) goes to an end.' [this poin t assumes, as always, that the goal of an intransitive verb of motion constitutes a direct object.]

attanā vippakataṃ attanā pariyosāpeti idaṃ ekakāritaṃ hetukattupadaṃ, ettha pana pari ava icc upasaggavasena akammakabhūtassa sodhātussa laddhakāritappaccayattā ekakammakaṃ eva sakāritapadaṃ bhavati,
(In) 'He himself finishes what he had done imperfectly,' the verb is causative with a single causative suffix. Here given that the root *so*, which is an intransitive verb with the prefixes *pari* and *ava*, has a causative suffix, it is a causative with one object.

attanā vippakataṃ parehi pariyosāvāpeti, idaṃ dvikāritaṃ hetukattapadaṃ, ettha ca pana pari ava icc upasaggavasena akammabhūtassa sodhātussa laddhakāritappaccayadvayattā dvikammakaṃ sakāritapadaṃ bhavati,
(In) 'He has what he had done imperfectly finished by others' the verb is causative with a double causative suffix, and (and) here given that the root *so*, which is an intransitive verb with the prefixes *pari* and *ava*, has a double causative suffix, it is a causative with two objects.

The phrase *attanā vippakataṃ parehi pariyosāvāpeti* is from the Vinaya (Vin III 155), and Aggavaṃsa provides a detailed analysis:

ettha bhikkhū ti hetukattupadaṃ ānetabbaṃ,
here 'monk' is to be supplied as the subject of the causative

attanā vippakatan ti ettha ca attanā ti vippakaraṇakiriyāya kattukārakavacakaṃ karaṇavacanaṃ,

in ' what he had done imperfectly,' he [=himself]' is an instrumental expressing the factor of action consisting in the agent of the action 'doing imperfectly,'

vippakatan ti kammakārakavācakaṃ upayogavacanaṃ,

'Done imperfectly' is an accusative expressing the factor of action which is the object (of the verb),

ettha pana attanā ti avyāpadabhūtena sayaṃsaddena samānatthaṃ vibhatyantapaṭirūpakaṃ avyayapadaṃ sayaṃsaddasadisaṃ vā tatiyāvibhatyanta-avyayapadaṃ, tathā hi attanā pariyosāpetī ti vuttavacanassa sayaṃ pariyosāpetī ti attho bhavati attanā pāṇātipātī ti ādisu viya,

but here 'himself' (can be taken as) an adverb with the appearance of a case ending, with the same meaning as the word (*sayaṃ*) 'on his own,' which is an adverb; or, again, it (can be taken as) an adverb with the third [instrumental] case ending, like the word 'on his own,' such that the meaning of the phrase he himself finishes' is 'he finishes on his own,' in the same way as phrases such as 'he himself killed,'

parehi pariyosāvāpetī ti ettha pana parehī ti kammakārakavacakaṃ karaṇavacanan ti gahetabbaṃ sunakhehi pi khādāpenti ettha sunakhehi padaṃ viya, ettha hi, yathā rājāno coraṃ sunakhe khādāpentī ti upayogavasena attho bhavati tathā bhikkhu attanā vippakataṃ pare jane pariyosāvāpetī ti upayogavasena attho bhavati,

in 'he has completed by others' one should understand 'by others' as an instrumental expressing the factor of action consisting in the object, in the same manner as the word (*sunakhehi*) 'by dogs' in the clause 'they have dogs eat.' * Here, just as in 'kings have dogs eat a bandit' ['dogs' = *sunakhe*] the meaning is that of an accusative.

[* the canonical original is: *ekacco passati coraṃ āgucāriṃ rājāno gahetvā... sunakhehi khādāpente*, someone sees kings capture a bandit, a criminal... (and) having him eaten by dogs (A I 47–8)]

dhāturūpakasadda (denominative)

This conjugation is called in Sanskrit *nāmadhātu*, 'whose root is a noun.' They can also be formed from adjectives, adverbs, onomatopoeias, etc. Denominatives of this kind occur in Pali: *kathā*, story → *kathāyati*; tell or recount; *udāna*, breathing upwards or inspiration (the title of a text in the Canon) → *udāneti*, make an inspired utterance. Aggavaṃsa's term is *dhāturūpakasadda*, word whose root is a metaphor, exemplified by *saṃgho pabbatāyati*, the monastic order "mountains". This is explained as *saṃgho pabbato iva attanaṃ ācarati*, the monastic order conducts itself like a mountain: that is, it is unmoving, impressive, etc.; *samuddāyati*, from *samudda*, ocean, is given as a similar example. From *putta*, child → *puttīyati*, treat (someone) like a child. A Denominative root is not always, strictly speaking, a metaphor, but it is the imaginative extension into the verbal domain of a noun, and the use of a nominal theme (*pāṭipadika*) as a root.

Denominatives conjugate as verbs in –*a*– with the affixes -*ya*, -*ăya*, -*ĭya*, or as verbs in –*e*– (examples from Sadd 587):

NOUN, ETC.	MEANING	DENOMINATIVE	MEANING
namas	honor	*namassati*	do honor, revere
mettā	friendliness	*mettāyati*	be friendly
ciraṃ	a long time	*cirāyati*	hesitate, delay
hirĭ	shame, shyness	*hirĭyati*	feel shame, be shy
dukkha	suffering, pain	(i) *dukkhīyati* (ii) *dukkhāpeti*	(i) feel pain (ii) cause pain
patti	gain, profit	*pattīyati*	desire, seek profit
ghurughuru	the sound 'ghuru'	*ghurughurāyati*	snore, grunt
kiḷikiḷi	the sound kili	*kiḷikiḷāyati*	tinkle, jingle

noun	verb	meaning	explanation	translation
ciccita	*ciccitāyati*	sizzles	*saddo ciccitaṃ iva attānaṃ ācarati*	a sound (behaves) seems like 'ciccita'
ati+hattha	*atihatthayati*	overtakes on an elephant	*hatthinā atikkamati*	he overtakes (with) on an elephant
chatta	*chattīyati*	acts as a parasol	*achattaṃ chattaṃ iva attānaṃ ācarati*	something which is not a parasol acts as one
putta	*puttīyati*	treats as a son	*aputtaṃ puttaṃ iva ācarati, puttīyati sissaṃ ācariyo*	a teacher treats his pupil as a son, [i.e.] behaves towards him, who is not his son, as if he were his son

devo ca vassati devo ca gaḷagaḷāyati,
the (sky-)god rains, the (sky-)god thunders (Th 189, from sound *gaḷagaḷa*),
ye 'maṃ kāyaṃ mamāyanti andhabalā puthujjanā / vaḍḍhenti kaṃasiṃ ghoraṃ,
blind ordinary people who cherish this body fill up the dreadful charnel ground (Th 575, from *mama*, mine),
dukkhitaṃ maṃ dukkhāpayase,
you are causing me to suffer, I who am (already) suffering (Ja IV 452, causative from *dukkha*).

Desideratives and Intensives both require *abbhāsa*, 'Doubling' or reduplication of the root syllable. They can in principle be formed from any root, although in practice in Pali only certain standard verbs are so used regularly. As well as reduplicating the root syllable they add the affixes *-sa-* → *-cha-/-kha-* (desiderative) and *-ya-* (intensive - not all verbs).

Desideratives are *tumicchattha*, with the meaning 'wanted for oneself' (cf. Sadd 822):

SANSKRIT	
root	desiderative
gup	*jugupsate*
cit	*cikitsati*
vi-cit	*vicikitsati*
man	*mīmāṃsate*
śak	*śikṣati*
śru	*śuśrūyate*
bhuj	*bubhukṣati*
pā	*pipāsati*
tij	*titikṣate*
dā	*ditsati*

PALI				
root	meaning	present	desiderative	desiderative meanings
gup	protect	*gopeti*	*jigucchati*	seek to protect oneself against, avoid, detest
cit	think about	*cinteti*	*tikicchati*	want to think about , treat (medically), cure
vi-cit	think	*vicinteti*	*vicikicchati*	want to think about, worry, be in doubt
man	think	*maññati*	*vīmaṃsati*	want to think, question, investigate
sak	be able	*sakkoti*	*sikkhati*	want to be able, train, learn
su	hear	*suṇoti* *suṇāti*	*sussūsati*	want to hear, listen, pay attention
bhuj	eat, enjoy	*bhuñjati*	*bubhukkhati*	want to eat, be hungry
pā	drink	*pibati* *pivati*	*pipāsati* *pivāsati*	want to eat, be thirsty
tij	be sharp	*[-]*	*titikkhati*	want to be sharp, firm, endure
dā	give	*dadāti*	*dicchati*	want to give

bhojanaṃ va jighacchato, like food to one who wants to eat (D II 266, from √*ghas*, eat), *hitasukhataṃ jigiṃsamāno*, desiring welfare and happiness (D III 154, from √*hṛ* → Sanskrit *jihīrṣati* → Pali *jigiṃsati*), *tassa te savakā na sussūsanti*, his followers do not want to listen to him (D I 230, from √*śru*).

Intensives are not designated by a standard term in Pali. They are also called Frequentatives in western grammars, since they express the idea that the action of the verb is done intensely or frequently. They are not made from polysyllabic roots, or from those beginning with a vowel, or from those of the 8th (*cur*) class. It is not possible or necessary to give rules for forming intensives in Pali. The Sanskrit rules are complex, the orthographic changes in Pali add further difficulty, and the intensive occurs but rarely.

SANSKRIT		PALI				
root	intensive	root	meaning	present	intensive	meanings
kram	*caṅkramyate*	*kam*	walk, go	*-kamati*	*caṅkamati*	goes often, walks back and forth
lap	*lālapyate*	*lap*	talk	*lapati*	*lālappati*	talk intensively, prattle, blather
jval	*jājvalate*	*jal*	burn, shine	*jalati*	*daddaḷhati**	burn, shine brightly

* Aggavaṃsa gives also *daddallati* (Sadd 826)

Intensive adjectives are also found: from √*cal*, *cañcala*, unsteady, from √*muh*, *momūha*, very foolish, from √*lup* (or *lubh*) *lolupa*, greedy, and *loluppa*, greed, from √*jṛ*, *jajjara*, very old.

atha kho Bhagavā sayaṇhā samayaṃ paṭisallinā vuṭṭhito... abbhokāse caṅkamati,
then the Blessed One arose from his seclusion in the early morning and walked back and forth in the open air (D III 80),
pekkhataṃ yeva ñātīnaṃ passa lālapataṃ puthu / ekameko va maccānaṃ go vajjho viya niyyati,
see, while the relatives look on and babble greatly, each and every mortal is lead away like a cow to slaughter (Sn 580),
ediso ahu ayaṃ samussayo jajjaro bahudukkhānaṃ alayo,
such was this body, (now) rapidly aging, a home for many kinds of suffering (Thī 270).

3.3. *kitanta*, words ending in -*kit*, etc. (participles), *tvādiyanta*, words ending in -*tvā*, etc. (absolutives), *tumanta*, words ending in -*tum* (infinitive)

(i.e. Non-conjugated forms)

Non-conjugated verbal forms are of two kinds: those which decline (participles and derived nouns) and those which are indeclinable (absolutives, infinitives)

(i) Declined forms: Participles

Participles, absolutives and infinitives are in Pali members of the class of suffix, *paccaya*, and of its subclass *kitanta*, from Sanskrit *kṛdanta*, ending in a *kṛt* suffix. The other subclass is *taddhita*, and the two are referred to in English as primary and secondary suffixes respectively. *kitanta* suffixes are added directly to a verbal root while *taddhita* are added to *kitanta* and other forms already derived from a root. There are very many of both kinds: Aggavaṃsa devotes a full chapter to each, a total of 72 pages in Smith's edition. The following are some examples of *kit* suffixes:

root	suffix(es)	*kitanta*	class of word	meaning
gam	(prefix *ā*- +) -*tukā*	*āgantuka*	adjective	added, adventitious
kar (= *kṛ*) → *kuru*	-*māna*	*kurumāna*	present middle/ passive participle	doing/being done
gam (= **gm*)	-*ti*	*gati*	action noun	going, destiny
ji → *jay*	-*ant*	*jayant*	present active participle	conquering
dis (= *dṛś* → *darś*) → *dass*	-*ana*	*dassana*	action noun	seeing, sight
ñā	-*tabba*	*ñātabba*	future passive participle	to be known
pā	-*eyya*	*peyya*	future passive participle	to be drunk, drinkable
car	-*iyā*	*cariyā*	action noun	conduct
dā → *dad*	-*ta*	*datta*	past passive participle	given
nī → *nāy*	-*aka*	*nāyaka*	adjective, agent noun	leading, leader
labh	-(*i*)*tvā*	*labhitvā*	absolutive	having obtained
phus (= *spṛś*)	-*ya* (→ *sa*)	*phussa*	absolutive	having touched
mar (= *mṛ*)	-*tyu*	*maccu*	action noun/ abstract noun	dying, death
dis (= *diś*)	(*i*)*tuṃ*	*desitum*	infinitive	to teach

Present Active Participle

Verbs which decline in *-a* form present participles by suffixing to the present stem *either*

(i) the endings *-ant/-an*, with variations as in changeable stems, *or*

(ii) the ending *-anta*, declined as in *-a* stems for masculine and neuter, and as in *-ī* stems for feminine.

There is a rare form in *-āna*, which declines as an *-a/-ā* stem.

Verbs which decline in *-e* or *-o* form the present participle analogously to verbs in *-a*, except for the nominative singular, where there is only one possibility.

from √*gam*, go:

SINGULAR	masculine	alternatives	feminine	neuter*
nominative	*gacchaṃ*	*gacchanto*	*gacchantī*	*gaccham* or *gacchantaṃ*
accusative	*gacchantaṃ*	*gacchantaṃ*	*gacchantiṃ*	*gaccham* or *gacchantaṃ*
instrumental	*gacchatā*	*gacchantena*	*gacchantiyā*	*gacchatā*
dative	*gacchato*	*gacchantāya*	*gacchantiyā*	*gacchato*
ablative	*gacchatā*	*gacchantā*	*gacchantiyā*	*gacchatā*
genitive	*gacchato*	*gacchantassa*	*gacchantiyā*	*gacchato*
locative	*gacchati*	*gacchante*	*gacchantiyā* or *gacchantiyaṃ*	*gacchati*
vocative	*gacchaṃ*	*gacchanta*	*gacchanti*	*gaccham* or *gacchantaṃ*
PLURAL				
nominative	*gacchanto*	*gacchantā*	*gacchantiyo* or *gacchantī*	*gacchanti* or *gacchantāni*
accusative	*gacchanto*	*gacchante*	*gacchantiyo* or *gacchantī*	*gacchanti* or *gacchantāni*
instrumental	*gacchantehi*	*gacchantebhi*	*gacchantībhi*	*gacchantehi*
dative	*gacchataṃ*	*gacchantānaṃ*	*gacchantīnaṃ*	*gacchataṃ*
ablative	*gacchantehi*	*gacchantebhi*	*gacchantībhi*	*gacchantehi*
genitive	*gacchataṃ*	*gacchantānaṃ*	*gacchantīnaṃ*	*gacchataṃ*
locative	*gacchantesu*		*gacchantīsu*	*gacchantesu*
vocative	*gacchanto*	*gacchantā*	*gacchatiyo* or *gacchantī*	*gacchanti* or *gacchantāni*

* alternatives as masculine in oblique cases

from √ diś, teach:

SINGULAR	masculine	alternatives	feminine	neuter*
nominative	*desento*		*desentī*	*desentaṃ*
accusative	*desentaṃ*		*desentiṃ*	*desentaṃ*
instrumental	*desetā*	*desentena*	*desentiyā*	*desetā*
dative	*deseto*	*desentāya*	*desentiyā*	*deseto*
ablative	*desetā*	*desentā*	*desentiyā*	*desetā*
genitive	*deseto*	*desentassa*	*desentiyā*	*deseto*
locative	*deseti*	*desente*	*desentiyā* or *desentiyaṃ*	*deseti*
vocative	*desento*		*desenti*	*desentaṃ*
PLURAL				
nominative	*desento*	*desentā*	*desentiyo* or *desentī*	*desenti* or *desantāni*
accusative	*desento*	*desente*	*desentiyo* or *desentī*	*desenti* or *desantāni*
instrumental	*desentehi*	*desentebhi*	*desentībhi*	*desentehi*
dative	*desetaṃ*	*desentānaṃ*	*desentīnaṃ*	*desetaṃ*
ablative	*desentehi*	*desentebhi*	*desentībhi*	*desentehi*
genitive	*desetaṃ*	*desentānaṃ*	*desentīnaṃ*	*desetaṃ*
locative	*desentesu*		*desentīsu*	*desentesu*
vocative	*desento*	*desentā*	*desentiyo* or *desentī*	*desenti* or *desantāni*

* alternatives as masculine in oblique cases

SINGULAR	masculine	alternatives	feminine	neuter*
nominative	*karonto*		*karontī*	*karontaṃ*
accusative	*karontaṃ*		*karontiṃ*	*karontaṃ*
instrumental	*karotā*	*karontena*	*karontiyā*	*karotā*
dative	*karoto*	*karontāya*	*karontiyā*	*karoto*
ablative	*karotā*	*karontā*	*karontiyā*	*karotā*
genitive	*karoto*	*karontassa*	*karontiyā*	*karoto*
locative	*karoti*	*karonte*	*karontiyā* or *karontiyaṃ*	*karoti*
vocative	*karonta*		*karonti*	*karontaṃ*
PLURAL				
nominative	*karonto*	*karontā*	*karontiyo* or *karontī*	*karonti* or *karontāni*
accusative	*karonto*	*karonte*	*karontiyo* or *karontī*	*karonti* or *karontāni*

instrumental	karontehi		karontīhi	karontehi
dative	karotaṃ	karontānaṃ	karontīnaṃ	karotaṃ
ablative	karontehi		karontīhi	karontehi
genitive	karotaṃ	karontānaṃ	karontīnaṃ	karotaṃ
locative	karontesu	karontesu	karontīsu	karontesu
vocative	karonto	karontā	karontiyo or karontī	karonti or karontāni

* alternatives as masculine in oblique cases

Present Middle Participle

The ending *-māna*, with a preceding *-a* if necessary, is added to the present stem. Verbs in *-e* change this to *-aya*, verbs in *-o* either change the vowel or do not have this participle. It declines as an *-a* stem. Many present middle participles are identical in form to the present passive participles of the same verb, but in meaning they are the same as the active.

√*labh* → *labhate* → *labhamāna*   √*gam* → *gacchate* → *gacchamāna*
√*sam-vid* → *saṃvijjate* → *saṃvijjamāna*   √*bhāṣ* → *bhāsate* → *bhāsamāna*
√*diś* → *desayate* → *desayamāna*   √*man* → *maññate* → *maññamāna*

Present Passive Participle

The ending *-māna* is added to the present passive stem. The participle declines as an *-a/-ā* stem. It is important to be aware of sound changes, such as *-dy-* → *-jj-*, *-ty-* → *-cc-*, *-ny-* → *ññ*.

ROOT	PRESENT (PASSIVE) STEM	PASSIVE PARTICIPLE
nī	nīyati, niyyati	nīyamāna or niyyamāna
han	haññati	haññamāna
vac	ucyati → vuccati	(v)uccamāna
kṛ	kīryati → *kīrrati	kīramana
dṛś	dissati	dissamāna
yudh	yujjhati	yujjhamāna
yuj	yuñjĭyati	yuñjĭyamāna
kṛ	karĭyati or kayĭrati	karĭyamāna or kayĭramāna
hṛ	harīyati	harīyamāna
chind	chindīyati	chindīyamāna

The past, present and future participles correspond, roughly, to the past, present and future tenses, although there are some differences. Past participles are very often used, as in English, as adjectives without reference to time. Aggavaṃsa explains (Sadd 852):

vattamāne vippakatavacane mānantā, (the suffixes) *māna* and *anta* (are used) to express an unfinished action in the present.

vattamāne kāle vippakatavacane vattabbe sabbadhātūhi māna anta icc ete paccayā honti: saramāno rodati, gacchanto gaṇhāti, gacchanto so Bhāradvājo addasa Accutaṃ isiṃ,
the endings *māna* and *anta* are (used) for all roots when it is necessary to express an unfinished action in present time: remembering he/she weeps, (going, he takes) he goes and gets, (while) going, Bharadvaja saw the sage Accuta.

As the example with the aorist *addasa* shows, the 'present' of the present participle is the time of the main verb, or better is in the continuous/progressive/imperfective aspect, and so his first example could be expanded:

saramāno rodi remembering, he/she wept
saramāno rodati remembering, he/she weeps
saramāno rodissati remembering, he/she will weeps

tena kho pana samayena Devadatto... dhammaṃ desento nisinno hoti,
at that time Devadatta was seated, teaching Dhamma (Vin II 199),

addasaṃsu kho pañcavaggiyā bhikkhū bhagavantaṃ dūrato āgacchantaṃ,
the group of five monks saw the Blessed One coming from afar (Vin I 8),

tassa evaṃ jānato evaṃ passato kāmāsavā pi cittaṃ vimuccati...,
the mind of the person who knows this and sees this is freed from the Corruption of Desire (A I 165).

sā kho pan' esā, bhikkhave, taṇhā kattha uppajjamānā uppajjati, kattha nivisamānā nivisatī?
This desire, monks, when it arises where does it arise, and when it stops where does it

stop? (D III 308).

sā kho pan' esā, bhikkhave, taṇhā kattha pahīyamānā pahīyati, kattha nirujjhamānā nirujjhati?

This desire, monks, when it is abandoned where is it abandoned, and when it is destroyed where does it stop? (D II 310)

evaṃ pi kho, Bhaggava, Sunakkhatto Licchaviputto mayā vuccamāno apakkam' eva imasmā dhammavinayā,

then Bhaggava, Sunakkhatta son of the Licchavis (after) being spoken to by me in that way left this Dhamma and Discipline (D III 6).

Past Participles

The Past Active Participle is a rare form, used with some verbs only. It is made by adding *-vant* or *-āvin* to the past passive participle stem, declined like nouns or adjectives with *-vant* and *-in* endings:

√*vas* → *vusita* → *vusitavant*, √*bhuj* → *bhutta* → *bhuttāvin*

yo pi so bhikkhu arahaṃ khīṇāsavo vusitavā...,

that monk who is an Arahant, whose corruptions are destroyed, who has lived the [noble] life (M I 4).

seyyathāpi Ānanda gahapatissa... manuññaṃ bhojanam bhuttavissa bhattasammado hoti...,

just as Ananda, when a householder has eaten an excellent meal he feels drowsy... (D II 195).

Past Passive Participles are extremely common. They decline as *-a/-ā* and stems are formed

(i) by adding *-ta*, *-ita* or *-na* to the unstrengthened root, √*bhū* → *bhūta*, √*bhās* → *bhāsita*, √*jṝ* → *jiṇṇa*, or

(ii) by adding *-ita* to the present stem, √*gam* → *gacchita* (or *gata*), √*pad* → *-pajjita* (or *-panna*), √*muc* → *muñcita* (or *mutta*). This is the case with causatives: √*gam* → *gamayati* → *gamita*, √*ruh* → *ropeti* → *ropita*.

They can be used as the main verb (with √*bhū*, √*as* or somesuch implicit or explicit). Like present participles, they can express both tense and aspect, and are also used as simple adjectives regardless of time:

sannipatito bhante bhikkhusaṅgho,
Sir, the order of monks has assembled (D II 76),

addhā idaṃ tassa Bhagavato vacanaṃ imassa ca bhikkhuno suggahītaṃ ti,
surely this saying of the Blessed One was well-grasped by that monk (D II 124),

tāya ca pana te vācāya Devadatto kupito ahosi,
and when you said that Devadatta became angry (M I 394),

Kusāvatī Ānanda rajadhānī dasahi saddehi avivittā ahosi divā c' eva rattī ca,
the royal city Kusavati, Ananda, was not without [√*vi-vic*] the ten sounds day or night (D II 147),

uḷārā kho te ayaṃ Sāriputta āsabhī vācā bhāsitā, ekaṃso gahito sīhanādo nadito,
great is this bull-like thing you have said, Sariputta, a lion's roar roared with certainty! (D II 82).

parinibbute Bhagavati saha parinibbānā mahābhūmicālo ahosi,
when the Blessed One attained nirvana, at the same time as (his) nirvana there was a great earthquake (D II 156).

Some verbs can have both active and passive uses: from √*anu-pa-āp*, attain:

tisso vijjā anupattā, the three knowledges have been attained (M II 105) and *samaṇo khalu bho Gotamo... Venāgapuraṃ anupatto,*
the ascetic Gotama has arrived at Venagapura (A I 180),

ye te bhante ahesuṃ atītaṃ addhānaṃ arahanto sammāsambuddhā, sabbe te... supatiṭṭhacittā... sammāsambodhiṃ abhisambujjhiṃsu, ye pi bhante bhavissanti anāgataṃ addhānaṃ arahanto sammāsambuddhā, sabbe te... supatiṭṭhacittā... sammāsambodhiṃ abhisambujjhissanti, Bhagavā pi bhante etarahi arahaṃ sammāsambuddho... supatiṭṭhacitto... sammāsambodhiṃ abhisambuddho, sir, those Arahants, Fully-Awakened Ones in the past all... with minds firmly set... awakened to Full Awakening, and, sir, those Arahants, Fully-Awakened Ones in the future all... with minds firmly set... will awaken to Full Awakening, and the Blessed One, sir, now, an Arahant, a Fully-Awakened One... with mind firmly set... is awakened to Full Awakening (D II 83).

The past passive participle can be used as a noun:

bhikkhu abhikkante paṭikkante sampajānakārī hoti ālokite vilokite... sammiñjite pasārite... saṃghāṭipattacīvara-dharaṇe... asite pite khāyite sāyite... uccāra-passāvakamme... gate ṭhite nisinne sutte jāgarite bhāsite tuṇhībhāve,

the monk remains mindful in going forward and going back, in looking forward and looking around... in bending and stretching, in carrying/wearing his outer garment, bowl and robe, in eating, drinking, chewing and savoring, in the acts of defecating and urinating, in moving, standing still, sitting, asleep, awake, speaking and remaining silent (D II 292).

All of the words describing actions and postures are past passive participles in *-ita*, with three exceptions: *dharaṇa* (carrying/wearing) is an action noun in *-ana* from √*dhṛ*, *kamma* (act) is a noun, and in *tuṇhībhāva* (state of being silent) *-bhāva* is a noun.

Future Participles

Future Active and Future Middle Participles are very rare. Some examples are:

mataṃ marissaṃ rodanti ye...,

those who weep for someone who is dead or who is going to die (Ja III 214)

[√*mṛ* → future stem *mariss-*, here with *-ant* suffix changed to *-a*],

kā tiṭṭhasi mandam ivāvalokaṃ / bhāsesamānā va giram na muñcasī ti,

who are you who stand looking languidly, as if about to speak but saying nothing? (Ja V 404).

More common are forms using *-esin*:

...bhūtā vā sambhavesī vā, sabbe sattā bhavantu sukhitattā,
whether they exist or are going to exist, may all beings be happy (Sn 147),

bhave vāhaṃ bhayaṃ disvā bhavañ ca vibhavesinaṃ,
I, having seen the fear in existence and the condition of those who are going to cease to exist (M I 330).

Future Passive Participle (Gerundive) (*kicca*)
kicca is one example, from √*kṛ*, used by synecdoche as a term for them all. The Future Passive Participle is called future, but it is more often used in sentences with past or present verbs, and it can, like the future conjugation, be non-temporal, in stating general truths or duties, etc. It is often said to be prescriptive, but it need not imply necessity or obligation: for the verb √*kṛ*, to do, for example *kātabba* can mean must be done, should be done, but also can be done (i.e. is permitted) do-able (i.e. is possible). Many future passive participles have stable adjectival meanings unconnected with any verbal mode: from the verbs √*ram* and √*mad* for example, are derived the adjectives *ramaṇīya* lovely and *madanīya*, enchanting. It is formed

(i) by adding the ending -*(i)tabba* either to the root, usually in guṇa, or to the present stem:

śru → sotabba	*pad → pajjati → pajjitabba*	*spṛś → phoṭṭhabba*
gam → gantabba	*vas (i) → vatthabba* or	*dṛś → daṭṭhabba*
nī → netabba	*(ii) → vasati → vasitabba*	*sthā → (caus.) ṭhapetabba*
vid → veditabba	*bhū → (caus.) bhāvetabba*	

*kṛ → (*kartabba → kattabba) → kātabba.*

(ii) by adding the ending *-anīya* (sometimes *-aneyya*) to the root, usually in guṇa:

ram → rāmaṇīya	*kṛ → karaṇīya*	*dṛś → dassanīya or dassaneyya*
khad → khādanīya	*bhuj → bhojanīya*	*mad → madanīya.*

(iii) by adding the endings *-ya* or *-iya* to the root, usually strengthened, with some special rules; final *ā* → *e* (sometimes with *-yya*); and *-t-* is inserted after some short vowels:

han → *haññа*	*pūj* → *pūjiya* or *pujja*	*kṛ* → *(kṛtya* → **kitya)* → *kicca*
dā → *deyya*	*labh* → *(labhya)* → *labbha*	*nī* → *neyya* (*-nīya* after prefixes)
pā → *peyya*	*bhū* → *(bhavya)* → *bhabba*	*rakṣ* → *rakkhiya*.

Examples of various future passive participles from √*kṛ*:

na ekaccassa parikammaṃ kātabbam, na ekaccena parikammaṃ kārapetabbaṃ,
no service is to be performed for anyone, and no service should be caused to be performed by anyone (Vin I 50),
tattha te yāvajīvaṃ ussāho karaṇīyo,
you should make a lifelong effort in this respect (Vin I 58),
dvay' ajja kiccaṃ ubhayañ ca kāriyaṃ,
today there are two duties, both of which must be done (Vv 80, 7),
kayyaṃ bhavatā vatthaṃ,
you should make (some) clothes (Sadd 862),
na okāso kāretabbo,
he should not (seek to) obtain an opportunity (to speak) (Vin II 5).

future passive participles can be used as an impersonal passive:

dāni na tena ciram jīvitabbaṃ bhavissati,
now he does not have long to live (it is not to be lived long by him) (D II 22),
asantiyā āpattiyā tuṇhībhavitabbaṃ,
if there is no offence, silence is to be maintained (Vin I 103).

the future passive participle *bhabba* (√*bhū* → *bhav* + *ya*) is used with dative or infinitive to mean able to, capable of, permitted to, etc.

abhabbo kho Yaso kulaputto hīnāyāvattitvā kāme paribhuñjitum,
Yasa the son of good family, is incapable of returning to the lower life to enjoy the pleasures of the senses (Vin I 17),
viññāṇaṃ abhijānaṃ parijānaṃ virajāyaṃ pajahaṃ bhabbo dukkhakkhayāyā ti,
knowing and understanding consciousness, being without passion towards it and renouncing it one is capable of ending suffering (S III 27).

Aggavaṃsa's three main examples of the use of *kicca* suffixes are those shared by the Imperative and Optative conjugations (Sadd 862):

(i) *pesana*, exhortation:
kattabbaṃ idaṃ bhavatā ti anuyuttassa ajjhesanaṃ,
requesting/ordering a servant: '(please) do this, my good man.'

(ii) *atisagga*, (non-)authorization:
kim idaṃ mayā kattabban ti,
what should I do now?'
upasampannena bhikkhunā sañcicca pāṇo jīvitā na voropetabbo ti ādinā nayena paṭipattinidassana-mukhenanuññā,
decreeing (a rule) as a means of showing (correct) practice, in a way like this: 'a bhikkhu with Full Ordination should not consciously deprive a living being of life.'

(iii) *pattakāla*, opportunity:
sampattasamayo, tassa ārocane... bhojanīyaṃ bhojjaṃ bhavatā,
when the time has come, announcing this... 'Sir, the meal is (ready) to be eaten (by you).

He adds two more:

(iv) *avassaṃ*, inevitability
kattabbaṃ me bhavatā kammaṃ,
you will do this task for me.

(iv) *adhamiṇa*, debtor:
dātabbaṃ me bhavatā sataṃ iṇaṃ,
Sir, you owe me a debt of a hundred (coins).

(ii) Declined forms: derived nouns

Verbal roots are analytically basic, and the vast majority of Sanskrit and Pali nouns can be derived from verbs, so one could say that all nouns are verbal nouns. Common nominal endings are *-a*, *-an*, *-i*, *ŭ*, *-tā*, *-ti*, *-yu*, etc.

root	meaning	suffix(es)	word	meaning
pa-grah	stretch out	*a* (with lengthening of root vowel)	*paggāha*	exertion
kṛ	do	*an*	*kamma(n)*	deed
pra-ṇi-dhā	aspire	*i* (with loss of final vowel)	*paṇidhi*	aspiration
gam (gṃ)	go	*ă* (with loss of final vowel/syllable)	suffix -*gă*, e.g. *antagă*	going to the end
gam	go	*ti*	*gati*	journey, destiny
mṛ	die	*(t)yu*	*maccu*	death

Two classes of nouns formed from verbs can govern a case in the manner of a verb: action nouns in -*ana* and agent nouns in -*tar*.

Action nouns in -*ana*

root	meaning	+ *ana*	meaning
gam	*go*	*gamana*	going
dṛś	*see*	*dassana*	seeing, sight

sādhu kho pana tathārūpānaṃ arahataṃ dassanaṃ hoti,
good indeed is it to see such Arahants! (Vin I 35),
asīti gāmikasahassāni idh' upasaṃkantāni bhagavantaṃ dassanāya,
eighty thousand village headmen have come here to see the Blessed One (Vin I 180).

Agent nouns in -*tṛ (tar)*
-*tar* is added to the root with various transformations (citing the nominative singular):

√gam → gantā, √śru → sotā, √dṛś → daṭṭhā, dassetā, √smṛ → saritā, √śās → satthā.

(paṇḍito) yoniso pañhaṃ kattā hoti, ayoniso pañhaṃ vissajjetā, parassa kho pana yoniso pañhaṃ vissajjitaṃ... abbhanumoditā hoti,
(one wise person) asks questions carefully, (another) answers questions carefully, (another) is glad when someone else answers a question thoughtfully (A I 103),
addasāsiṃ sugataṃ... adantānaṃ dametāraṃ,
I saw the Happy One,... the tamer of the untamed (Thī 135),

santi hāvuso... bhikkhuṃ pañhaṃ pucchitāro khattiyapaṇḍitā,
there are, friends, wise khattiyas who ask a monk a question (S III 6),

On rare occasions, an agent noun can act, as in Sanskrit, as a periphrastic future:
ye... nirodhaṃ appajānantā, āgantāro punabbhavaṃ,
those who do not know cessation will come to rebirth (Sn 754).

(iii) Indeclinable forms: Absolutive

Pali grammarians call words in this class *tvādiyantapadāni*, words with the endings *-tvā*, etc. Western scholars have called them indeclinable (past) participles, (past) gerunds, and absolutives. None of these three terms seems entirely appropriate. Although *tvādiyanta*-s are indeclinable, they are not participles and do not always refer to the past. The word gerund in English has traditionally applied to action nouns which have, like the present participle, the suffix -ing: winning is not everything. Certain uses of the *tvādiyanta* do resemble those of the present participle. How the term absolutive came into use is not clear, but it is perhaps the least misleading term to use. OED says that 'the absolute form of a word [is] that in which it is not inflected to indicate relation to other words in a sentence.' Pali *tvādiyanta*-s are not inflected, since the *-tvā* ending is the instrumental case of an old action noun in *–tu*, and so, like every instrumental case, they have already been declined. Many aspects of the way absolutives are used which might otherwise be surprising can be more easily understood if it is borne in mind that the form has this quasi-nominal, adverbial nature.

Absolutives are formed:

(i) by adding *-tvā* (*-tvāna*) or *-itvā* (*itvāna*), or rarely *-tuna*, to the root (occasionally in guṇa) or to the present stem:

√chid → chetvā or *chinditvā(na)*, *√gṛh* (*gaheti*) *→ gahetvā(na)*, *√kṛ → katvā(na)*, *dā → datvā(na)* or *daditvā*

(ii) by adding *-ya* to the root or present stem (in both cases usually but not always with compound verbs), with an inserted *-t-* if necessary:

√pa-hā + ya → pahāya, *√prati-i + tya → paṭicca*, *√ni-sad + ya → nisajja*, *kṛ → (kṛtya) kicca*

In most cases the absolutive is used to express a previous action by the subject of the sentence, and is to be understood as a verb in the same tense and mood as the main verb. But this is not always the case. Aggavaṃsa classifies the main uses of *tvādiyanta* suffixes thus (Sadd 311–13 [851–2]):

(i) where the agents of the absolutive and main verb are the same and the absolutive refers to the past (*samānakattukānaṃ dhātūnaṃ pubbakāle tvādisaddapayogo*), citing
ummaggā nikkhamitvāna Vedeho nāvam āruhi,
the Vedehan emerged from the tunnel and boarded the ship (Ja VI 445),
bhutvāna bhikkhu bhikkhassu,
enjoy yourself, monk, (then) seek alms! (S I 8).

Some more examples:
atha kho Bhagavā Pāṭaligāmiye upāsake bahud eva rattiṃ dhammiyā kathāya sandassetvā samādapetvā samuttejetvā sampahaṃsetvā uyyojesi,
then the Blessed One, after he had (spent) much of the night teaching, encouraging, inciting and gladdening lay-followers from Pataligama with a Dhamma talk, allowed them to go (D II 86),
so taṃ dhammaṃ sutvā Tathāgate saddhaṃ paṭilabhati,
he hears the Dhamma and acquires faith in the Tathagata (D I 62–3),
sakadāgāmino sakid eva imaṃ lokaṃ āgantvā dukkhass' antaṃ karissanti,
Once-Returners will come back to this world once and then make an end of suffering (D II 93),
yaṃ nūnāhaṃ sāmaṃ pattacīvaraṃ paṭiyādetvā kesamassuṃ ohāretvā kāsayāni vatthāni acchādetvā ārāmaṃ gantvā bhikkhūhi saddhiṃ saṃvaseyyan ti,
what if I were to prepare a robe and bowl for myself, have my hair and beard shaved, put on yellow clothes, go to the park and live with the monks? (Vin I 86).

(ii) where the agents of the absolutive and main verb are the same but the absolutive refers to the same time (*samānakattukānaṃ samānakāle tvādisaddapayogo*), citing
andhakāraṃ nihantvāna udito 'yaṃ divākaro, this sun has arisen, destroying the darkness, *akkhīni parivattetvā passati*, turning his eyes he sees, *nisajja adhīte*, he studies sitting down, *ṭhatvā katheti*, he speaks standing up.

Some more examples:

atha kho bhagavā pubbaṇhasamayaṃ nivāsetvā pattacīvaram ādāya rājagahaṃ pāvisi, then the Blessed One got up in the morning, and taking (with him) his bowl and robe, entered Rajagaha (Vin I 38)

(*ādaya* and other absolutives used in stereotypical cases such as this may be regarded as equivalent to prepositions).

The sentence cited under (i), *so taṃ dhammaṃ sutvā Tathāgate saddhaṃ paṭilabhati*, could also be regarded in this light.

(iii) where the agents of the absolutive and main verb are the same but the absolutive refers to the future (*samānakattukānaṃ parakāle tvādisadda-payogo*), citing

dvāram āvaritvā pavisati, he enters and closes the door,

dhan ti katvā patito daṇḍo, the stick fell and made a 'Dhan' sound.

(iv) where the agents of the absolutive and main verb are different (*asamānakattukānaṃ tvādisaddapayogo)*, citing:

pisācaṃ disvā c' assa bhayaṃ hoti, when he saw the goblin he was afraid,

paññāya c' assa disvā āsavā parikkhīṇā, and in him, seeing with wisdom, the Corruptions are destroyed (M I 160, etc.).

Some more examples:

tassa bhikkhave bhikkhuno bhāsitaṃ na abhinanditabbaṃ na paṭikkositabbaṃ. anabhinanditvā appaṭikkositvā tāni padavyañjanāni uggahetvā sutte otaretabbāni Vinaye sandassetabbāni,

monks, what that monks says is not to be rejoiced at nor rejected. (You) should learn these words and syllables without rejoicing or rejecting, and bring them down into (consideration with) Sutta and compare them with Vinaya (D II 124),

itarena (Jūjakena) āgantvā codiyamānā kahāpaṇe dātum asakkontā Amittatāpanaṃ nāma dhītaraṃ tassa adaṃsu,

[lit. requested by that other one (Jujaka) when he came back] when he came back Jujaka demanded the money, but as they could not give it to him they gave him their daughter Amittatapana (instead) (Ja VI 521).

In most cases any words governed by the absolutive come before it, but not all:

na kho me paṭirūpaṃ yo haṃ anāmantetvā upaṭṭhāke anapaloketvā bhikkhusaṃghaṃ parinibbayeyyaṃ,

it would not be suitable if I pass into final nirvana without speaking to those who have served me, and without taking my leave of the Order of Monks (D II 99).

There is a rare absolutive in *-aṃ*, called *ṇamul* in Sanskrit:

atha kho te… sattā rasapaṭhaviṃ hatthehi ālumpakārakaṃ upakkamiṃsu paribhuñjituṃ,

then, these beings started to eat the earth-essence taking (big) mouthfuls of it with their hands (D III 85),

so tattha phen' uddehakaṃ pacati,

he burns there [in hell] heaping up foam (A I 141).

Traces of what seems to be an Eastern dialect absolutive in *-ttā* (or *-tā*) also exist:

abhijānāti nu kho bhante Bhagavā iddhiyā manomayena kāyena Brahmalokaṃ upasaṃkamitā?

Sir, does the Blessed One remember having gone to a Brahma-world by magical power, in a mind-made body? (S V 282),

sarasi tvaṃ Dabba evarūpaṃ kattā yathāyaṃ bhikkhunī āha ti,

Dabba, do you remember having acted in the manner this bhikkhuni alleges? (Vin III 162).

(iv) Indeclinable forms: Infinitive

Infinitives are accusative or dative cases of the old action noun in *-tu*, as the absolutive is its instrumental. The accusative suffix *-tuṃ*, preceded by a vowel if necessary, is by far the most common; there are rare dative infinitives in *-taye*, *-tave*. Pali Grammarians call Infinitives *tumantapadāni*, words which end in *tum*:

sabbāni tumantapadāni catutthyatthe vattanti. tvaṃ mama cittam aññāya nettaṃ yācituṃ āgato ti ettha viya. yācitun ti yācanatthāyā ti attho,

All words ending in *-tum* have the sense of the fourth (dative) case, as in 'knowing (what was in) my mind you have come to ask for my eyes.' *yācitum* has the meaning of 'for the sake of, asking for.' (Sadd 309-10)

Infinitives can be formed from transitive and intransitive verbs, from causatives or double causatives:

(i) by adding *-tuṃ* to the root, usually in guṇa

nī → netuṃ	*(b)hū → hotuṃ*	*dṛś → daṭṭhuṃ*
pra-āp → pattuṃ	*śru → sotuṃ*	*vas → vatthuṃ*
*kṛ (→*kartuṃ) → kattuṃ → kātuṃ*	*jñā → ñātuṃ*	*gam → gantuṃ*
spṛs → puṭṭhuṃ		

(ii) by adding *-ituṃ*, *-etuṃ* or *-otuṃ* to the present stem of verbs in *-a*, *-e*, and *-o* respectively:

bhū → bhavituṃ	*pra-āp* $\rightarrow_1$ *pāpuṇituṃ*	*gam → gacchituṃ*
bhuj → bhuñjituṃ	$\rightarrow_2$ *pappotuṃ*	*diś → desetuṃ*
gṛh → gahetuṃ	*pra-viś → pavisituṃ*	*jñā → jānituṃ*
jīv → jīvituṃ	*kṝ → kirituṃ*	

gṛh	*→ gāheti → gāhetuṃ*	*kṛ*	*→ kāreti → kāretuṃ*
	→ gāhāpeti → gāhāpetuṃ		*→ kārāpeti → kārāpetuṃ*
yuj	*→ yojeti → yojetuṃ*	*rakṣ*	*→ rakkheti → rakkhetuṃ*
	→ yojāpeti → yojāpetuṃ		*→ rakkhāpeti → rakkhāpetuṃ*

The infinitive is used with verbs in any tense or mood, and can be either active or passive:

bhikkhū nāsakkhiṃsu vitthārena pātimokkhaṃ uddisituṃ,
the monks were not able to recite the Patimokkha at length (Vin I 112),
dhammacakkaṃ pavattetuṃ gacchāmi Kāsinaṃ puraṃ,
I have come to the city of the Kasis to set in motion the wheel of the Dhamma (Vin I 8),
ekamekena pi amatadvārena sakkuṇissāmi attānaṃ sotthiṃ kātuṃ,
by any one door to the deathless I will be able to make myself safe (M I 353),
tena hi bhikkhave saṅgho Sudhammassa bhikkhuno anudūtaṃ detu Cittaṃ gahapatiṃ khamāpetuṃ,
so, monks, may the Order give the monk Sudhamma an accompanying messenger to obtain forgiveness from Citta the householder (Vin II 19),
samuddaṃ visakumbhena yo maññeyya padūsituṃ,
whoever might think to pollute the ocean with a pot of poison... (Vin II 203)

anujānāmi bhikkhave therena bhikkhunā bhattagge anumoditun ti,
I ordain, monks, that thanks be given in a refectory by a monk who is an elder (Vin II 212).

The infinitive can be used with various verbs and prepositions:

rājā arahasi bhavituṃ,
you ought to be a king (Th 822),

ye samaṇesu sakyaputtiyesu pabbajanti, na te labbhā kiñci kātuṃ,
there is nothing to be done against those who have gone forth among the Sakyan ascetics (Vin I 75),

pañcahi bhikkhave aṅgehi samannāgato saddhivihāriko alaṃ paṇāmetuṃ,
monks, when someone who shares a cell has five qualities it is sufficient to turn him away (Vin I 54-5).

The ending *-kāma*, desiring to, can be added to the infinitive with its final *-ṃ* dropped:

atha kho Māro pāpimā Bhagavato bhayaṃ... uppādetukāmo,
then Mara, the evil one, was eager to cause fear to arise in the Blessed One (S I 104),

Rājā... Ajātasattu... Vajjī abhiyātukāmo,
king Ajatasattu wants to attack the Vajjis (D II 72).

4 nipāta

Particles, Negation, Adverbs

The word *nipāta* means falling, and a *nipāta* is a word which falls into language whole and complete, not needing grammatical transformation. All of them, especially the sub-category which western grammar calls adverbs, are sometimes called *avyayībhāva*, not subject to change.

4.1 *samuccaya-vikappanādi,* Particles (effecting) Conjunction, Disjunction, etc. (Sadd 886f.)

samuccaya-vikappana-paṭisedha-pūraṇattham asatva-vācakā nepātikā, *nipāta* words are used for conjunction, disjunction, negation/prohibition, or as fillers, and do not denote any substantial existent (i.e. something which can be the subject of a sentence, whether personal or impersonal):

(i) *samuccaya*, conjunction: *ca*, and. Horses and elephants can be (i) *assā ca hatthino ca*, (ii) *assā ca hatthino*, or (iii) *assā hatthino ca.*

(ii) *vikappana*, disjunction: *vā*, or. Horses or elephants can be (i) *assā vā hatthino vā*, (ii) *assā vā hatthino*, or (iii) *assā hatthino vā.* (*ca* can also, in context, mean but, and *vā* can also, in context, mean and.)

(iii) *paṭisedha*, Negation, Prohibition (*na*, *no*, *mā*, *a-*, *alaṃ*, *halaṃ*)
negation: *na v' āhaṃ paṇṇaṃ bhuñjāmi*, I will not eat this leaf [medicine].
no dubbhāsitaṃ bhaṇe, he should not say bad things,
anavajja, blameless,
privation: *abhāva*, non-existence, *aputtaka*, without children,

prohibition: *mā haṃ kāko viya dummedho kāmānaṃ vasaṃ anvāgaṃ*, I must not come under the power of desires, like the dim-witted crow,
alaṃ me buddhena... dhammena... saṅghena, I've had enough of the Buddha,... the Dhamma,... and the Sangha!
halaṃ dāni pakāsituṃ, away with explaining!
alaṃ etaṃ sabbaṃ, all this is enough!

(iv) *pūraṇatthaṃ duvidhaṃ: padapūraṇañ ca atthapūraṇañ ca*, (A *nipāta* used) as a filler can be of two kinds: filling up a verse or sentence or filling out the meaning:

(iv.a) *padapūraṇaṃ bahuvidhaṃ*, *nipāta*-s used to fill up a verse or sentence are of many kinds:
these particles join words together without expressing a specific meaning (*asati atthavisesābhidhāne vācāsiliṭṭhatāya*). Most of them are translatable as then, indeed, certainly, or somesuch: *atha*, *atho*, *assu*, *ā*, *enaṃ*, *kahaṃ*, *kīva*, *khalu*, *kho*, *carahi*, *tato*, *naṃ*, *pana* (also but), *yagghe*, *yathā* (just as), *vata*, *vatha*, *ve*, *sudaṃ*, *seyyathīdaṃ* (that's to say), *have*, *have*, *hi* (for, because).

(iv.b) *atthapūraṇaṃ duvidhaṃ: vibhattiyuttañ ca avibhattiyuttañ ca*, those used to fill out the meaning are of two kinds, i.e. those which can be used with or to replace case- and verbal endings, and those which cannot:
vibhattiyutta, those which are used with nominal or verbal endings, include
sakkā, *labbhā*, it is possible [indeclinable verbal forms]
bhiyyo, more, to a greater degree, [adverbial accusative]
saha/vinā, with/without [these usually take the instrumental case]
sammā/micchā, rightly/wrongly [i.e. manner]
- *tuṃ*, *-tave*, [indeclinable infinitive endings]
- *(i)to* [ending with the meaning] from
- *(i)to* [ending with the meaning] situated in/at (place or state), (*ekato*, *pacchato*, *padato*, *purato*, *sīsato*)

in this sense also *kuhiṃ*, *kva*, *tattha*, *tatra*, *tahiṃ*, *yatra*, *yattha*, *yahiṃ*, *yadā/tadā*, when/then [situated in time and/or space]
(also for place: *ajjhattaṃ/bahīraṃ*, *upari*, *oraṃ/paraṃ*, *pacchā/pure*, *samantā*, *samantato*, *sammukhā/parammukhā heṭṭhā*, etc.
avibhattiyutta, those which are not so used include:

app eva nāma	perhaps (+ opt.)
addhā	surely
kāmaṃ	at will, as it pleases
eva	indeed, only
kacci nu/nanu	surely, I hope
kathaṃ	how
kiṃ (su)	why [or to mark a question]
evaṃ, iti	thus
yāva/tāva	as far as / thus far
evaṃ, sādhu, āma	yes
puthu/visuṃ	separately, apart
nu (kho)	indeed
sace, yadi	if
ce	if [enclitic]
handa	lets now, alas
-tvā(na), -tuna	[absolutive ending]
yatra hi nāma	in as much as
(a)pi	[emphasis] *
su, sudaṃ	[emphasis]
yan nūna	what now if? (+ opt.)

kiñcāpi	although
yathā/tathā	just as, just so, thus
evaṃ (eva)	just so, thus
seyyathāpi (nāma)	just as [introducing simile]
seyyathīdaṃ	thats to say, i.e
aho/nāma	[stating praise or blame]
sādhu	good, well done
kira, kila	it seems, so it is said
suṭṭhu/duṭṭhu	well/badly
aññatra	otherwise
puna(ṃ)	again
dhuvaṃ	certainly
tu	indeed, but
-dhā	times
tathā pi	even so, nevertheless
je/re	[contemptuous address]
pag eva	how much more so
iṅgha	[encouragement] look!
aṅga	[irony, sarcasm]
viya/iva	as, like

* also used in a concessive sense, usually after participles

Although the semantic value of these particles may sometimes seem small, they contribute to the sound and rhythm of the sentence, especially in verse.

4.2 *bhāvanapuṃsaka* a neuter (commenting on) the verb, *kriyāvisesaṇa* (specifying the action of the verb), Adverbs

Many of the words cited by Aggavaṃsa as examples of *nipāta* would be classified as adverbs by western grammar. There is no such category in Pali or Sanskrit. The category of *kiriyāvisesaṇa* (specification of the action of the verb) contains a sub-category corresponding to that of adverb; words used adverbially in the neuter accusative are called *bhāvanapuṃsaka* (neuter [specifying a] state); *itthambhūta*, being so, is used alone and in compounds for the accusative or instrumental cases used as adverbs of manner.

Adverbial forms can be made by adding a suffix to a pronominal or nominal stem:

suffix	word	meaning
-tra	*tatra* *atra* *aññatra*	there here elsewhere
-ttha	*tattha* *ittha* *aññattha*	there here elsewhere
-thā	*yathā* *tathā* *aññathā*	just as, like thus otherwise
-thaṃ	*kathaṃ* *itthaṃ*	how? in this way

suffix	word	meaning
-hiṃ	*kuhiṃ* *tahiṃ}* *tahaṃ}*	where (to) there
*-to**	*pācīnato* *ito* *saṅkhepato*	from the east from here briefly
-so	*chandaso*	(i) in verse (ii) at will
	yoniso	from its origin, profoundly
	bhiyyoso	even more
-rahi	*etarahi* *carahi*	nowadays in that case

* this suffix can be used with nouns to form their abl. sing.

Nouns or adjectives in all oblique cases can be used adverbially:

accusative	*dukkhaṃ* *kāmaṃ*	unhappily, with difficulty at will, as one wishes
instrumental	*dhammena* *anupubbena*	properly, rightly, truly gradually, regularly
dative	*cirāya* *ajjatanāya*	at length today
ablative	*ārā* *samantā*	far, distant from all sides, complete
genitive	*cirassa* *divādivassa*	long, at length at noon, in (broad) daylight
locative	*dūre* *aṭṭhāne*	far out of place, unsuitably

5 *upasagga*
Prepositions and Verbal Prefixes

upasagga, addition, is so-called because words in this category add something, semantically or otherwise, to the simple verb or noun, whether conjoined with it or as a separate word.

visati upasaggā anekatthā hutvā nāmākhyātavisesakārakā bhavanti. upecca nāmañ ca ākhyātañ ca sajjanti lagganti tesam atthaṃ visesentī ti upasaggā.

There are twenty *upasagga*-s, with various meanings, which specify (the meaning of) nouns and verbs. Applying to nouns and verbs they approach and adhere to them, specifying their meaning, thus they are called *upasagga* (Sadd 886, cf. 880f.)

5.1 *vīsati upasaggāni*, Twenty Prepositions and Verbal Prefixes

ati	beyond, too much, very much
adhi	towards, up to
anu	following, after
apa	away from
api	on, over
abhi	towards, over
ava or *o*	down, away
ā	near to, away
u(d)	up, out of, away from
upa	towards, be subordinate to

du(r)	bad, wrong
ni	down, out
nī	away, out
pa	towards, onward
paṭi	back to, opposite
parā	on, over
pari	round, about,completely
vi	apart, separate
sam	together
su	well, right, very

Only the following five are at all common as separate words, prepositions: *anu*, following, after (+ accusative), *apa*, away from (+ ablative), *abhi*, towards, over (+ accusative), *ā*, near to, away (+ablative), *paṭi*, back to, opposite (+ accusative).

5.2 *nāma-*, *tvādiyanta-upasagga*, Nouns and Absolutives used as Prepositions

Nouns in an oblique case and absolutives can be used as prepositions or post-positions, as separate words or in compounds:

noun or absolutive	takes	meaning	derivation
agge	genitive	in front, at the top	locative of *agga*, top
accayena	genitive	after (the passing of)	instrumental of noun from √*ati-i*, go beyond
atthaṃ, *atthāya*, *atthā*	genitive	for the sake of, for the benefit of	accusative, dative, ablative cases of *attha* (Sanskrit *artha*)
atthāya	accusative	standing on, using	from √*ā-sthā*
anurūpaṃ, *anurūpena*, *anūrūpato*	genitive	conforming to, corresponding to	accusative, instrumental, ablative of *anurūpa*, suitable
antaraṃ, *antarena*, *antarā*	accusative, genitive	in, in between, amidst	accusative, instrumental, ablative of *antara*, inside
anvāya	accusative	after, because of	absolutive of √*anu-i*, go after
antikaṃ, *antike*	genitive	near, in presence of	accusative, locative of *antika*, near
abbhantaraṃ	locative	inside	accusative of *abbhantara*, interior
abbhantare	genitive	within, among	locative of of *abbhantara*, interior
avidūre	genitive	near	locative of *a-vidūra*, not remote
āgamma	accusative	owing to, with reference to	absolutive of √*ā-gam*, come near, follow
ādāya	accusative	with	absolutive of √*ā-dā*, take
ārabbha	accusative	starting with, referring to	absolutive of √*ā-rabh*, begin
uddissa	accusative	intended for, concerning	absolutive of √*ud-diś*, point to, allot
upanidhāya	accusative	setting beside, comparing	absolutive of √*upa-ni-dhā*, put near
upanissāya, *nissāya*	accusative	depending on	absolutives of √*upa-ni-śri*, lie down
upādāya	accusative	attached to, starting from, with reference to	absolutive of √*upa-ā-dā*, take
kāraṇā	genitive	by means of, because of	ablative of *kāraṇa*, cause

noun or absolutive	takes	meaning	derivation
ṭhapetvā	accusative	except, besides	causative absolutive of √*ṭṭhā*, make stand (apart)
dūre	ablative	far from	locative of *dūra*, far
paccayā	genitive	because of	ablative of *paccaya*, cause
paṭicca	accusative	because of	absolutive of √*paṭi-i*, fall back on
paṭṭhāya	ablative	from (space and time)	absolutive of √*pa-ṭṭhā*, send away
majjhe	genitive	in the middle of	locative of *majjha*, middle
vivicca	instrumental	separate from, far from	absolutive of √*vi-vic*, separate
santikaṃ, *santike*	genitive	into, in the presence of	accusative, locative of *santika*, presence
sandhāya	accusative	with reference to	absolutive of √*saṃ-dhā*, put together
samīpe	genitive	near to	locative of *samīpa*, near
sammukhā	genitive	face to face, in presence of	ablative of *sammukha*, face to face
hetu	genitive	because of	accusative of *hetu*, cause

6 *samāsa* Compounds

6.1 *samāsapadāni,* Compound Words

(Aggavaṃsa deals with compounds in Chapter 23, from where the selections given here are mostly taken.)

samāsapadāni, words in a compound, are opposed to *vyāsapadāni*, words in separation and to *vākyapadāni*, words in a sentence, as synthetic linguistic processes in general are opposed to analytic. Compounds are characterized by *ekapadatta*, the fact of being one word, and *ekavibhattitā*, the fact of having one inflection (in relation to other words in the sentence). The final member of a compound, and hence the compound as a whole, is usually declined as an *–a* stem, with number, case and gender depending on the context. Usually a compound is related syntactically to other words in the sentence as a single unit. There are, however, many exceptions to this rule.

tattha duvidhaṃ samasanaṃ: saddasamasanaṃ atthasamasanañ ca, compounding is of two kinds, compounding of words and compounding of meanings:
saddasamasanaṃ luttasamāse labbhati, samaṇabrahmaṇā ti ādisu, compounding of words occurs with the elimination (of endings) in compounds such as 'ascetics and brahmins,'
atthasamasanaṃ aluttasamāse dūrenidānaṃ, gavampati... ti labbhati, compounding of meanings occurs without the elimination (of endings), in compounds such as 'Story of the Remote (Past),' 'Lord of Cows'.

Two egregious examples of compounds without the elimination of endings are the words translated as Active and Middle Voice, Sanskrit *parasmaipada*, *ātmanepada*, Pali *parassapada*, *attanopada*, word(s) for another, word(s) for oneself, in which the first elements retain their dative endings. This contrasts with usual forms such as *ātma/atta*, oneself, *para*, (an)other + *hita*, benefit → Sanskrit *ātmahita*, *parahita*, Pali *attahita*, *parahita*, benefit for oneself, benefit for another.

(*samāso*) *sabhāvato niccasamāso aniccasamāso ti duvidho*, a compound is by nature either permanent or impermanent.

Permanent compounds are:

(i) those with an accessory word (*upapada*) in final position: *kammaṃ karotī ti kammakāro*, he does a deed → he is a deed-doer,' *attato jāto ti attajo*, he is born from oneself → he is a son, and proper names such as *ariṃ dametī ti Arindamo*, he conquers his enemies → (he is) Arindama

(ii) those with an absolutive (*tvādiyanta)* in initial position, *aññamaññaṃ paṭicca sahite dhamme uppādetī paṭiccasamuppāda*, it gives rise to Existents together, in dependence on each other → (it is) Dependent Co-arising.

Impermanent compounds, which are the vast majority, are made up ad hoc, and are characterized by *ekapadatta*, constituting a single word, only temporarily.

6.2. *samāsavidha*, Categories of compound

No set of English terms for Sanskrit and Pali compounds is generally accepted, although the Sanskrit words for the three main kinds, *tatpuruṣa*, *karmadhāraya* and *bahuvrīhi* are now in OED as English words. There are eight main kinds of compound:

English term	Pali name	meaning
copulative	*dvanda*	pair
descriptive determinative (including) numerical	*kammadhāraya digu*	[unknown] two-cow
dependent determinative (including) prepositional	*tappurisa* *upasagganipātapubbaka*	his man (= the king's servant) beginning with a *nipāta* or *upasagga*
possessive, exocentric, attributive	*bahubbīhi*	of whom there is (who has) much rice
adverbial	*avyāyībhava*	(in an) unchanging state
syntactical	[this category comes from western scholarship]	

These eight categories can be reduced to two basic kinds, copulative and determinative:

copulative (*dvandva*) compounds are simple collocations of words.

The category of the determinative can be subdivided thus:
the descriptive (*kammadhāraya*) includes the numerical (*digu*),
the dependent (*tappurisa*), includes the prepositional (*upasagga-nipātapubbaka*),
both kinds can have adverbial (*avyayībhāva*) and possessive (*bahubbīhi*) uses

Copulative compounds:

if the words were uncompounded there would almost always be *ca / vā*, and/or, to connect them. The compound as a whole can be declined variously: as neuter singular, as singular in the gender of the final member, as plural in the gender of the final member. It is not possible to decide how many persons or things a *dvandva* refers to apart from its context.

copulative compound in the nominative case	members of the compound	meaning
sīhavyagghadīpī	*sīha + vyaggho + dīpī*	lion(s), tiger(s) and leopard(s)
jānapadanegamā	*jānapada + negama*	countrypeople and townspeople
jarāmaraṇaṃ	*jarā + maraṇa*	old age and death
udayabbayaṃ	*udaya + vyaya*	rise and fall
pītisukhaṃ	*pīti + sukha*	rapture and happiness
dhammavinayo	*dhamma + vinaya*	the Teaching and the Monastic Rule
(sā) daharasapaññā	*dahara +sapañña*	(she is) young and/but wise
dvittipattā	*dvi + ti + patta*	two or three bowls

Just as a word can be repeated separately in a sentence for various reasons, so also in dvandvas:

samasama, the same [modern South and Southeast Asian English same-same]
gāmagāmena, village by village
punappunaṃ, again and again

Determinative compounds can be used as nouns, adjectives or adverbs, and are formed from various combinations of parts of speech. They are called determinative because the first member determines or qualifies the second, that is, the first makes the compound as a whole a sub-category of the second. The major subdivision is between Descriptive (*kammadhāraya*) and Dependent (*tappurisa*) Determinatives:

In Descriptive Determinatives the first member describes the second.

The two members of a descriptive determinative would , if used as separate words, be in the same case, unless the first is an adverb and so indeclinable. A goldfish is one kind of fish, dog-tired is one way or degree of being tired, sky-blue is one kind of blue.

pubbapuriso, (former person) ancestor (D I 93),

assosi Bhagavā uccāsaddaṃ mahāsaddaṃ, the Blessed One heard a high sound, a great sound (Vin II 111), *ucchiṭṭhodakam pi pattena nīharanti*, they carried in their bowls water which had been spat out (Vin II 115).

When the initial member is a numeral, it is called *digu kammadhāraya*
saṃkhyāpubbo kammadhārayasamāso digusañño hoti: dve gavo digu. A *kammadhāraya* compound with a number initial is called a *digu*: two cows → two-cows.

samāhāradigu tāva: cattāri saccāni → *catusaccaṃ*, *asamāhāradigu*, *dasasahassāni cakkavāḷāni* → *dasasahassacakkavāḷāni*, a digu can bring things together (into a single concept, declined in the singular neuter), the four truths → fourfold Truth, [or] it need not do so, ten thousand world-spheres → ten-thousand-world-spheres (declined in the singular or plural, according to the gender of the final member).

Digu kammadhārayas are especially common in referring to lists of psycho-physical categories:

tilakkhanāni	Three Characteristics
catusaccāni	Four Truths
pañcakkhandhā	Five Bundles
saḷayātanāni	Six Sense-Bases
sattabhojaṅgāni	Seven Constituents of Awakening
atthalokadhammā	Eight Conditions in the World

In Dependent Determinatives the first member depends on the second for its sense within the compound.

The two members of a Dependent Determinative would, if used as separate words, be in different cases, and the case of the first would depend on the second. A side-door (door-at-the-side) is one kind of door, fact-finding (finding facts) is one kind of finding, a crewcut is one kind of cut (itself a synecdoche for haircut).

so bhagavā... vijjācaraṇasampanno... lokavidū... purisadammasārathi, that Blessed One is... possessed of knowledge and good conduct.. a knower of the world(s),.. a trainer of people in need of training (D I 49),

sīlaparibhāvito samādhi mahapphalo, concentration developed with morality is of great fruit (D II 81).

The final member can be a short word not used outside compounds, such as *-ññu* from √*jñā*, to know (*kataññu*, 'knowing what has been done' = grateful), *-dhara* from √*dhṛ*, to carry, (*antimadehadhārī*, one who bears his last body).

Prepositional compounds (*upasagganipātapubbaka*) are so called because they are Dependent Determinatives whose first element is a preposition or verbal prefix which governs the second member. This is the opposite of the relation between the first and second members in other Dependent Determinatives, since if the members of a Prepositional compound were separate words (sometimes only a theoretical possibility), the first would determine the case of the second:

Prepositional compound	if members were separate	meaning
ākumāra	*ā kumārehi* [ablative]	[known even] to children
paccakkha	*paṭi akkhe* [accusative]	in front of the eyes, immediate
adhikumārī	*adhi kumāriyāyaṃ* [locative]	(towards) about a young woman
abhidakkhiṇa	*abhi dakkhiṇaṃ* [accusative]	towards the right
viraja	*vi(nā) rajena* [instrumental]	without dust, stainless
anuloma	*anu lomaṃ* [accusative]	with the hair = properly, rightly

Adverbial compounds (*avyayībhāva*), are of two kinds, acording to whether they have an *upassagga* or a *nipāta* as initial member and so that which has *padhāna*, predominance, within the compound.

(i) with a preposition as initial member (*upassaggapaṭhamo*)
upa + *nagara* → *upanagaraṃ* = *nagarassa samīpaṃ*, close to town
ā + *pāṇa* + *koṃi* → *āpāṇakotiyaṃ* = *ā pāṇassa koṭiyā*, to the limit of breath (till death)
nir + *masaka* → *nimmasaka* = *n' atthi masakā etthā ti* = without mosquitoes
anu + *ratha* → *anurathaṃ* = *rathassa pacchā*, behind the cart

(ii) with a particle as initial member (*nipātapubbako*)
yathā + *vuḍḍha* → *yathāvuḍḍhaṃ* = *vuddhānaṃ paṭipāṭi* [or] *ye ye vuḍḍhā*, in order of age, according to age
tiro + *kuḍḍa* → *tirokuḍḍaṃ* = *kuddānaṃ tiro*, outside the walls
pure + *bhatta* → *purebhattaṃ* = *bhattassa pure*, before the meal

Some more examples:

yathābhūtaṃ	as it really is
paṭisotaṃ	against the stream, wrongly
vuttapakāraṃ	in the manner of what was (just) said, as before
rājasāsanato	in accordance with the kings orders
madhurassaraṃ	in a honey (-sweet) voice
ativelaṃ	beyond the limit, excessively
*adiṭṭhapubbaṃ**	in a way unseen before
yebhuyyena	mostly, usually
anupubbena	gradually

* *pubba* is usually placed at the end of compounds.

Possessives (*bahubbīhi*) are not are not a different kind of compound. They are determinative compounds ending in a noun, which are used and declined as adjectives. They are for this reason also called attributive, and, because as adjectives they necessarily refer to something outside of themselves, exocentric. Whatever is their final member, they almost always follow the *-a* declension, and as adjectives agree in number, gender and case with the noun they qualify. This means, for example, that a feminine noun at the end of a possessive used as an adjective qualifying a masculine noun becomes masculine, and vice-versa.

kiñcāpi kho 'mhi dukkhitā dubbalā gatayobbanā, [the nun Mettikā says] although I am suffering, weak and with youth gone (Thī 29),
Kondañño pattadhammo viditadhammo, Kondañña is one by whom the Dhamma is attained, and by whom the Dhamma is known (Vin I 12),
sabbaṃ bhedapariyantaṃ evaṃ maccāna jīvitaṃ, the end of everything is breaking up, such is the life of mortals (D II 120),
khīṇāsavā jutīmanto te loke parinibbutā, those in whom the Corruptions have wasted away, full of brightness, have reached nirvana in the world (Dhp 89).

Compounded words can also be used as possessive adjectives by the addition of the suffixes *(i)ka* or *(i)ya*. This is analogous to English noun compounds made into adjectives by adding the suffix –ed: white-coated, fair-haired, short-tempered, kind-hearted. In Pali sometimes the initial vowel in such adjectives is strengthened to guṇa.

words	compound type	compound	*(i)ka, (i)ya* adjective	meaning
anu + loma	prepositional	*anuloma*	*anulomika*	with the hair = properly, rightly
puna(r) + bhava	descriptive determinative	*punabbhava*	*ponobhavika*	leading to rebirth
ku + tittha	descriptive determinative	*kutittha*	*kuttithiya*	one who (follows a) bad path, member of another sect
aṭṭhaka + vagga	dependent determinative	*aṭṭhakavagga*	*aṭṭhakavaggiya*	belonging to the Chapter of Eights
*tiracchāna** *+ kathā*	dependent determinative	*tiracchānakathā*	*tiracchānakathika*	one who talks frivolously, a gossiper

* *tiracchāna* is from Sanskrit *tiryañc*, horizontal, and means going/one who goes horizontally, i.e. an animal. *tiracchāna-kathā*, talk about animals, is used as a synecdoche for unfruitful chatter, gossip.

Syntactical compounds, although a category deriving from western scholars, provides a useful rubric under which to gather compounds of four main types:

(i) those which have as first member a verb in a form other than an adjectival participle

viceyyadāna is made up of an absolutive from √*vi-ci*, to investigate, consider, and *dāna*, gift. So it means a gift (given) after consideration, a considered gift.

niggayhavādin is an absolutive from √*ni-gṛh*, to restrain, rebuke, with *vāda*, word, and the possessive *-in* suffix: one who speaks rebukingly, one who speaks in restraint (of others).

(ii) those which have as first member a past participle governing something outside the compound

idaṃ mayā navamāse aḍḍhamāsañca samaṇadhammassa katatthānaṃ, this is the place where the duties of an ascetic were done by me for nine and a half months (literally This is the place of the doing of an ascetic's duties by me) (Ja VI 588)

so tayā kathitamaggena taṃ gehaṃ gato, he went to the house by the way she had said (Ja VI 368)

(iii) those whose members when used separately would require a *ti* clause.

The simplest example of this type is when a letter of the alphabet or a word is cited rather than used, as in *īkara*, making (vowel-sound) "*ī* "

kālasaddo, the word *kāla* (time).

sādhusammatā, considered to be the good, would be *te sādhū ti sammatā*, they are considered "good"

kusalasaṃkhātaṃ, reckoned as meritorious, would be *kusalan ti saṃkhāyanti*, (people) reckon it to be 'meritorious'.

Some compounds start with the imperative *ehi*, from √ *ī*, go:

compound	element(s) added to *ehi*	meaning
ehipassika	imperative from √*paś*, *passa*, see + *ka*	(the Dhamma is) a "come, see!" thing
ehibhaddantika	*bhadanta*, sir + *ka*	(a monk invited with the words) "come, sir"
ehibhikkhupabbajjā	vocative *bhikkhu*, monk, and *pabbajjā*, ordination	the ordination (performed with the words) "come, monk"*

* This refers to the story in the Vinaya that the Buddha first ordained monks with the performative utterance 'come, monk.'

Aggavaṃsa explains that some compounds which look like Dependent Determinatives are not: e.g. in *(Buddhaṃ) saraṇagato*, gone to (the Buddha for) refuge, *Buddhaṃ* is the object of *gata*, with *saraṇa* [neuter, nominative] in a *ti* clause with *ti* elided: *Buddhaṃ saranan ti gato*, gone to the Buddha as (one's) 'refuge.'

(iv) those rare cases which contain a *ti* clause:

anaññātañ ñassāmī ti evaṃ paṭipannassa pavattaṃ indriyaṃ anaññātañ-ñassāmī-t'-indriyaṃ, 'the faculty which occurs in a person practising (with the thought) 'I will come to know what is unknown' is the I-will-come-to-know-what-is-unknown-faculty,

Jotipālo ti nāmaṃ Jotipālo-ti-nāmaṃ, the name 'Jotipala' is Jotipala-name.

Most compounds cited so far have had only two members, but they can have more than two members, sometimes many more. The analysis of long compounds at every stage breaks them into two parts:

the three-part compound *adiṭṭhapubbamaraṇā*, she who had not seen death before, is a Descriptive Determinative, not-seen-before-death, used as a Possessive, by whom death was unseen-before.

a + *diṭṭha* is a Descriptive Determinative with two members, a past passive participle with the negative prefix,

[adiṭṭha] + *pubba* is a Descriptive Determinative with two members, *adiṭṭha* + *pubba*,

{[a-diṭṭha]-pubba} + *maraṇa* is a Descriptive Determinative with two members, *adiṭṭhapubba* + *maraṇa*.

The four-part compound *alaṃkata-hatthi-kkhandha-gato* translated directly is decorated-elephant-back-gone, which is as a whole a Descriptive Determinative (*gata* at the end of compounds rarely means gone. It has prepositional force, meaning on, at, in, etc.):

alaṃkata + *hatthi* is a Descriptive Determinative with two members, *alaṃkata* + *hatthi*

[*alaṃkata-hatthi*] + *kkhandha* is a Dependent Determinative with two members, *alaṃkatahatthi* + *kkhandha*

{[*alaṃkata-hatthi*]*kkhandha*} + *gata* is a Dependent Determinative with two members, *alaṃkatahatthikkhandha* + gata the six-part compound *catur-assa-pokkharaṇī-pupphita-rukkha-paṭimaṇḍitaṃ* translated directly is four-cornered-lotus-pond-flowering-tree(s)-made-beautiful. It is a Dependent Determinative used as an adjective.

catur + *assa* is a *digu* Descriptive Determinative used as a Possessive, with two members, *catur* + *assa*

[*catur- assa*] + *pokkharaṇī* is a Descriptive Determinative, with two members *caturassa* + *pokkharaṇī*

pupphita + *rukkha* is a Descriptive Determinative, with two members *pupphita* + *rukkha*, contained within

{[*catur-assa*]*pokkharaṇī*} + [*pupphita-rukkha*], a Copulative with two members *caturassapokkharaṇī* + *pupphita-rukkha*,

⟨{[*catur-assa*]*pokkharaṇī*} - [*pupphita-rukkha*]⟩ + *paṭimaṇḍitaṃ* is a Dependent Determinative, with two members *caturassapokkharaṇīpupphitarukkha* + *paṭimaṇḍitaṃ*

Aggavaṃsa cites this example of Pali *kāvya*-style:

pavarasurāsuragaruḍamanujabhujagagandabbamakuṭakūṭacumbitaselasaṃghaṭṭitacaraṇo tathāgato, the Tathagata's feet resounded on rocks which had been gently touched by [lit.: 'at'] the tops of head-ornaments (belonging to) magnificent gods and anti-gods, garuda-birds, humans, snakes and celestial musicians

The analysis [from Kacc Be 173–4] is:

surā + *asurā* + *garuḍā* + *manujā* + *bhujagā* + *gandhabbā* is a Copulative with six members

pavarā + [*surāsuragaruḍamanujabhujagagandhabbā*] is a Descriptive Determinative

[*pavarasurāsuragaruḍamanujabhujagagandhabbānaṃ*] + *makuṭāni* is a Dependent Determinative

[*pavarasurāsuragaruḍamanujabhujagagandhabbamakuṭānaṃ*] + *kūṭāni* is a Dependent Determinative

[*pavarasurāsuragaruḍamanujabhujagagandhabbamakuṭakūṭesu*] + *cumbitā* is a Dependent Determinative

[*pavarasurāsuragaruḍamanujabhujagagandhabbamakuṭakūṭacumbitā*] + *selā* is a Descriptive Determinative

[*pavarasurāsuragaruḍamanujabhujagagandhabbamakuṭakūṭacumbitaselesu*] *saṃghaṭṭitā* is a Dependent Determinative [*pavarasurāsuragaruḍamanujabhujagagandhabbamakuṭakūṭacumbitaselasaṃghaṭṭitā*] + *caraṇā* is a Descriptive Determinative

[-*caranā yassa tathāgatassa*] *so 'yaṃ pavarasurāsuragaruḍamanujabhujaga-gandab bamakuṭakūṭacumbitaselasaṃghattitacaraṇo tathāgato* is a Possessive based on a Descriptive Determinative

7 *iti-sadda*

Direct and Indirect Speech

The word *iti*, usually abbreviated to *ti* in Pali, is used as an *avyayībhāva nipāta*, in western terms as an adverb of manner prefixed or, more often, suffixed to the word(s), phrase(s) or clause(s) to which it applies. (When followed by a vowel *iti* can → *icc*, *iti eva* → *icceva*, and also (for reasons not known) *ti eva* appears often in manuscripts as *tveva*). Its most common use is to record words which would in English be called direct speech. Before *ti* vowels are lengthened and *ṃ* → *n*.

> *sakkā pana, bhante, aññampi diṭṭheva dhamme sandiṭṭhikaṃ sāmaññaphalaṃ paññapetuṃ imehi sandiṭṭhikehi sāmaññaphalehi abhikkantatarañ ca paṇītatarañ cā ti? sakkā, mahārāja. tena hi, mahārāja, suṇohi, sādhukaṃ manasi karohi, bhāsissāmī ti. evaṃ, bhante ti kho rājā Māgadho Ajātasattu Vedehiputto bhagavato paccassosi.* 'but can you, sir, indicate a visible result of the ascetic life in this life which is greater and more refined than these visible results of the ascetic life?' 'I can, great king. So listen, great king, and pay careful attention (while) I speak.' 'Yes, sir,' agreed the Magadhan king Ajatasattu Vedehiputto (D I 62).

Sometimes the words which occur in the *iti* clause are not intended to be direct representations of speech or thought, but rather the *iti* clause gives the rationale for some action:

> *andhakāre vā telapajjotaṃ dhāreyya cakkhumanto rūpāni dakkhintī ti*, or might bring a lamp into the darkness, so that those who have eyes will (be able to) see [thinking 'those...'] (Vin I 16).

Aggavaṃsa (Sadd 317) notes that *iti* has many meanings (*anekatthapabhedo*), and gives these examples:

hetu, cause, reason: *ruppatī ti kho bhikkhave tasmā rūpan ti vuccatī ti ādisu*, in such sentences as 'It is vexed, and so it is called 'body,'

parisamāpana, bringing to completion: *tasmā-t-iha me bhikkhave dhammadāyādā bhavatha mā āmisadāyādā, atthi me tumhesu anukampā, kinti me savakā dhammadāyādā bhaveyyuṃ no āmisadāyādā ti ādisu*, in such sentences as 'therefore, monks, be heirs of the Dhamma, not of material things. I have compassion for you, (thinking) how (exactly) might my Listeners become heirs of the Dhamma, not of material things?',

ādi, beginning with, such as: *iti vā iti evarūpā visūkadassanā pativirato ti ādisu*, in such sentences as [following a list of various kinds of entertainment] dispassionate towards unseemly spectacles of such and such a kind,

padatthavipariyāya, variation in the meanings of (near-synonymous) words: *Māgandiyo ti tassa brahmanassa saṃkhā samaññā paññatti vohāro nāmaṃ nāmakammaṃ nāmadheyyaṃ nirutti vyañjanam abhilāpo ti ādisu*, in such sentences as '"*Magandiya*" is an appellation, designation, idea, customary term, name, naming, title, manner of speaking, expression, saying for that brahmin',

pakāra, manner: *iti kho bhikkhave sappaṭibhayo bālo appaṭibhayo paṇḍito sauppaddavo bālo anuppadāvo paṇḍito*...[etc.] *ti ādisu*, in such sentences as 'thus, monks, a fool is someone from whom derives fear, a wise man is someone from whom there does not, a fool is someone from whom derives misfortune, a wise man is someone from whom there does not [etc.],'

avadhāraṇa, affirmation: *atthi idappaccayā jarāmaraṇan ti iti puṭṭhena satā Ānanda atthī ti 'ssa vacanīyaṃ, kimpaccayā jarāmaraṇaṃ iti ce vadeyya jātipaccayā jarāmaraṇam ti icc 'ssa vacanīyan ti ādisu*, in such sentences as 'Ananda, were a wise person questioned in this way, 'Does old-age-and-death exist because of a specific cause?', he would say 'It does.' If [the interlocutor] were to speak in this way, 'from what as cause is there old-age-and-death?' he would reply in this way: 'old-age-and-death exists because of birth as cause' [the commentaries contrast this with situations where a question is to be set aside because it cannot be answered]

nidassana, illustration: *atthī ti kho Kaccāna ayam eko anto, n' atthī ti kho Kaccāna ayaṃ dutiyo anto ti ādisu*, in such sentences as '"it exists," Kaccana, this is one extreme, 'It does not exist," Kaccana, this is a second extreme'

A related use is at the beginning of adverbial compounds: *iti Kaccāyanaṃ*, thus Kaccayana.

Appendix 1

PALI GRAMMATICAL TERMS

akammaka	verb without an object, intransitive
akārāgama	augment *a* used with some past tenses of verbs
akkhara	letter, syllable
aghosa dhanita	voiceless aspirated
aghosa sithila	voiceless unaspirated
ajjatanī	aorist
antaṭṭha	semi-vowel
attanopada	middle voice
atthapūraṇa nipāta	particle which fills out the meaning of a sentence
adhikaraṇa	locative case
anajjatanī	imperfect
(an)abhihita	(un)expressed (agent or object)
anutta-, aniyatakāla	not restricted to a specific time (applies to imperative and optative)
apādāna	ablative case
appadhānaliṅga	whose gender is subordinate, adjective
abbhāsa	reduplication
abhidheyya-liṅga	whose gender is that which it signifies, noun
avadhi	ablative case
avyaya	indeclinable
avyayībhāva	adverbial compound
asatva	not denoting a substantial existence (i.e. which could be the subject of a sentence)
ākhyāta	verb
ādhāra	locative case
ālapana	vocative case

āmantaṇa	vocative case
itthiliṅga	feminine gender
uttama purisa	last (third) person = I, we
upayoga	accusative case
upasagga	preposition, verbal prefix
ekavacana	singular
okāsa	locative case
oṭṭhaja	labial
kaṇṭhaja	guttural
kattā	grammatical and logical subject of active verb, logical subject of passive verb
kamma	object of a verb
kammakattā	an agent who is (also) an object
kattukamma	secondary agent of causative verb
kammakattukiriyāpada	verb which expresses an object-agent (reflexive)
kammuno kiriyāpada	passive voice
kammadhāraya	descriptive determinative compound
karaṇa	instrumental case
kāra	letter, syllable (e.g. *lakāra* = the letter 'la')
kāraka	factor of action
kārita	causative
kāla	tense
kālātipatti	conditional
kicca	'to be done', future passive participle (gerundive)
kitanta	words with a suffix (from the list beginning with) *kit* (participles, absolutives and infinitives)
kiriyāvisesa	adverb
kriyā, kiriyā	action of a verb
kiriyāvisesaṇa	specification of the action of the verb, esp. adverb

gaṇa	verbal class, metrical group
guṇa	intermediate strength in vowel gradation
guṇanāma, guṇapada	word for a quality, adjective
guṇipada	word for that which has qualities, noun
ghosavat dhanita	voiced aspirated
ghosavat sithila	voiced unaspirated
catutthī	dative case
chaṭṭhī	genitive case
tatiyā	instrumental case
taddhita	secondary derivative
tappurisa	dependent determinative compound
tāluja	palatal
tumanta	infinitive
tumicchattha	with the meaning wanting (for oneself), desiderative
tvādiyanta	indeclinable (past) participle, gerund, absolutive
dantaja	dental
digu	numerical compound
dutiyā	accusative case
dvanda	copulative compound
dvikammaka	(verb) with two direct objects
dhātu	verbal root
dhāturūpakasadda	denominative
napuṃsakaliṅga	neuter gender
nāma	noun, adjective, pronoun, numeral
nāmanāma	noun
nāsikā	nasal
niggahīta	nasalization, the letter ṃ
nipāta	particle, including conjunctions, adverbs
nissaka	ablative case

paccatta	nominative case
paccaya	verbal suffix
paccuppanna(kāla)	present (time)
pañcamī	imperative mood; ablative case
paṭisedha	negative, privative, prohibitive
paṭhamapurisa	first person of verbs = he, she, it, they
paṭhamā	nominative case
pada	word, syllable, phrase, sentence
padhānalinga	whose gender is superordinate, noun
parassapada	active voice
parokkhā	perfect tense
pātipadika	nominal theme
puthuvacana	plural
pubbakiriyā	gerund
pūraṇa	filler
pūraṇapada nipāta	particle which fills up a sentence, without expressing a specific meaning
purisa	person
pulliṅga	masculine gender
bahubbīhi	possessive, exocentric compound
bahuvacana	plural
bhāva	state, simple notion expressed by verb
bhāvakiriyāpada	verb which expresses a state-of-being, impersonal passive
bhāvanapuṃsaka	adverb (in neuter singular)
bhavissantī	future tense
bhumma	locative
majjhimapurisa	second person = you
matta (= mora)	the length of time it takes to pronounce a short vowel
muḍḍhaja	cerebral, retroflex
lakāra	verbal tense or mood (according to the Pāṇinian scheme)
liṅga	gender; nominal stem

vāccaliṅga	whose gender is that of the word which it qualifies, adjective
vaṇṇa	phoneme
vattamāna	present tense
vākya	sentence
vācogadhapada	(type of) word contained in language
vikappana	disjunction (e.g. *vā*)
(no)vikaraṇa(-paccaya)	verbal suffix
vibhatti, vibhatyanta	inflectional suffix, for nouns and verbs
visesana	specification, e.g. adjective or some genitives
vuddhi (vṛddhi)	greatest strength in vowel gradation
vyañjana	consonant
vyaya	inflection
saṃyoga	conjunction (e.g. *ca*, *pi*)
sakammaka	verb with one or more objects
sakāra	sibilant
saṃkhyā	number
saṃkhyāpadhāna	cardinal number used as a noun
saṃkhyāpūraṇa	ordinal number
saṃkhyeyyapadhāna	cardinal number used as an adjective
sattamī	optative mood; locative case
sadda	word
saddasattha	grammar
sandhi	conjunction of final and initial letters, or of letters within a word
sabbanāma	pronoun, pronominal adjective
samāsa	compound
samuccaya	conjunction (e.g. *ca*, *pi*)
sampadāna	dative case
sambandha	genitive case
sambodhana	locative case
sara	vowel
sāmi	genitive case
suddhakattukiriyāpada	verb which expresses an agent pure and simple
suddhakattā	an agent pure and simple

hakāra	spirant
hīyattanī	imperfect tense
hetukattukiriyāpada	verb which expresses a causal agent (= agent of a causative verb)
hetukattā	agent of causative verb

Appendix 2

ENGLISH GRAMMATICAL TERMS

ABSOLUTE CONSTRUCTIONS

The word absolute is from the Latin *absolūtus*, which means both separate from (absolute constructions being grammatically separate from the sentence) and complete (absolute constructions being complete in themselves). A construction is absolute if

(i) it contains a non-finite verb form, usually -ing or -ed (excluding the infinitive), or is verbless

(ii) it has an explicit subject which is not identifiable with anything in the main clause, and

(iii) it is not introduced by a subordinator.

In spoken English, absolute constructions are restricted to a few stereotypes such as God willing, weather permitting, present company excepted. Formal or written English can make them up ad hoc: retirement only a few years away, he decided to increase his pension payments; there being no further discussion, the jury voted; those objections notwithstanding, they went ahead as planned.

ADJECTIVE

The word *adjective* is from *ad-iectum*, thrown or placed next to. Adjectives can be single words, phrases or clauses. Older European grammars often classed adjectives with nouns, under the names *noun adjective* and *noun substantive*.

Adjectives answer one of the questions: What kind is it? How many are there? Which one is it? They can be formed in different ways:

as simple words: green, tall
derived from or identical to nouns: golden, quizzical, silver
derived from verbs, especially the present and part participles: smiling, escaping, beaten, guided.

Adjectives can be:
attributive, placed before what they qualify: He is a skilled plumber.
postpositive, placed after what they qualify: This needs a plumber skilled in repairing central heating pipes.
a predicative complement: Her brother is skilled in many kinds of plumbing.

Words classified as nouns are often used as adjectives (more precisely, they are used, like adjectives, as attributive modifiers): house → house-boat, tractor → tractor-driver, mouse + dropping (verb → noun) → mouse-dropping chili (a Thai chili), studio → studio apartment.

However, adjectives can have comparative and superlative forms (big, bigger, biggest) whereas nouns used as adjectives, or adjectives derived from nouns, cannot: a studio apartment but not *a studioer apartment, a golden cup but not *a goldener cup.

Adjectives can be modified by an adverb, whereas nouns used as adjectives cannot: a very good car but not *a very sports car.

When an adjective qualifies a pronoun it almost always follows it: those present at (the play), but not *present those; anyone worthy (of respect), but not *worthy anyone. Occasional exceptions can be found.

When an adjective is used postpositively it can be seen as a short version of a clause (the only thing likeable in this = the only thing which is likeable in this). Used as predicates they follow the verb, which will be the copula or a linking verb. A verbal phrase containing a participle used adjectivally usually follows the noun.

ATTRIBUTIVE PRECEDING	PREDICATIVE	ATTRIBUTIVE FOLLOWING
a well-done steak	the steak is well-done	I prefer my steak well-done
[What was this big thing?] I don't know, it was a big something	something is big (I don't know what)	something big
this easier task (is possible)	this task is easier	(do you want) a task easier than that?
tired women (during pregnancy)	women feel tired	women tired (by pregnancy should try to rest)
her smiling face	her face is smiling	her face smiling with joy

Words which look like adjectives may not be adjectives:

In the sentence This woman is like an angel the word like is an adjective, but in This woman dances like an angel it is an adverb. Accordingly, in translation into Pali the first would require an adjective for like, agreeing with woman in case, number, and gender, whereas the second would require an indeclinable word used adverbially.

Some pronouns are identical in form, but not in function, to pronominal adjectives, as this/these in the following: This is a book (pronoun), This book is mine (pronominal adjective), Whose books are these? (pronoun), These books are John's (pronominal adjective).

If the comparison of adjectives is counted as an inflection, then adjectives can also decline, with -er and -est in regular forms and unpredictable changes in irregular forms:

fast →	faster →	fastest
big →	bigger →	biggest
good →	better →	best
bad →	worse →	worst

ADVERB

Adverbs qualify—i.e. they describe, modify, intensify, limit, etc.—verbs, adjectives, other adverbs, phrases and clauses. They express relations of place, time, circumstance, causality, manner, or degree. They can be derived from other words, standardly by using suffixes such as -ly, or they can be independent words, which are often identical in form to adjectives or prepositions. The derived class is open, as new instances can be freely added, but the non-derived class is closed. Adverbs can qualify:

verbs: He runs quickly; They walked clockwise round the park.
adjectives: They are more interested in books; She is extremely beautiful.
adverbs: He drives too fast; You spoke very clearly.
clauses: We will probably have left by then; Frankly I haven't the faintest idea

Other suffixes are seen in words such as homeward(s), crab-fashion, lengthways, American-style.

Some adverbs join phrases or clauses: also, consequently, finally, hence, however, indeed, instead, likewise, meanwhile, nevertheless, next, nonetheless, otherwise, still, then, therefore, thus

Adverbs can be classified in many different ways. One common way is:

adverbs of time answer the question when?: then, now, formerly, earlier, later, yesterday, sometimes
adverbs of place answer the question where?: there, here, in front, behind, somewhere, upwards, downwards
adverbs of manner answer the question how?: happily, easily, loudly, softly, painfully, gladly
adverbs of degree answer the question how much? excessively, insufficiently, quite, scarcely, very, wholly, etc.

Like adjectives, adverbs can have comparative and superlative forms. Regular forms use -er and -est or the auxiliaries more and most:

fast → faster → fastest, slow → slower → slowest, quietly → more quietly → most quietly, thoroughly → more thoroughly → most thoroughly

Some irregular forms: good → better → best, bad → worse → worst, little → less → least

Many adverbs do not have comparative and superlative forms: almost, extremely, nearly, rather, too, etc.

ANALYTIC / SYNTHETIC LANGUAGES AND PROCESSES

Analytic languages predominantly (never completely) express syntactic relations within sentences by the use of small words or particles, while synthetic languages use such means as inflection and the use of compounds. English is a predominantly analytic language. Pali is a predominantly synthetic language. Languages which are predominantly analytic use on average only slightly more than one morpheme per word. Vietnamese has been estimated to have 1.06 morphemes per word. Predominantly synthetic processes, as are found in some Native American and Siberian languages, combine morphemes into single words which can be as long as, and equivalent to sentences. Pali compounds, unlike English, can have many members.

Although English is predominantly analytic, with roughly 1.68 morphemes per word, it also has synthetic processes:

	ANALYTIC	SYNTHETIC
NOUNS	the hair of the dog	the dog's hair or dog hair
PRONOUNS	Which person does this belong to?	Whose is this?
ADJECTIVES	not able to be found like a child, like an infant	unfindable childlike, infantile
COMPOUNDS	a stop for the door a place to walk on the side (of the road)	a doorstop a sidewalk
VERBS	walk → will walk say → used to say	walk → walked say → said

What is often cited as the longest word in English, antidisestablishment-arianism, has eight morphemes: anti-dis-e-stabl-ish-ment-arian-ism (the number might vary according to the view taken of the etymology of establish). An analytic equivalent could be: opposition to the view that the church should be made to stand no more as the church of state. This sentence has seventeen monosyllabic constituent words.

ARTICLES

Articles are two: definite the and indefinite a/an, pluralized as some. Questions of when and how articles are used or omitted are very complex, but since there are no articles in Pali it is not necessary to go into them here. As will be seen immediately by anyone trying to translate from a language like Pali, which does not use articles standardly, they can have a considerable influence on meaning. Traditional grammar has sometimes classed articles with adjectives, specifically with demonstrative adjectives; modern grammars sometimes treat them as determiners. Some regularities are:

Definite: the

The definite article refers to a specific individual or group, who or which is or are subject to some kind of pragmatic or conceptual identification:

Have you fed the cats? (i.e. our cats, the ones we are supposed to feed, etc.)

An unidentified animal climbed the Eiffel Tower yesterday. By late afternoon the beast had reached the fourth level (i.e. the individual previously referred to).

She likes to lead men by the nose (i.e. the only one, actual or metaphorical, they have)

Indefinite: a/an (some)

a is used before consonants, a tiger, a mountain, and consonant-sounding vowels, a European,

an is used before vowels, an elephant, and vowel sounds, an hour

The choice between a and an depends on the word immediately following, not on the noun qualified by the article: a big elephant, an enormous cat, an extremely small dog

The indefinite article is used for any member of a group: a dolphin, a teacher, an Indonesian

Definiteness, however, can be a difficult quality to decide, and on occasion, in the singular, a and the may be interchangeable, or replaced by other words:

A person / The person / Any person / Anyone / Everyone who wants to learn grammar must have stamina.

People who want to learn grammar must have stamina

perhaps: The people who want to learn grammar must have stamina;

but not: Some people who want to learn grammar must have stamina.

There are many specific rules relating to count versus non-count nouns, specific names (countries, languages, meals, geographical phenomena, etc.) where articles of either kind are necessary, possible, or impossible.

ASPECT

Aspect, unlike TENSE, does not concern the point in time at which the action of the verb occurs but whether, from the point of view of the speaker, it is incomplete or complete. The incomplete is also called continuous, progressive, imperfect, and the complete is also called perfect. There is also a third aspect, the indefinite, habitual, or simple. The incomplete and complete are used with past, present, and future tenses, but the indefinite is only used with the present tense.

There are four sub-divisions of aspect in each of the three tenses, past, present, and future:

past simple	We bought a car.	Birds sang.
past continuous	We were buying a car.	Birds were singing.
past perfect	We had bought a car.	Birds had sung.
past perfect continuous	We had been buying a car.	Birds had been singing.

present simple	We buy a car.	Birds sing.
present continuous	We are buying a car.	Birds are singing.
present perfect	We have bought a car.	Birds have sung.
present perfect continuous	We have been buying a car.	Birds have been singing.

future simple	We will buy a car.	Birds will sing.
future continuous	We will be buying a car.	Birds will be singing.
future perfect	We will have bought a car.	Birds will have sung.
future perfect continuous	We will have been buying a car.	Birds will have been singing.

In many cases the simple present expresses the indefinite habitual aspect and the present continuous must be used to express present time: We buy a car (every three years) but We are buying a car (now). Birds sing (as a general truth, whereas dogs bark), but Birds are singing (now), You hurt my feelings (whenever we discuss that issue), but You are hurting my feelings (now).

Note that the PRESENT PERFECT and PRESENT PERFECT CONTINUOUS tenses sound like past tenses, but are not. We have bought a car refers primarily to a present condition of us, viz. having completed the action of buying a car, usually but not necessarily in the recent past. We have been buying a car likewise refers to a present state, viz. our having begun but not yet completed the action of buying a car. For any verb X, the present perfect or perfective aspect means: I am (you are, etc.) now in the condition of having X-ed. In Pali, past passive participles are used frequently as adjectives with present verbs, and while the appropriate translation will depend on context, the principle that such participles do not specify time without an auxiliary or an obvious inference from context is an important one.

BAHUVRĪHI

A compound composed of an adjective and a substantive so as to form, principally, a possessive adjective, like the word *bahuvrīhi* itself, which means much-rice, and is used as an adjective, much-riced, i.e. well-off; also generally, forming a compound that is a part of speech different from its head member. They are sometimes called Possessive.

In English, such noun compounds are often made into adjectives by adding the suffix –ed: white-coated, fair-haired, short-tempered, kind-hearted. These are straightforwardly adjectives. There are also many genuine bahuvrīhis, which do not alter the last member when used as adjectives:

BASED ON KARMADHĀRAYA	BASED ON TATPURUṢA
free-range (eggs)	lakefront (house)
blackmarket (goods)	seaside (fun-fair)
slow-motion (film)	potluck (dinner)
east-coast (accent)	bedroom (table)
uptown (restaurant)	trashcan (lid)
saber-tooth (tiger)	bite-size (cookies)
fast-forward (button)	bird's-eye (view)

CASE

Case is the inflection of a declined word which expresses its relation to another word or words in a sentence. It is not central to English but it is to Pali. Pali has eight cases, which require different endings to a word. English usually translates these with the use of prepositions. There are three cases in English:

1. The subject or the subjective case, used for the subject of a sentence and the complement of the verb to be or other linking verb.

2. The object or the objective case, which itself has three forms, as
   (i) the direct object of a verb
   (ii) the indirect object of a verb,
   (iii) the object of a preposition.
3. The possessive case, which indicates relations, typically of ownership or belonging, but also of other kinds.

In the subject and object cases, nouns do not change their form

SUBJECT	VERB (AL PHRASE)	DIRECT OBJECT	INDIRECT OBJECT	PREPOSITIONAL OBJECT
The vicar	sent	a letter	to Miss Brown	by courier.
The letter	upset	Miss Brown.		
Miss Brown	refused to send	a letter	to the vicar	by any method.

but pronouns do:

SUBJECT	VERB (AL PHRASE)	DIRECT OBJECT	INDIRECT OBJECT	PREPOSITIONAL OBJECT
He	sent	a letter	to her	by courier.
It	upset	her.		
She	refused to send	one	to him	by any method.
Who	sent	what	to whom	and how?

The possessive case in nouns is marked either by their use as adjectives preceding another noun, as a separate word or compounded, or by the use of apostrophe and/or the suffix -s.

ADJECTIVAL OR INFLECTED FORM	PREPOSITIONAL EQUIVALENT
train driver	driver of trains
watchmaker	maker of watches
sorcerer's apprentice	the apprentice of the sorcerer
John's cat	the cat owned by John
children's toys	toys of/for children
the Smiths' house	the house of the Smiths

In pronouns there are inflected forms for which prepositional equivalents are rarely used:

ADJECTIVAL OR INFLECTED FORM	PREPOSITIONAL EQUIVALENT
my watch, your garage	the watch of (belonging to) me, the garage of (belonging to) you
his comb, her toothbrush	the comb of (belonging to) me, the toothbrush of (belonging to) her
our distress, their profit	the distress of/to us, the profit of/for them
whose is this book?	to whom does this book belong?, who possesses this book?

CAUSATIVE

The category of causative is not used very often in expository accounts of English grammar, although it is common in linguistic analysis. Causative is a syntactic and not semantic category: different kinds of instigation of action are covered by the term: He smashed the glass; She got her brother to go; I'll have a plumber come, etc.

There are three main ways to form a causative:

(i) when an intransitive verb can also be used transitively, the transitive use is its causative:

The bell rang → You rang the bell; The dog hides → I hide the dog; The wood split in two → I split the wood; She is worried about money → Financial problems worry her.

(ii) in a few cases, the causative is formed by inflecting the verb

The tree falls → I fell the tree (= cause it to fall).

The carpet lies on the floor → We lay the carpet on the floor (= cause it to lie).

The temperature rises → She raises the temperature (causes it to rise).

They sit down → I seat them at the table (= cause/invite/etc. them to sit).

Causative verbs can be formed, sometimes ad hoc, by adding a suffix to a noun or adjective: stiff → stiffen, loose → loosen, harmony → harmonize, winter → winterize, null → nullify, code → codify

(iii) the majority of causatives are formed by using an auxiliary verb, such as make, get, have, let

The tree fell → He made the tree fall.

An electrician came → I got an electrician to come.

She left early → We let her leave early.

They ran to the store → We had them run to the store.

There are many verbs which might qualify as auxiliaries in a causative or quasi-causative construction: allow, assist, convince, employ, encourage, force, help, hire, inspire, let, permit, require, etc. Different verbs and different kinds of object require different constructions:

She can make the computer work, She gets the computer working, She has her computer fixed, She has the store fix the computer, she allows him to look at her computer, etc.

There can be double causatives:

The doctor came → I had the doctor come → My wife had me have the doctor come.

Prices might rise → She might raise prices → Circumstances might make her raise prices.

The dead man hung from the tree → The vigilantes hanged the man from the tree → Hatred made the vigilantes hang the man from the tree.

CLAUSE

A clause has, explicitly or implicitly, a subject, and a predicate containing a finite verb. A phrase has no finite verb, and lacks either a subject or a predicate, although it may contain a clause which does. A clause can be either a main (independent) clause, i.e. = a sentence, or a subordinate (dependent) clause.

[Some linguists hold that there can be non-finite clauses, with an infinitive preceded by to, gerunds ending in -ing or past participles ending in -ed: To start you off let's try 100mg a day, Reading books is her great passion, Fatigued by the heat he had a siesta. Traditional grammar, followed here, sees these as phrases.]

A main clause can itself constitute a sentence, but a subordinate clause cannot, since it is always connected and subordinate to a superordinate main clause. Because main clauses can stand alone they are also called independent. Subordinate clauses, because they cannot stand alone, are dependent. Subordinate clauses are introduced by a word which connects them to the main clause, such as a subordinating conjunction, an interrogative or relative pronoun. Their grammatical function can be that of noun, adjective or adverb.

AS NOUN:	
Why she left then puzzles me.	
His main failing is that he does not recognize his failings.	
Whoever tries to learn an ancient language will face many challenges.	
Where we will be tomorrow is anyone's guess.	
She said nothing about what she saw.	
I will give it to whomever deserves it.	
AS ADJECTIVE:	AS ADVERB:
The dog that we saw yesterday is dead.	If she comes I will ask her.
Children who live in slums are unfairly disadvantaged.	They were late because the traffic was bad.
They saw the boy who later disappeared.	After I came home I fell straight asleep.
I like to drink coffee which is strong and sweet.	Did you come here so that you could learn grammar?
No-one can predict the day when death will arrive.	When the going gets tough the tough get going.

COMPOUND

(see also BAHUVRĪHI, KARMADHĀRAYA, TATPURUṢA)

In English grammar the word compound is used in a number of ways not corresponding to terms used by Pali grammarians. These include:

COMPOUND SUBJECT	My father and I went fishing.	Cadets Smith, Jones, and Wesson spoke first.
COMPOUND OBJECT	I caught a carp and a perch.	They told a wild and improbable story.
COMPOUND VERB I (two verbs + conjunction)	He tried but failed.	We are hoping and praying she will come back.
COMPOUND VERB II (verb + auxiliary)	He had hoped to learn it.	They will have been studying for three years.
COMPOUND SENTENCE (two clauses + conjunction)	She may come tomorrow, or maybe she won't come till next week.	

The relevant sense for Pali is that in which compound refers to a sequence of words put together to form a single syntactic and semantic unit, in one of three ways

(i) as one word: bluebird, downtown, dragracing, pipedreams, smokescreen, dogsbody
(ii) with a hyphen: well-intentioned, hump-backed, get-together, put-down, go-between
(iii) as two words functioning as one: milk shake, pest control

The choice between them is not obligatory: fastfood, fast-food and fast food are all acceptable as compound nouns or adjectives: I don't like fastfood; This is a fast-food restaurant; Let's get fast food

English uses such compounds with more frequency than is sometimes recognized, and makes them from a wider range of parts of speech than do Pali and Sanskrit, but they are not treated as a separate category of grammar and not subjected to systematic analysis. Beginners in Pali and Sanskrit often find compounds difficult, but English speakers have in fact, like Molière's M. Jourdain and prose, been speaking compounds all their lives.

ELEMENTS OF THE COMPOUND	USED AS	EXAMPLES
noun + preposition + noun	adjective or adverb	face-to-face
noun + adverb	noun	passer-by
noun + adjective	adjective	sky-blue, dog-tired, worldwide, godlike,
noun or verb + noun	noun or adjective	bathroom (cabinet)
noun + verb	noun	hair-do
adjective + adjective	adjective	red-hot, livelong*
adjective + verb + adjective	adjective	happy-go-lucky
adjective + noun	noun or adjective	goldfish (bowl), old-hat (ideas), grandfather (clock)
adverb or adjective + agent noun	noun	newcomer, oldtimer
adverb + adverb	adjective	upside-down, inside-out
adverb + verb	noun	underpass
adverb + adjective	adjective	long-lost, hard-won, newborn, well-paid
adverb + noun	noun	overview, wellbeing
pronoun + noun	noun	she-dog, he-man
verb + noun	noun	call-girl, jump-rope
verb + noun	adjective	lack-luster
verb + preposition + noun	adjective	fly-by-night
verb + preposition/adverb	noun	hide-out, farewell, go-between, put-on
preposition + noun	adjective	underage

* this was originally two adjectives, which became understood later as verb + adjective

CONJUGATION

The word conjugation comes from a Latin word meaning 'join,' and refers to the joining together of all verbal forms deriving from the same root, according to their different tense, mood, and person. Verbs, as also nouns and pronouns, have two numbers: singular and plural. Those verbal forms which are not normally used as any other part of speech are subject to conjugation, which means they must be marked, explicitly or implicitly, for PERSON, NUMBER, and one or more of TENSE, ASPECT and MOOD. They are in either the ACTIVE or the PASSIVE VOICE, and can be CAUSATIVE. English has two classes of verb: (i) the regular or weak, and (ii) the irregular or strong.

(i) In regular or weak verbs, there are only three forms of conjugation:

(i-a) adding -s to the base verb in the third person singular present tense:

walk → walks, build → builds

(i-b) adding -ing to the base verb to make the present participle and gerund, and sometimes doubling the final consonant (less so in American than British English):

walk → walking, build → building, travel → traveling or travelling

(i-c) adding -ed or -d to form the simple past tense and past passive participle, sometimes changing final -d to -t, and sometimes doubling the final consonant:

walk → walked, build → built, travel → traveled or travelled

(ii) In irregular or strong verbs the present participle is always formed with -ing, but there are many other kinds of conjugation. The first person singular is usually the same as the infinitive or base form:

INFINITIVE	FIRST PERSON	THIRD PERSON	PRESENT PARTICIPLE	PAST TENSE	PAST PARTICIPLE
grow	grow	grows	growing	grew	grown
speak	speak	speaks	speaking	spoke	spoken
do	do	does	doing	did	done
be	am/are	is/are	being	was/were	been

CONJUNCTION

Conjunctions can be used to join words, phrases and clauses. They can be divided into three groups: co-coordinating conjunctions, subordinating conjunctions and paired conjunctions:

Co-coordinating conjunctions are: and, but, for, nor, or, so, yet. They co-ordinate

words: She is slight yet strong.

phrases: I like going to the movies and reading books.

clauses: I love eating durian but it's difficult to find in Peoria.

In all cases they must come between what they conjoin.

Common subordinating conjunctions are: after, although, as, because, before, how, if, once, since, than, that, though till, until, when, where, whether, while

They co-ordinate clauses, and often, but not always, come between the clauses they conjoin:

Once this course is over I'll never study linguistics again.

We don't watch television because it's so commercialized.

They can also join phrases to clauses:

While talking to her he could forget his financial problems.

I always feel uneasy when driving in New York.

Some paired conjunctions are: both ... and, either ... or, neither ... nor, not only ... but also, so ... as, whether ... or

They can conjoin

words: You seem both arrogant and frightened.

phrases: They will be either sleeping in the dorm or studying in the library.

clauses: It makes no difference whether you come with us to the store or go out for a walk by yourself.

There are also conjunctive adverbs, which join two clauses. Some of them are:

also, consequently, finally, furthermore, hence, however, incidentally, indeed, instead, likewise, meanwhile, nevertheless, next, nonetheless, otherwise, still, then, therefore, thus

These are distinguished from conjunctions because they need a semi-colon when used by themselves:

He told me not to go, but nevertheless I think I will. He told me not to go; nevertheless, I think I will.

We should go get a pizza first and then go to the movie. We should go get a pizza first; then we can go to the movie.

DECLENSION

The word declension derives from a Latin word meaning *bend*, and refers to variation in the form of a noun or pronoun, according to their different cases, or case-relationships with other words. The declension of nouns and pronouns involves three variables, which only appear clearly in Pronouns:

NUMBER (singular or plural), he/she/it or they
GENDER (masculine, feminine, neuter) he or she or it
CASE (subject, object, possessive), he or him or his

DEPENDENT DETERMINATIVE (compound); see TATPURUṢA

DESCRIPTIVE DETERMINATIVE (compound); see KARMADHĀRAYA

DIRECT SPEECH

Direct Speech presents actual or presumed words or thoughts of someone, using inverted commas. The tense and pronoun of the quoted speech remain those used by the reported speaker:

He said, 'I don't have the money,' but he did.	You said, 'I don't have the money,' but you did.
He says, 'I don't have the money,' but he does.	You say 'I don't have the money,' but you do.
He will say, 'I don't have the money,' but he will.	You will say, 'I don't have the money,' but you will.

DVANDVA

Dvandva or Copulative compounds in English are not usually made of more than two members, A + B: twenty-two, thirty-three; gray-green, blue-black, topsy-turvy

GENDER

Gender is rare, and in modern English always natural: that is, the words denote things which are themselves of the gender. This is unlike many languages, such as French or Pali, where words denoting non-gendered things or ideas are assigned a grammatical gender. In English there are the pronouns he, she, it (and their cases), and agent nouns such as governor/governess, master/mistress, waiter/waitress.

GRAPHEME

A grapheme is a written or other recorded symbol. The relationship between graphemes and phonemes in English is extraordinarily variable:

fantasy/phantasy cool/chemist, chiropractor/chair, thought/thou, scoff/cough, mud/blood

American and British spellings afford many examples: center/centre, colour/color, plow/plough

George Bernard Shaw invented the word *ghoti to highlight this: it is pronounced fish: gh as in enough, o as in women, and ti as in any word ending in -tion, e.g. ignition

INDIRECT SPEECH

Indirect speech converts actual or presumed words into a clause following a verb and the conjunction that, which can be explicit or implicit. In indirect speech tense and mood are determined by the perspective of the reporting speaker:

He said (that) he didn't have the money, but he did.	You said (that) you didn't have the money, but you did.
He says (that) he doesn't have the money, but he does.	You say (that) you don't have the money, but you do.
He will say (that) he doesn't have the money, but he will.	You will say (that) you don't have the money, but you will.

There are also indirect questions: I wonder whether she will come; He did not know when the party was to begin.

It is possible, particularly in narrative fiction, to use a mode of expression which is halfway between direct and indirect speech, when the narrator gives what purport to be a person's thoughts or words, but from the narrator's point of view:

> She glanced around the conference room. The balding man in the corner would have to be watched carefully, but the woman on the left could be trusted.
>
> In direct speech this would be: She glanced around the conference room and thought "The balding man in the corner will have to be watched carefully, but the woman on the left can be trusted."
>
> In indirect speech: She glanced around the conference room, and thought that the balding man in the corner would have to be watched carefully, but that the woman on the left could be trusted.

INFINITIVE

The infinitive is so-called because it is unlimited or unspecific to any person, number, tense, etc. It has more uses in English than Pali, and consists of the base or root of the verb, with the preposition to, used as an infinitive particle, which can be omitted in certain cases. The root is the form listed in the dictionary and is usually identical to the first person singular of the present tense (a notable exception being the verb to be). Infinitives and infinitive phrases can take direct and indirect objects, and be used as nouns, adjectives or adverbs:

	infinitive is
To LOVE one's children is the best thing in life.	a noun, the subject of the sentence
The best way to be happy is TO FORGET about it.	a noun, the subject-complement
I don't want TO SLEEP right now.	a noun, the object of the verb want
She is studying Pali TO UNDERSTAND the texts better.	a noun (dative of purpose) or an adverb modifying study
Gourds TO EAT are better than ornamental gourds.	like ornamental, an adjective modifying the noun gourd
I prefer the train TO TRAVEL to work.	an adjective modifying the noun train
She is eager TO PLEASE.	an adverb modifying the adjective eager

Infinitives can be active or passive: I want to see the Eiffel Tower and The Eiffel Tower is easy to see. Passive infinitives with an auxiliary + past participle, to be done, to be killed, are often used to translate one of the uses of the Pali future passive participle, also called a gerundive.

With auxiliary verbs and some others, often of perception, the infinitive form can be used without the preposition to. For example, auxiliary verbs usually come immediately before their infinitive:

> We can (could) go; You had better try; I may (might) sleep; He must buy some new shoes; They need not worry; She shall (should) give that some thought; He will (would) study more if he had time; We dare not try

Verbs, especially of perception, usually place the object between the main verb and the infinitive:

> He feels the rain fall on his head; I heard the police car give chase; She listens to the choir sing; They watch the sun fall over the sea; Didn't you notice him say that? She will see you arrive; I like to smell the coffee brew; I helped him pack

INFLECTION

English retains some forms of inflection, but it is not a central category in English grammar, apart from historical philology. It is, however, vital in Pali. Inflection comes from a Latin word meaning *bend*, and refers to modification of the form of words to express different grammatical relations into which they enter. There are two forms of inflection: declension and conjugation. In modern English, nouns, pronouns (and perhaps the comparative and superlative of adjectives) are subject to declension, verbs to conjugation. All other words are uninflected.

INTERJECTION

Interjections are, literally, thrown between, but also in front of, words, phrases, clauses and sentences with no grammatical relation to them. Their purpose is usually to convey emotion, and/or to serve as fillers, and they may or may not have any semantic content. Oh! has no meaning in the dictionary and little anywhere else outside of a specific context, phrases such as Excuse me; Well let's see, are rarely meant literally. Interjections are prone to changes in fashion, as any dictionary entry will show: OED, for example, has such old expressions as Marry! Fiddlesticks!. Some swear words, of four or more letters, are perennial favorites.

KARMADHĀRAYA

A compound in which the first member describes the second, as highway (adjective + noun), steamboat (attributive noun + noun). Such compounds are called Descriptive Determinative. They can be formed from various combinations of parts of speech. The first member determines or qualifies the second; that is, the first makes the compound as a whole a sub-category of the second - a goldfish is one kind of fish, dog-tired is one way or degree of being tired, sky-blue is one kind of blue.

COMPONENT WORDS	COMPOUND USED AS	EXAMPLE
adjective + noun	noun or adjective	blackbird, quicksilver
adjective + adjective	adjective	clean-shaven, squeaky-clean
adverb + adjective	adjective	slow-moving
noun + adjective (comparison)	adjective or noun	canary-yellow, lily-white

METATHESIS

The transposition of sounds or letters in a word, such as in British → American English centre → center, metre → meter, or in Sanskrit *jihma* (crooked) → Pali *jimha*.

MOOD

Mood refers to kinds of conjugation which express the function for which the verb is used, e.g. as a statement, command, wish, counterfactual supposition, etc. Traditional Grammar, based on Latin, has three moods or modes INDICATIVE, IMPERATIVE and SUBJUNCTIVE:

The INDICATIVE is the most widely used mood. It expresses statements, predication, opinions etc. in any of the three tenses: You studied Pali. You study [are studying] Pali. You will study Pali

The IMPERATIVE is used for commands, requests, etc. Its form is identical to the second person indicative, used without a pronoun: Study Pali!

The SUBJUNCTIVE is used for an action or state as conceived (and not as a fact). It expresses a wish, command, exhortation, or refers to a contingent, hypothetical, or prospective state of affairs: Were she to study Pali. It is advisable that she study Pali. Would that she study Pali. If she were to have studied Pali.

A mood sometimes seen as a sub-category of the SUBJUNCTIVE and sometimes as a separate category is the OPTATIVE. As its name suggests it is used to express wishes. In Pali the mood standardly called OPTATIVE is used for many of the functions classed in English as SUBJUNCTIVE.

MORPHEME

A MORPHEME IS the smallest unit of language perceived to be meaningful. Words can have more than one morpheme, as in act-or/act-ress, treat-ment, child-like, in-conceiv(e)-able, dis-like, un-convinc(e)-ing, a word of one or more syllables can be a morpheme, as in cat, dog, are, happy, a single letter can be a morpheme, as is the plural marker s, in cat-s, dog-s.

NEGATION

Negation is effected

(i) with words, by a negative (from Latin *nego*, deny, refuse), or privative (from Latin *privo*, deprive, prevent) prefix or suffix. Logically, negation is the mere denial that something is characterized in some way, whereas privation is the assertion that something is deprived of or without something formerly or properly possessed. Grammatically both can denote simply the absence of some quality.

Examples: ab-normal (not normal), a-cephalic (having no head), de-contaminate (remove contamination), dis-inherit (deprive of inheritance), in-applicable (not able to be applied), mis-appropriate (appropriate improperly), non-appearance (failure to appear) un-compromising (without compromise), hope-less (lacking hope), smoke-free (smoking not permitted). Some words have more than one negative: immoral ≠ amoral (both = not moral), some words with negative form have no positive counterpart: disheveled, unkempt. Sometimes negatives are compounded: ne'er-do-well

(ii) with words, phrases, clauses or sentences by negatives such as no (adjective), not (adverb), nothing (pronoun), never (adverb), etc.
Examples: phrases can use both absolute negatives, not understanding grammar, no big deal, never ceasing, nothing to the contrary, none of the bears, etc., and also words which are loosely or proximately negative, hardly over 15, scarcely adequate. Clauses and sentences are usually marked for negation by not, which can be abbreviated to n't in some auxiliary verbs (isn't, daren't, doesn't, don't, haven't, mightn't, wouldn't, etc.), or by another word, often an adverb or pronoun: I have seldom seen such a bad grammar.

In simple sentences such as It is raining or It is not raining, the negative and positive clauses are straightforwardly opposed in meaning. More complex negations often depend on word order, and the positive versions will be different: I specifically did not say that ≠ I did not say that specifically. The relation between grammatical and logical negation can be ambiguous, particularly in written English where intonation cannot be used: the positive counterparts to I did not see my mother yesterday are many: but my brother did, but I spoke to her on the phone, but I saw my father, but I saw her today.

NON-CONJUGATED VERBAL FORMS

Of the verbal forms which do not conjugate, some decline and some do not. Participles are used as adjectives, and hence as nouns: the going rate, the dear departed. They decline as adjectives or nouns, all these comings and goings. Infinitives are indeclinable, however used: to read books is good, she likes to read.

NOUN

The word *noun* comes from Latin *nomen*, meaning *name*. Older European grammars often classed nouns with adjectives, under the names *noun substantive* and *noun adjective*.

A word or group of words is used as a noun, noun phrase, or noun clause if it can function as
(i) the subject of a sentence: The plumber arrived.
(ii) the object of a verb: We need a plumber.
(iii) a predicative complement: Her brother is a plumber.

Nouns can be classified by type:

Common (shared by many things): table, chair, wristwatch, mountain, type, example

Proper (belonging to an individual or specific group): Penelope, the Bulls, Saturday, the Triads

Concrete (objects of sense-perception): rock, ocean, elephant, crossroads, stink, noise

Abstract (objects of thought): compassion, wonder, difficulty, memory, democracy

Collective (denotes a group): pride (of lions), tribe (of people), committee, team

Countable: cat, dog, hope, problem, universe, spoon

Non-countable: courage, arrogance, hydrogen, kitchenware, education (Non-countable nouns are sometimes pluralized, as a shorthand for 'kinds of' or 'forms of': His various arrogances can be traced to the same source. The store has various kitchenwares.)

Many words which are normally classified otherwise can function in the same way as nouns, and there are noun-phrases and noun-clauses:

SENTENCE	USUAL CLASS OF THE NOUN
The Blues won the championship.	adjective
The ins and outs of this are beyond me.	prepositions
The ifs and buts in the argument make it difficult to follow.	conjunctions
Going to the dentist makes me afraid.	verb (participle used as gerund)
The Ayes outnumber the Nays 51 to 9 [= those who voted Yes or No].	interjection
To err is human, to forgive divine.	verb (infinitive)
Their farewells were soon made.	verb + adverb compounded

NUMBER

There are two numbers, singular and plural. (Sanskrit, but not Pali, has a further number, the dual, used for two people or things, in any of the three persons.) Number is most often seen by the addition of the suffix -s in the plural, cat → cats, dog → dogs, with differences in pronunciation, cats, dogz, and orthography, hoof → hooves, pony → ponies. There are other suffixes, child → children, ox → oxen. Plural can also be shown by vowel changes, woman → women, mouse → mice, tooth → teeth.

NUMERAL

It is essential in grammar to distinguish between NUMBER, which refers to singular and plural, and NUMERALS. Numerals are divided into cardinal and ordinal numbers, both of which can be used as nouns or adjectives.

Cardinal means *principal* or *chief*, and is applied to members of the series 0, 1, 2, 3, etc. When used as nouns, cardinals are usually common nouns, answering the question how many? They are therefore called counting numbers. There is a sub-category sometimes called nominal, as in things like zip codes or competitors in a race, where the number acts as a name: Seventeen is way behind the others

Ordinal refers to an order or place in the series first, second, third, etc.

	CARDINAL	ORDINAL
NOUN	Three threes are nine.	the fifth of November
	She's in her late twenties	three-fourths
	Chicago, Illinois 60637	an interval of a third
ADJECTIVE	fourteen elephants	the third man
	a hundred and one Dalmatians	second-best

OBJECT

The word *object* derives from Latin, meaning *thrown in front of* or *in the way of*, and it is used for a word, phrase, or clause immediately dependent on or 'governed by', a verb. Like *subject* it is a spatial metaphor, suggesting that objects are what verbs meet in the course of completing their action. The first thing they meet (logically, not necessarily in order of words) is a direct object, and if they meet something to which or for which the direct object is intended, this is their indirect object. The direct object is the person or thing receiving the action of a transitive verb; the indirect object is the person or thing to whom or for whom the action of a verb is done. She tells a story is a complete sentence, where story is the direct object of he verb tells. In answer to the question to whom? it might be expanded to She tells a story to her children, where her children is the indirect object. Word order is irrelevant to the grammatical relationships: She tells her children a story is, depending on context, identical, but it is also easy to imagine contexts in which the same words, with the same grammatical relationships, would serve a slightly different purpose: To her children she tells a story, (but to others she says nothing).

Another way of saying this is that the direct object receives the action of the verb, and the indirect object receives the direct object.

When the indirect object precedes the direct object, it is likely that prepositions such as to or for will be omitted

SUBJECT	VERB	DIRECT OBJECT	INDIRECT OBJECT
We	give	money	to charities
I	cooked	sea cucumbers	for the bishop
They	attribute	their misfortunes	to witchcraft

SUBJECT	VERB	DIRECT OBJECT	INDIRECT OBJECT
She	won't tell	them	any secrets
He	gave	a dog	a bone
I	told	the audience	a few jokes

Less commonly, a verb may take an indirect object alone, although there will be a direct object implicit: She told me, We give to charities regularly.

PARTICIPLE

Participles are so called because they participate in the nature of both verbs and adjectives. They are used with auxiliary verbs in verbal phrases, have tense, and, in transitive verbs, can govern direct and indirect objects. In English there are two participles, usually called present and past, though more accurately continuous/imperfect and complete/perfect.

(i) The present is formed by adding -ing to the verb, which loses a final e, and may double a final consonant (there are differences between British and American English in this regard):

VERB	PRESENT PARTICIPLE	USED VERBALLY	USED AS ADJECTIVE	USED AS NOUN
go	going	The company is going to the dogs.	The company is a going concern.	Going to the pawnshop now is not wise.
travel	traveling (Br. travelling)	He was traveling to Paris.	He was a traveling salesman.	Traveling light is the best.
tell	telling	She is telling him off.	That was a telling remark.	She is giving him a good telling-off.

(ii) While the present (continuous) participle in -ing is regular, the past (perfect) participle admits of much variation. In weak/regular verbs both past tense and past participle are formed with the suffix -ed, sometimes with alterations in spelling, as when verbs end in -y. Sometimes -ed can become -t.

reject → rejected, upholster → upholstered, try → tried, pay → paid, deal → dealt, spell → spelled or spelt

In irregular/strong verbs, many different inflections are possible:

VERB	PAST TENSE	PAST PARTICIPLE
speak	spoke	spoken
grow	grew	grown
burst	burst	burst
come	came	come
ring	rang	rung

The past tense in both transitive and intransitive verbs is finite, in the active voice:

In the sentence The play moved her the past tense moved is transitive, i.e. takes a direct object (her) and is finite in that it includes reference to the time, relative to the present, when the action of the verb is done. The intransitive verb rise does not take a direct object, so one cannot rise something or be risen by something. So in the past tense there is the finite form The dough rose.

But the past participle in

(i) transitive verbs is non-finite and in the passive voice:

The past participle moved can be used for any time but only in the passive voice: She was moved by the play, She had been / is / will be / will have been / etc. moved by the play.

(ii) intransitive verbs is also non-finite but must be in the active voice:

The past participle risen can be used for any time but only in the active voice: The dough has / is / will be / etc. risen.

PARTICLE

Particle, from Latin *particula*, a small part, is used for various small, uninflected words, such as the negative particle not, the infinitive particle to (to think; to walk), and for many adverbs and prepositions that combine with verbs to form phrasal verbs (turn off, give up, care for). The term pragmatic particle is sometimes used for fillers and discourse markers which have little or no meaning: oh, well, yes, no, you know, actually, anyway.

PERIPHRASIS

The word means circumlocution, and can be used in the same way. In grammar a periphrastic construction has some form of the simple verb and an auxiliary, as distinct from a formation from the verb-stem alone.

PERSON

There are three persons, which denote or indicate

(i) the person(s) speaking (first person: I/we)

(ii) the person(s) spoken to (second person: you)

(iii) the person(s) or thing(s) spoken of (third person: he/she/it/they).

(Greek grammarians called such persons, which include the impersonal it, *prosopoi*, masks, which was translated into Latin as *personae*.)

PHONEMES

Phonemes are the smallest units of sound perceived as significant to meaning in any one language. Naturally these vary greatly between languages and between dialects of the same language. It is said that languages can contain from 2 to 25 vowels, and 5 to more than 100 consonants. English has at least 13 vowel-sounds and over 30 consonant-sounds, despite the fact that the standard alphabet taken over from Latin has 5 vowel- and 21 consonant-graphemes.

The word bat has three phonemes, /b/ /a/ /t/, the last of which distinguishes it from bad, /b/ /a/ /d/

The word pit has three phonemes, /p/ /i/ /t/, the second of which distinguishes it from pot, /p/ /o/ /t/

PHRASE

A PHRASE is a word or grammatically linked group of words lacking a finite verb, which fulfils the syntactic function of a noun, adjective or adverb in a clause or sentence.

A VERBAL PHRASE is either the whole predicate of the sentence without the subject, or a verb with an auxiliary verb or verbs.

A PHRASAL VERB has a preposition as part of its meaning.

Single words can, analytically, be called phrases, but these examples use groups of words:

NOUN PHRASES	ADJECTIVE PHRASES
THE MARX BROTHERS made FUNNY MOVIES.	This water is FREE FROM FLUORIDE.
I like THE MARX BROTHERS.	Men WITH BIG HATS look silly.
ROMANTIC LOVE is a DANGEROUS THING.	She feels excited about THE COMING year.
ADVERB PHRASES	**PREPOSITIONAL PHRASES**
QUITE HONESTLY, I don't know what an adverb phrase is.	Adjectival: A bird IN THE HAND is worth two IN THE BUSH.
She can run EXTREMELY FAST.	I'm feeling UNDER THE WEATHER.
They get up VERY EARLY IN THE MORNING.	Adverbial: He put the gun back IN ITS CASE.
There's nothing new UNDER THE SUN.	
VERBAL PHRASES	**PHRASAL VERBS**
The cat SAT ON THE MAT.	SEE HIM OFF, Rover!
The cat WAS SLEEPING.	The plane TOUCHED DOWN.
People in glass houses SHOULDN'T THROW STONES.	I can't MAKE THIS OUT.

PREDICATE see **SUBJECT**

PREPOSITION

Prepositions are so called because in Latin, from where the term derives, and also in English, they standardly come before that to which they apply. There are also post-positions, which are included in the same category. Prepositions, which can be single words or phrases, express a relation between some part of a sentence and what is called the Prepositional Complement. The Prepositional Complement is typically a noun or noun phrase, a nominal clause beginning in a wh- word, or a nominal clause using the present participle -ing form:

COMPLEMENT CLASS	PREPOSITION	COMPLEMENT
noun	The fruit is in	the bowl.
	They drove all over	the country.
	He left in search of	enlightenment.
noun phrase	I like to go to	football games.
	We must struggle against	dishonest politicians.
	He worked for the sake of	his children's education.
wh- clause	They will dress up as	whatever character you want.
	Bitterness was evident throughout	what she said.
	About	what will she be speaking?
-ing form	You can only achieve that by	working hard
	He is surely above	doing something like that
	She works full-time in addition to	doing all the housework

Words used as Prepositions can also be used as adverbs, and adjectives:

WORD	USED AS PREPOSITION	USED AS ADVERB	USED AS ADJECTIVE OR IN ADJECTIVE PHRASE
across	She came ACROSS the room.	How long is it to get ACROSS?	In today's crossword the ACROSS clues are hard.
between	Santa Barbara is BETWEEN Los Angeles and San Francisco.	Such a distance lies BETWEEN us.	The BETWEEN-wars period was hard in Europe.
down	The skier fell DOWN the hill.	Can you come DOWN?	The accused was arrested on the DOWN train.
over	She is OVER the moon about it.	How soon can you come OVER.	The party will soon beOVER?

PREFIX

Prefixes, which may or may not be found as independent words, are usually combined with words without hyphenation. Prefixes are placed before what they apply to, suffixes after. They perform several semantic functions:

FUNCTION	PREFIX	EXAMPLES
reversative, privative	de-	decenter, desegregate, debug
	dis-	disappear, distrust
	un-	unravel, unplug, unscrew
pejorative	mal-	malfunction, maltreat
	mis-	misinterpret, misjudge, misplace
	co-	co-drive, cooperate, coexist
degree, size	hyper-	hyperventilate, hyperbolize
	out-	outclass, outgrow, outlive,
	over-	overact, overestimate, oversimplify
	super-	superheat, superimpose, superpose
	under-	undercut, underfeed, undervalue
opposition, rivalry	contra-	contraindicate
	counter-	counterattack, countercharge
place, relation	inter-	interbreed, intercalate, internationalize
	sub-	subedit, submerge, subserve
	trans-	transmigrate, transplant, transship
time, sequence	fore-	forecast, foreclose, foresee,
	pre-	prearrange, preexist, prefabricate
	re-	rearrange, rebroadcast, recall

PRONOUN AND PRONOMINAL ADJECTIVE

Pronouns (the word is from *pro-nomen*, in place of a noun) are words which substitute for or refer to nouns, noun-phrases, noun-clauses, or even whole sentences. Where nouns and most adjectives describe their referent, pronouns and pronominal adjectives simply point to it.

Pronouns function in the same way as nouns, and pronominal adjectives in the same way as adjectives. In English pronouns can be personal, demonstrative, relative, interrogative, indefinite, possessive and reflexive. Pronominal adjectives, also called determiners (see below), can be demonstrative, relative, and interrogative.

CATEGORY		PRONOUN	ADJECTIVE (DETERMINER)
personal	I, you, he, she, it, they		
demonstrative	this, that, these, those	This is a big cat. I like these, but not those.	This big cat I like these apples but not those oranges.
relative	who, whom, whose, which, that	I like speeches which are short The girl to whom I spoke	I liked it, which feeling surprised me It depends whose car it is
interrogative	who, whom, whose, which, what	What do you want? Whose is it?	What car do you want? Whose car is it?
indefinite [*]	anyone, anything, whoever, whatever	Do you want anything? Whatever you say.	Any way is good. Whatever way you want.
possessive	mine/my, your/your, his, hers/ her, its, ours/our, theirs/their	This coat is mine. Hers is the blue coat.	My coat is this one. Her coat is blue.
reflexive/ intensive	myself, yourself, himself, herself, itself, ourselves, themselves	He did it himself. We ruined ourselves. I gave myself two days.	[intensive] I myself saw it happen. I saw the Dean herself.

[*] There are other indefinite pronouns, many of which can also be used, sometimes with slight changes, as adjectives/determiners: all, another, any, anybody, anyone, anything, each, everybody, everyone, everything, few, many, nobody, none, one, several, some, somebody, someone.

Personal pronouns are so called because they refer to the three persons, singular and plural, of the verb.

Demonstrative pronouns and adjectives are so called because they point to things, verbally. English this usually points to something close by, that to something farther away, in fact or in thought.

Relative pronouns relate a part or all of a subordinate (relative) clause to a main clause. That to which they refer is called the antecedent, whether or not they precede or follow the relative clause.

Interrogative pronouns ask questions: Who said that? Whose car has been stolen?

Indefinite pronouns do not refer to a specific antecedent: Whoever wishes to enter here must be a mathematician. Invite whomever (singular, whoever plural) you want. Anything will do.

Possessive pronouns indicate possession, belonging, etc.

Reflexive pronouns refer back to the subject of the sentence or clause.

Intensives place greater emphasis on what immediately precedes them.

Personal and relative pronouns are among the very few words which decline in English. Only the third person singular has gender. The third person singular retains the three genders, masculine, feminine and neuter, of Greek, Latin, German, etc.

SUBJECT	I	you	he	she	it	we	they	who
OBJECT	me	you	him	her	it	us	them	who, whom*
POSSESSIVE	my	your	his	her	its	ours	their	whose

* the use of the object-case, accusative ending -m is fast disappearing from modern English.

In the following examples of relative pronouns, the antecedent and the relative pronoun are underlined. In the final two examples, the antecedent is the whole main clause.

<u>I</u> am the one <u>who</u> said that.
<u>We</u> are the people <u>who</u> did that.
This is <u>the person whom</u> you saw.
These are <u>the people who</u> you saw.
<u>The police chief, whose</u> authority was threatened, ordered his men to fire.
<u>The protesters, whose</u> only crime was to sit in the road, were fired on.
<u>Our teacher, to whom</u> we all give thanks, has announced his retirement.
<u>Large pay rises, for which</u> we all hope, are rarely to be had.
<u>He finally smiled, which</u> made me glad.
<u>The potatoes were black, which</u> made us anxious.

Relative clauses function for the most part as adjectives, modifying a noun, a noun phrase, or sometimes a whole clause. That which they modify is called the antecedent:

<u>The woman who</u> gave me the book.
There are <u>many people who</u> would like to do that.
<u>I saw the woman crying, which</u> made me sad.

Choosing between an adjective and a relative clause is a matter of style rather than semantic difference:

The brown table is large and square *or* The table which is brown is large and square.

Both sentences have the form X is Y, and both can be analyzed (a)X is Y [b+c]. In the first sentence (a) is the adjective brown; in the second it is the relative clause which is brown.

In traditional grammar, pronominal adjectives were so called because they function as adjectives. Some modern linguists prefer to subsume them into the wider category of determiner, along with other adjectives, the articles a/an, the, and numerals. Examples are: all, another, any, both, each, enough, every, few, many, no, several, some. A numeral used attributively or predicatively with a noun is a determiner: one grammar is enough, this person is first in line. Other words analogous to the sequence of numerals also function as determiners: former, last, latter, next, previous, subsequent, etc. It is easy to distinguish between a pronoun and a determiner: pronouns can be replaced by nouns, determiners cannot: This is a nice cat → Felix is a nice cat, but I like this cat → *I like Felix cat.

SENTENCES

A sentence has, explicitly or implicitly, a subject, and a predicate containing a finite verb (i.e. one which has past, present or future tense). Some linguists think that the subject-predicate structure, in the more general form of Topic-Comment, is a universal structure of language: the subject/topic picks out something from the world, and the predicate/comment says something about it. Both subject and predicate can be single words or phrases or clauses. Sentences are most easily defined by punctuation: they begin with a capital letter and end with a full stop (period), a question mark, or an exclamation mark.

A sentence is called:

SIMPLE if it has one main clause but no subordinate clause: The king died yesterday.

COMPOUND if it has two or more main clauses joined by a coordinating conjunction, comma or semi-colon but no subordinate clause: The king died yesterday and today the queen died of grief.

COMPLEX if it has one main clause and one or more subordinate clauses: When the king died, the queen, who loved so him dearly, died of grief.

COMPOUND-COMPLEX if it has two or more main clauses with one or more subordinate clauses: The king, who reigned for forty years, died yesterday and today the queen, who loved him so dearly, died of grief.

SUBJECT AND PREDICATE

The word *subject* derives from Latin, meaning *thrown under*, and like the concept of substance (*stand under*), it is a spatial metaphor of supporting or grounding something, in this case a sentence. The word *predicate* derives from Latin, meaning *to speak forth*, *proclaim*, *assert*. In relation to sentences and at its simplest, it means everything else in a sentence other than the subject. Sometimes it is restricted to the main verb and its object or complement.

SUBJECT	PREDICATE
Birds	sing
Most birds	sing in the morning
Cats and bears	like eating fish
The brownish, mangy dogs	searched for food in the trash
Whoever wants to learn Pali	must work long and hard

The subject can be implicit, as in imperative sentences: the subject of Get out of here!, Pass the salt!, Think carefully!, is you. The subject or predicate can be omitted in questions and answers:

Who poisoned Mr. Jones? Mr. Smith.

What did Mr. Smith do? Poisoned Mr. Jones.

In both cases the answers are shortened forms of Mr. Smith poisoned Mr. Jones.

There are sentences in which the grammatical subject of the verb is not the real subject. The previous sentence was an example. Its subject is sentences and not there. Some sentences can have a grammatical subject but no real subject: It is raining, It is difficult to learn Grammar. Buddhists would say that this is true of I am thinking.

SYNTACTICAL COMPOUNDS

Syntactical compounds are those where one or more of the constitutive members is in a syntactic form other than that of substantive (that is, it is not a noun, adjective, pronoun, numeral): a Johnny go-lightly, an all-you-can-eat lunch, a yes-man, a go-getter

TATPURUSHA

A compound in which the first element qualifies or determines the second, while the second retains its grammatical independence as noun, adjective, or participle. *Bookcase* consists of a substantival attribute + substantive. Such compounds are called Dependent Determinative. They can be formed from various combinations of parts of speech, except that the first member cannot be an adjective or adverb. The first member determines or qualifies the second: side-doors are one kind of door, fact-finding is one kind of finding, a crewcut is one kind of cut (itself a synecdoche for haircut).

CASE OF FIRST ELEMENT	ELEMENTS OF THE COMPOUND	EXAMPLES
accusative	noun + adjective	all-knowing
instrumental	noun + noun	handball, football
dative	noun + noun	table-cloth, wine-glass, shower-curtain
ablative	noun + noun	orange-juice, moonlight
genitive	noun + noun	kitchen-door, pony-tail, waterfall
locative	noun + noun, noun + adjective	backdoor, basketball, homespun

TENSE

Tense refers to the finite forms of a verb, which indicate past, present, or future time. Strictly speaking, English verbs have only two tenses, past and present, as only they are formed by inflecting the verb; other tenses, including the future, have to be formed with auxiliary verbs. An auxiliary (helping) verb helps the main verb to function as a finite verb.

PAST	PRESENT	FUTURE
We sold sea-shells.	We sell sea-shells.	We will sell sea-shells.
She felt unwell.	She feels unwell.	She will feel unwell.
They left.	They leave.	They will leave.

VERB

The word *verb* derives from Latin *verbum*, meaning word in general, but also the subcategory of words expressing action, as opposed to *nomen*, name or noun. The dichotomy was derived from Greek *rhema*, saying, and *onoma*, naming. Verbs have transitive and intransitive forms. The word transitive is from Latin, meaning carry over or move (as in English transit).

Transitive verbs express actions which pass over to an object, needing a direct object to complete their sense.

Intransitive verbs express actions which do not pass over to an object, and which cannot take a direct object. They can also refer to events or states of being.

Many verbs in English, and in Pali, can be used transitively and intransitively. In the following sentences a direct object is necessary to complete the sense of the transitive verb, whereas in sentences with intransitive verbs nothing in addition to the subject and verb is necessary grammatically. In both cases adjuncts may contain vital semantic information, but are not necessary to syntax

SUBJECT	PREDICATE		
	TRANSITIVE VERB	DIRECT OBJECT	ADJUNCT
The book	moved	me	to tears.
He	enjoys	cycling	at night.
Compassion	heals	all wounds	however slowly.
She	has	(the) courage	of a lion.
We	will deliver	it	tomorrow.
Too much sticky rice	makes	people	fat.

	INTRANSITIVE VERB	ADJUNCT
She	sleeps	very soundly.
I	moved	to Guatemala last year.
They	worry	too much.
The noise	stopped	immediately.
We	arrived	at the meeting very late.

There is a well-known story about the 18th century English lexicographer Samuel Johnson which illustrates the difference between transitive and intransitive verbs. Nowadays the verb smell can be used in both ways: I smell the flower, the flower smells nice. At that time, however, in Johnson's view, it could only be transitive. He arrived at a party and took off his overcoat, at which the hostess remarked Dr. Johnson, you smell! He replied No, madam, you smell, I stink.

Intransitive verbs also express events, Mistakes happen; The king died; Under Mussolini the trains ran on time; or states of being, I am sick; She is becoming old; We feel unloved. The last three examples contain a subject complement, a word deriving from Latin meaning *fill up* or *complete*. A complement is any word, phrase, clause, or mixture of them which completes any other word, phrase, clause, or mixture of them, and makes it or them a complete syntactic unit of the relevant kind. Subject complements usually follow the verb to be, or other linking verbs such as appear, become, feel, seem, smell, etc. The verb to be, when used in this way, is called the copula, which in Latin means to fasten together. The subject complement can be an adjective, a noun, an adjective phrase, or noun phrase:

	ADJECTIVE	NOUN	ADJECTIVE PHRASE	NOUN PHRASE
be	Our car is blue.	This is madness!	She is very clever.	We are old-fashioned grammarians.
seem	They seem rich.	She seems (to be) the spokesperson.	You seem overly cautious.	It seemed a good idea at the time.
become	He became tiresome.	This is becoming a nuisance.	I became extremely happy.	We became ministers of the king.

VOICE

Voice is an ubiquitous term in modern accounts of English, Pali, and other grammars, but it is more problematic linguistically and historically than it might seem. It is not clear when and why the Latin *vox* came to be so used (the standard earlier terms being *genus* and *significatio*), nor when the use began in Romance languages (German retains *Genus*). It is used to indicate the relationship between the subject of the verb and the action of the verb.
In the active voice the subject performs the action, in the passive voice the subject receives the action:

Active: The thief stole the jewelry.

Passive: The jewelry was stolen by the thief.

Transitive verbs have both active and passive voices, intransitive verbs can only be active. In English the passive voice is made by using the verb to be as an auxiliary, with the past participle of the verb.

Active Transitive verbs can become passive:

I shot the sheriff → The sheriff was shot by me

They bought a house → A house was bought by them

She baked a cake → A cake was baked by her.

But Active Intransitive verbs have no passive:

The sheriff died from gunshot wounds → *The sheriff was died from gunshot wounds

The house decayed rapidly → *The house was decayed rapidly

She had seemed to be a good cook before she baked a cake → ?

In analyzing voice, in English and Pali, a useful distinction can be made between the grammatical subject and the logical subject.

The active voice of a verb is that in which the logical subject (i.e. the agent) of the action is the same as the grammatical subject of the verb: in The woman cooks the rice, the woman is the logical and grammatical subject.

The passive voice of a verb is that in which the logical object of the action is made the grammatical subject of the sentence. In Rice is cooked by the woman rice is the logical object, that which receives the action of the verb, but it appears as the grammatical subject, while the logical subject, the woman, is made into a grammatical adjunct. Adjuncts are not syntactically necessary: The jewelry was stolen is a complete sentence, however important the adjunct in The jewelry was stolen by Brian Cartwright might be in practice. Thus:

Active voice		
agent	verb	object
The woman	cooks	rice.
grammatical subject		grammatical object
logical subject		logical object

Passive Voice		
patient	verb	agent
Rice	is cooked	(by) the woman.
grammatical subject		grammatical adjunct
logical object		logical subject

There are some cases in English where the verb seems midway between active and passive: The rice cooked, the water boiled, The wood burned.

In the same way as the active voice, the passive can be used in different moods:

INDICATIVE	past tense	Pali was studied by you.
	present tense	Pali is studied by you.
	future tense	Pali will be studied by you.
IMPERATIVE	May Pali be studied by you!	
SUBJUNCTIVE / OPTATIVE	Were Pali to be studied by you.	
	Would that Pali could be studied by you.	
	Pali might be studied by you.	

Appendix 3

METER

Some technical terms:

chandas - meter, prosody	*mattā* - measure = *kāla* - instant
vutta - meter	*vaṇṇa* - syllable
gāthā - verse (of four quarters)	*gaṇa* - group (of syllables)
pāda - quarter-verse	*lahu* - light, short syllable = 1 measure, marked as ∪
yati - pause, caesura, marked as ||	*garu* – heavy, long syllable = 2 measures, marked as —

The study of meter (*vutta*), or prosody (*chandas*), starts from the principles of vowel and syllable length given in section 1.2 concerning the Law of Morae. The words *mora*, *mattā*, and *kāla* all refer to the length of time it takes to pronounce a syllable:

A short syllable is one in which a short vowel is followed by nothing or by one consonant. This is one *mattā* and light, *lahu*, and is standardly indicated by the symbol ∪.

A long syllable is one in which there is a long vowel, or a short vowel followed by two consonants. This is two *mattā* and heavy, *garu*, and is standardly indicated by the symbol — .

Many meters have a break, called by the Latin name *caesura*, which is often in meaning as well as in meter, and which is indicated here by the symbol ||.

In discussions of Pali meter, especially in older works, one often finds the vocabulary of Greek and Latin meter, where Pali and Sanskrit poetics use syllables as a code:

	SANSKRIT/PALI	SYLLABLE LENGTH	GREEK NAME	MEANING OR EXPLANATION
groups of 2 syllables	*gaga* or *gā*	— —	spondee	from a solemn verse used at drinking rituals
	la ga	∪ —	iambus	light and playful, from the story of Iambé
	ga la	— ∪	trochee	running, tripping
	lala or *lā*	∪ ∪	pyrrhic	from a dance at Pyrrhus
groups of 3 syllables	*ma*	— — —	molossus	
	ya	∪ — —	bacchic	
	ra	— ∪ —	cretic	
	sa	∪ ∪ —	anapaest	reversed (dactyl)
	ta	— — ∪	antibacchic	opposite of bacchic
	ja	∪ — ∪	amphibrach	short at both (ends)
	bha	— ∪ ∪	dactyl	finger, with 3 joints: long, short, short
	na	∪ ∪ ∪	tribrach	3 short (syllables)
groups of 4 syllables	*	∪ ∪ ∪ ∪	proceleusmatic	inciting, animating

* There seems to be no code-syllable(s) for this *gaṇa*. The *Vuttodaya* calls it either *akhilalahu*, wholly short, or *sabbalahu*, all short.

There are two ways in which the number and length of syllables in each line constitute a recognized meter:

(i) syllabic (*vaṇṇavutta*) meters are defined by both the order and length of syllables (*vaṇṇā*). For example, the *upavajirā* variety of the eleven-syllable *tuṭṭhubha* meter has four groups (*gaṇa*): short-long-short, long-long-short, short-long-short, long-long ∪ — ∪ | — — ∪ | ∪ — ∪ | — —. This is an invariable form.

(ii) quantitative (*mattāvutta*) meters are defined primarily by the number of measures (*mattā*), although there may be secondary rules in individual meters concerning the number and/or order of syllables in certain groups. For example,

In both kinds of meter:
an initial vowel followed by two consonants can be counted short
a short final vowel can be counted long

any syllable can be shortened (*systole*) or lengthened (*diastole*) because of the meter (*metri causa*).

Some examples:

The easiest meter, which is by far the most common in Pali and Sanskrit texts, is usually known by the Sanskrit name *śloka*. This means literally 'verse' in general, but is applied to one kind of *anuṭṭubh* (Sanskrit *anuṣṭubh*) meter. Each *śloka* must contain four feet (*pāda*) of eight syllables, and the only restrictions on syllable length are in the fifth, sixth and seventh places. In its basic form there are two patterns allowed: ∪ — ∪ , short-long-short, or ∪ — —, short-long-long. A further restriction is that whichever pattern is chosen for the first *pada*, the other must be chosen for the second *pada*, and then the third must be the same as the first and the fourth the same as the second, and so on. The same pattern of feet within stanzas must then be repeated.

∪ — — ∪ — ∪

sīlaṃ samādhi paññā ca vimutti ca anuttarā
morality, concentration, wisdom and unsurpassed release

∪ — — ∪ — ∪

anubuddhā ime dhammā Gotamena yasassinā
have been awakened to by the renowned Gotama.

∪ —— ∪ — ∪

iti Buddho abhiññāya dhammaṃ akkhāsi bhikkhunaṃ
Knowing this, he told the monks the Dhamma

∪ —— ∪— ∪

dukkhass' antakaro Satthā cakkhumā parinibbuto
the Teacher, ender of suffering, he who sees, who is completely quenched (D II 123)

The following lines use three varieties of the 11-syllable *tuṭṭubha* (Sanskrit *triṣṭubh*) meter. The first and third are in *indavajirā*, — — ∪ | — — ∪ | ∪—∪ | — —, the second is in *upaṭṭhitā* — — ∪ |∪ — ∪ | ∪ — ∪ | — —, and the fourth is in *upavajirā*, ∪ — ∪ |— — ∪ |∪— ∪ |— —:

— — ∪ | — — ∪ | ∪ — ∪ | — —
gantvāna Buddho nadiyaṃ Kakutthaṃ
The Buddha went to the Kakuttha river

— — ∪ | ∪ — ∪ | ∪ — ∪ | — —
accodisatodikavippasannaṃ
which was clear, with pure and pleasant water

— — ∪ | — — ∪ | ∪ — ∪ | — —
ogāhi Satthā sukilantarūpo
(then) the Teacher, his body very tired, bathed

∪ — ∪ | — — ∪ | ∪ — ∪ | — —
tathāgato appaṭimo va loke
the Tathāgata, with no equal in the world (D II 135).

The following lines use two varieties of the 12-syllable *jagatī* meter. The first, second and fourth padas are in *vaṃsaṭṭha*, ∪ — ∪ | — — ∪ | ∪ — ∪ | — ∪ —, and the third is is *indavaṃsa*, — — ∪ | — — ∪ | ∪ — ∪ | — ∪ —.

∪ — ∪ | — — ∪ | ∪ — ∪ | — ∪ —
tathāgataṃ buddham asayhasāhinaṃ
To the Tathagata, the Buddha, who bears the unbearable

∪ — ∪ | — — ∪ | ∪ — ∪ | — ∪ —
duve vitakkā samudācaranti naṃ
two thoughts occur:

— — ∪ | — — ∪ | ∪ — ∪ | — ∪ —
khemo vitakko paṭhamo udīrito
the first which arises is safety

∪ — ∪ | — — ∪ | ∪ — ∪ | — ∪ —
tato viveko dutiyo pakāsito
then the second to appear is seclusion (It 32)

The *vetālīya* meter is quantitative, and has fourteen measures in its first and third lines, and sixteen in its second and fourth. All lines must end with the same two groups long-short-long, short-long (short)*, — ∪ — | ∪ — (∪) |. The preceding portion of the first and third feet are made up of six measures, that of the second and fourth by eight measures, freely chosen.

* A short final syllable is counted long.

∪ ∪ —∪ ∪ |— ∪ —| ∪—
supinena yathā pi saṅgataṃ
Just as what is encountered in a dream

∪ ∪— — ∪ ∪|—∪ —|∪∪
paṭibuddho puriso na passati
a person does not see when woken up

—— ∪ ∪|—∪ — | ∪ —
evam pi piyāyitaṃ janaṃ
so beloved people

— — —∪ ∪|— ∪ —|∪∪
petaṃ kālakataṃ na passati
a person does not see when they are dead and gone (Sn 807)

The *opacchandasika* meter has 16 measures in the first line and 18 in the second. All lines must end in the two feet — ∪ — |∪ — —. In the first these are preceded by 6 measures and in the second 8. Thus verse 5 from the Theragāthā:

— — ∪ ∪|— ∪ —|∪ — —
yo duddamayo damena danto
He who was hard to tame has been tamed by the taming,

— — — ∪∪|—∪—|∪ — —
Dabbo santusito vitiṇṇakaṅkho
Dabba (the worthy one) is happy, doubts overcome,

⏑ ⏑ — ⏑ ⏑ | — ⏑ — | ⏑ — —
vijitāvi apetabheravo hi
victorious, with fear gone,

— — — ⏑ ⏑ | — ⏑ — | ⏑ — —
Dabbo so parinibbuto ṭhitatto
that Dabba is completely awakened, steadfast.

Further work in Pali meter is hampered by the fact that the terminology used in different sources is both under-developed and inconsistent. For further reading see Appendix 4, Bibliography.

Appendix 4

BIBLIOGRAPHICAL ESSAY

For more than a hundred years the main organization for the dissemination and study of Pali texts in the west has been the Pali Text Society. Their website is palitext.com.

The indigenous Pali grammatical tradition has been studied most extensively in recent times by Ole Pind:

'Studies in the Pāli Grammarians I,' *Journal of the Pali Text Society* vol. XIV, 1989: 33–81.

'Studies in the Pāli Grammarians II.1,' *Journal of the Pali Text Society* vol. XIV, 1990: 175–218.

'Pāli Grammarians: The Methodology of the Pāli Grammarians,' in *Sauhṛdyamaṅgalam, Studies in Honour of Siegfried Lienhard on his 70th Birthday*. Stockholm 1995.

'Pali Grammar and Grammarians from Buddhaghosa to Vajirabuddhi: A Survey,' Bukkyô Kenkyū XXVI (Buddhist Studies) 1997: 23–88.

A list of titles of Pali grammatical works is given in D. L. Barua, 'Some Works on Pali Grammar, Rhetoric and Prosody,' *Indian Culture* 1948–9, 15: 194–202.

H. Scharfe, *Grammatical Literature*, vol. V, 2 of J. Gonda (ed.) *History of Indian Literature*. Wiesbaden: Harrassowitz 1977.

Modern roman script editions of Pali grammars are sadly few. Pride of place must go to

H. Smith, *Saddanīti*, Lund: C.W.K. Gleerup, 1928–66 (6 vols.)., republished in 3 vols. London: Pali Text Society 2001.

Kaccāyana, the standard textbook in Asian Pali curricula, traditional and modern, has been edited at least three times:
James D'Alwis, *An Introduction to Kaccāyana's Grammar of the Pali Language*. London: Williams and Norgate 1863.
E. Senart made an edition and partial translation in *Journal Asiatique* 6ᵉ serie Tome XVII, 1871: 193–540 (also published separately).
S. C. Vidyabhusana, *Kaccāyana's Pali Grammar (edited in Devanagari characters and translated into English)*. Calcutta: Hari Charan Manna 1901.
Bālāvatāra, (partial) ed. and transl. L. Lee, *The Orientalist* 1892, 2: 71–3, 97–8, 198–9, 210–12.
ed. (nagarī characters) and Hindi transl. Swami Dwarikadas Shastri, Varanasi, Bauddha Bharati, 1996.
Saddabindu: 'Minor Pāli Grammar Texts: the Saddabindu and its "new" subcommentary,' F. Lottermoser, *Journal of the Pali Text Society* vol. XI, 1987: 79–109.

Web sites and disks have many more texts, although the quality of editorial work is variable: the Vipassanā Research Institute (vri.dhamma.org) online and in their Chaṭṭhasaṅgāyana CD, and the Sri Lanka Tipitaka Project, (jbe.gold.ac.uk), offer versions of *Abhidhānappadīpikā, Bālavatāra, Dhātu-mañjusā, Dhātupāṭha, Kaccāyana, Moggallānavuttivivaraṇapañcikā, Moggallāna-vyākaraṇa, Padamañjari, Padasādhana, Rūpasiddhi, Saddanīti, Saddabindu and Vākyamālā*. The traditions of Pali grammatical analysis and pedagogy in Sri Lanka and mainland Southeast Asia have been continuous and still flourish, in so far as grammatical study does anywhere. In Thai, with quotations from Kaccāyana, Moggallāna and Aggavaṃsa, see Supaphan na Bangchang, *Waiyakarana Bali* (BE 2538 = AD 1995, ISBN 974-580-609-9).

There are too many European grammars to list here; the following examples are mostly in English.

(i) The following are more in the nature of a primer:

O. Frankfurter *Handbook of Pali*. London: Williams and Norgate 1883.
A. P. Buddhadatta Thera *The New Pali Course Part I*. Colombo: The Colombo Apothecarie's Co., 1949.
L. De Silva, *Pali Primer*. Igatpuri: Vipassanā Research Institute, 1995.

J. Gair and W. S. Karunatilleke, *A New Course in Reading Pāli*. Delhi: Motilal Banarsidass, 1998.
A. K. Warder, *Introduction to Pali*. London: Pali Text Society 1963 (latest revision 2001).

(ii) the following are more in the nature of a reference grammar:

J. Minayeff (I.P. Minaev), *Pāli Grammar*, published first in 1872, then translated from Russian to French to English 1882, Rangoon (reprinted Delhi: Bahri Publications 1990, with errors).
W. Geiger, *A Pali Grammar*, translated into English by Batakrishna Ghosh (1943), revised and edited by K.R. Norman (latest ed.) 2000. This is still the standard work, the reference point for all others.
C. Duroiselle, *A Practical Grammar of the Pāli Language*, first published 1906, revised by U. Dhamminda 1997 (available at tipitaka.net).
M. Mayrhofer, *Handbuch des Pāli I. Teil: Grammatik, II. Teil: Text und Glossar*. Heidelberg: Carl Winter Universitätsverlag, 1951.
O. von Hinüber, *Das ältere Mittelindisch im Überblick*. Wien: Verlag Der Österreichischen Akademie der Wissenschaften, 1986.
A. Fahs, *Grammatik des Pali*. Leipzig: VEB Verlag Enzyklopädie, 1989.
V. Perniola, *Pali Grammar*, (republished) London: Pali Text Society 1997.
T. Oberlies, *Pāli: A Grammar of the Language of the Theravāda Tipiṭaka*. Berlin: de Gruyter, 2001.

(iii) other works:

By far the largest modern mine of Pali treasures is K. R. Norman, *Collected Papers, vols. I–VII*. London: Pali Text Society, 1991–2001. An Index to all seven volumes is given in *Journal of the Pali Text Society*, vol. XXVI, 2000: 169–231. Also indispensable are four of his translations, each of which has very full notes and a good Index: *Elders' Verses I*, *Elders' Verses II*, London: Pali Text Society 1969, 1971; *Group of Discourses*, London: Pali Text Society, 2nd ed. 2001; *The Word of the Doctrine (Dhammapada)*, London: Pali Text Society 1997.

M. A. Burston, *A Semantic Analysis of the Pali Case System*, Ph.D. thesis Cornell University, 1977 (available from Xerox University Microfilms, Ann Arbor Michigan).

C. Caillat, *Pour Une Nouvelle Grammaire du Pāli*. Torino: Istituto di Indologia della Università di Torino, Conferenze IV, 1970.

M. A. Deokar, *A Comparative study of the Pāṇinian Grammatical Tradition and the Three Grammars of Pali* [sic], D. Phil. thesis, University of Pune, 2002.

H. Hendriksen, *Syntax of the Infinite Verb-Forms of Pāli*. Munksgaard: Copenhagen, 1944.

O. von Hinüber, *Studien zur Kasussyntax des Pāli, besonders des Vinaya-Piṭaka*. München: Kitzinger, 1968.

————. *Selected Papers*. London: Pali Text Society, 1994.

————. 'Pāli: How do we see it eighty years after Geiger's Grammar?' in U. Everding and A. Tilakaratne (eds.) *Wilhelm Geiger and the Study of the History and Culture of Sri Lanka*. Colombo: Goethe Institute and Postgraduate Institute of Pali and Buddhist Studies, University of Kelaniya, 1999.

J. M. Peterson, *Grammatical Relations in Pāli and the Emergence of Ergativity in Indo-Aryan*. München: Lincom Europa, 1998.

O. H. de A. Wijesekera, *Syntax of the Cases in the Pali Nikayas*. Colombo: The Postgraduate Institute of Pali and Buddhist Studies, University of Kelaniya, 1936, reprinted 1993.

Articles are too numerous to list, but notable are:

S. Insler, 'Rhythmic Effects in Pali Morphology,' *Die Sprache* 1994: 36: 70–93.

E. Nolot, 'Studies in Vinaya Technical Terms I–III,' *Journal of the Pali Text Society* vol. XXII: 73–150.

'Studies in Vinaya Technical Terms IV–X, *Journal of the Pali Text Society* vol. XXV, 1993: 1–111.

S. M. Katre, 'On the history of ḷ in Pāli,' in R. Bhandarkar et al. (eds.) *B.C. Law Volume, Part Two*. Poona: Indian Research Institute, 1946.

Dictionaries of Pali are not yet satisfactory. The old warhorse is the Pali Text Society's *Pali-English Dictionary*, by T. W. Rhys Davids and W. Stede, published in 1921–25 and used by every Pali scholar since. In 1925 Stede wrote 'I realize now that I am only at the beginning of the

"Perfect" Dictionary. May I, within the next twenty years, see a second edition of the Pāli Dictionary which will come nearer to the ideal.' We have had to wait for a new millennium to see the first part of a second edition, made by Margaret Cone: *A Pāli Dictionary, Part I, A–Kh* (Pali Text Society 2001), which comes very much nearer to the ideal. R. C. Childers' *A Dictionary of the Pali Language*, first published in 1875, is still valuable, particularly for words from medieval literary texts which the *Pali-English Dictionary* chose to ignore. The *Critical Pali Dictionary*, started in 1924, has now reached the consonants, in vol. 3, so far to *kāmadhātu* in vol. III fasc. 7, 2001. M. Cone's 'Lexicography, Pali, and Pali Lexicography,' in *Journal of the Pali Text Society* vol. XXII, 1996: 1–34, is an informative and witty survey.

A. P. Buddhadatta *English-Pali Dictionary*, London: Pali Text Society 1979 (first published in 1955), remains useful.

Ñāṇamoli's *A Pali-English Glossary of Buddhist Technical Terms* (Kandy: Buddhist Publication Society 1994) has a list of grammatical terms at pp.123–34. This section is also available at tipitaka.net.

Meter

The only work specifically dedicated to Pali Meter is A. K. Warder, *Pali Metre* (Pali Text Society 1967), which is unfortunately very hard to use, especially for a beginner. The works of K.R. Norman cited above all contain a great deal of information on meter. Perhaps the greatest desideratum in this area is a modern edition of and commentary on the Pali treatise *Vuttodaya* . It is currently available in these forms:

The best and most recent edition is in Thai script, with the Pali text and extensive commentary and tabulation: วุตโตทยมัญชรี พระคันธสาราภิวงศ์ โรงพิมพ์ ธรรมสภา กรุงเทพฯ ๒๕๔๔ (= AD 2001).

G. E. Fryer, The Pali Text of the Vuttodaya, or 'Exposition of Metre,' *Journal of the Asiatic Society of Bengal*, IV, 1877: 371–410.

An edition in Roman script, with explanatory material mostly in Japanese, is 'Vuttodaya,' *Buddhist Studies (Bukkyō Kenkyū)* vol. III, 1973 pp.143–105.

J. Minayeff, 'Vuttodaya', *Mélanges Asiatiques* (St. Petersbourg: L'Académie Impériale des Sciences, VI, 1869: 195ff.

Helmer Smith's edition of the *Saddanīti* contains material on meter in vol. IV pp.1148–72. His edition of *Paramatthajotikā II* vol. III discusses the meters of the *Sutta Nipāta* on pp. 637–44.

For *Itivuttaka* there is

J. H. Moore, 'Metrical Analysis of the Pāli Itivuttaka, a Collection of Discourses of Buddha,' *Journal of the American Orientalist Society*, vol.28 1907: 317–30.

Ven. Ānandajoti's *An Outline of the Meters in the Pāli Canon* is available in pdf. form at www.buddhanet-de.net/ancient-buddhist-texts.

Sanskrit

There are many primers for learning Sanskrit. The best for revision purposes is M. Coulson's *Teach Yourself Sanskrit*, London: Teach Yourself Publishing, first edition 1976, 2nd edition (edited by R. Gombrich and J. Benson) 1992. The two classic grammars are by Whitney and MacDonnell, the former providing more detail, the latter a clearer synoptic view. For the Pāṇinian tradition there is P.–S. Filliozat's precise and lucid *Grammaire Sanskrite Pāṅinéenne*, Paris: Picard, 1988.

INDEX

Ablative case, 3, 10, 13, 14, 18, 28–30, 42, 47–49, 53
Absolute constructions, 37–41, 149
Absolutives, 6, 102, 114–17, 126–27, 130, 136
Accusative case, 4, 13–14, 18, 20–23, 25, 42, 44–45, 53, 56, 60, 77–78, 98, 117, 122, 124, 180; (absolute) 37, 39, 40
Active voice, 18–19, 77–78, 90, 93, 103, 107–9, 118, 130, 162, 167, 174–75, 186–87
Adjectives, 12–13, 15, 17, 19, 28, 31, 33, 41, 52–53, 57–58, 61–63, 65–68, 70, 73, 99, 101, 106–8, 110, 124, 132, 135, 138, 149–51, 153, 155–61, 166–74, 176–81, 183, 185
Adverbs (adverbial uses), 12, 19, 22–23, 26, 30–31, 33–34, 36, 37, 40, 53, 60, 62, 67–68, 98–99, 114, 121–22, 124, 131–32, 134, 141–42, 150–52, 159–60, 163, 166, 169–70, 175–77, 183
Alphabet, 136, 176; (Pali) 1–3,
Analytical languages, linguistic processes, 127, 152–53
Aorist tense, 14–15, 79–80, 87–89, 93, 106
Articles, 70, 153–54, 181
Aspect, 14–15, 106, 108, 154–56, 162

Bahuvrīhi (bahubbīhi) (Possessive) compounds, 17, 131, 135, 156

Cardinal numbers, 70–74, 172
Cases, 13–14, 18–37, 42, 77, 117, 124, 133, 156–58, 164
Causative(s), 21–22, 77, 79, 95–98, 100, 107, 118, 158–59, 162
Cerebral (Retroflex) consonants, 2–3, 7, 9, 10–11
Changeable noun stems, 52, 56–60, 103
Clause, 19, 37, 47, 64, 68, 136–37, 141, 149–52, 159–60, 163, 165, 169–71, 177, 182, 185
Complement, 150, 156, 166, 170, 177, 185
Compounds, 3–4, 17, 68, 73–74, 129–39, 152–53, 156, 160–61, 164, 168, 183
Conditional mood, 14–15, 79–80, 91–92
Conjugation, 14–16, 75, 79–101, 112, 162, 167–68
Conjunction, 12, 121, 159, 163–64, 181
Copulative compounds – see Dvandva
Consonants, 1–4, 7–12, 56, 59, 87, 154, 162, 173, 176

Dative case, 13–14, 18, 27–28, 41, 46–47, 53, 111, 117, 130, 166
Declension, 12–14, 18–74, 164, 167
Denominatives, 12, 79, 95, 99–101
Dentals consonants, 2–3, 7–9
Dependent determinative compounds – see Tatpuruṣa
Descriptive determinative compounds – see Karmadhāraya
Desideratives, 15, 79, 100–101
Direct and Indirect Speech, 141–42, 164–66
Dvandva compounds, 131–32, 164

Factors of action (*kārakā*), 42–51
Frequentatives, see Intensives
Future participles, 106, 109–12, 167
Future (tense), 14–15, 79–82, 90–91, 114, 116, 154–55, 181, 183–84

Gender, 15, 17–18, 61–63, 68, 129, 131, 133, 135, 164–65, 180
Genitive case, 13–14, 18–19, 27, 31–34, 36, 42, 50–51, 53, (absolute) 37–39
Grapheme(s), 165, 176
Gutturals consonants, 1–3, 7

Imperative mood, 14–15, 65, 79, 83–84, 112, 168, 182, 187
Indirect Speech – see Direct and Indirect Speech
Infinitives, 102, 111, 117–19, 122, 148, 159, 162, 166–67, 170, 175
Inflection, 12–16, 129, 151–52, 167
Instrumental case, 13, 18, 23–26, 42, 46, 53, 77–78, 98, 114, 124; (absolute) 39
Intensive verbs, 15, 79, 95, 100–101, 179
Interjections, 22, 167
Interrogative pronouns, 61–62, 67, 159, 179
Intransitive verbs – see Transitive and intransitive verbs

Karmadhāraya (kammadhāraya) (Descriptive Determinative) compounds, 131–33, 168

Labials consonants, 1–3, 7
Locative case, 13–14, 19, 31, 34–37, 42, 49–50; (absolute) 37–38

Metathesis, 2, 10, 85, 168
Meter, 168, 188–95
Mood, 14–15, 79–86, 91–93, 95, 115, 118, 162, 165, 168–69, 187
Mora, Law of, 3–4, 60, 81
Morpheme, 152–53, 169
Moods (of verbs), 14, 79, 93, 95, 115, 118, 162, 168–69, 187

Negation, 121–23, 169–70
Nominal paradigms, 52–60
Nominative case, 13–14, 18–20, 42–43, 56, 77–78; (absolute) 37, 40–43
Nouns, 12–14, 17–60, 62, 70, 99, 102, 109, 112–14, 117, 125–26, 135, 149–50, 154, 156–57, 159–60, 162, 164–68, 170–72, 176–78, 183–85
Number (i.e. singular, plural), 15–16, 18, 62, 68, 129, 135, 151, 162, 164, 166, 171–72
Numbers (i.e. numerals), 12, 52, 61, 70–74, 132, 164, 172, 181, 183

Object (Direct and/or Indirect), 13–15, 18, 20–21, 42–47, 49, 77–78, 93–94, 96–98, 137, 157, 159, 164, 166–67, 170, 172–74, 182, 184, 186–87

Optative mood, 14–15, 79–80, 84–86, 92, 112, 168–69, 187
Ordinal numbers, 70, 73–74, 172

Participles, 12, 15, 37, 40–41, 52, 58–59, 102–12, 114, 136–37, 150, 155–56, 159, 162, 167, 170, 173–75, 177, 186
Particles, 12, 121–23, 134, 152, 166, 175
Passive voice, 77–78, 93–94
Past participles, 106–9, 114, 136, 159, 167, 174–75, 186
Periphrasis, 14, 80, 114, 175
Person(s), personal endings, 4, 13, 15–16, 62–67, 75, 79, 81, 162, 166, 175
Personal pronouns, 61–67, 179–80
Phonemes, 165, 175–76
Phrase, 20, 25, 31, 37, 38, 40, 64, 141, 149–52, 159, 163, 167, 169–73, 176–78, 180–81, 185
Predicate, 19, 150, 159, 176, 181–82
Prefixes, 3–5, 9, 12, 23, 40, 75, 77, 87–88, 97, 111, 125–27, 133–34, 169, 178
Prepositions, 12–14, 23, 30, 33–34, 40, 116, 119, 125–26, 131, 133–34, 151, 156–58, 162, 166–67, 173, 175–77
Present participles, 58, 103–8, 114, 162, 177
Present tense, 16, 81–83, 155
Pronominal adjectives, 52, 61–68, 151, 178–81
Pronouns, 12–13, 52, 61–69, 150–51, 157–59, 162, 164–65, 167–68, 178–81, 183

Relative pronouns and clauses, 61–62, 68–69, 159–60, 179–81
Retroflex, *see* Cerebrals
Roots (verbal), 12, 15, 75–80, 87–90, 93, 95–97, 99–102, 106–7, 110–14, 118, 162, 166

Semivowel(s), 1, 3, 5, 7–8, 11
Sentence, 12, 18–19, 31, 41, 63, 77–78, 114–15, 121–23, 129, 149, 152–53, 156, 159, 167, 169–72, 176–78, 180–82
Subject, 13–15, 19, 23, 31, 41, 77–78, 93, 97, 115, 121, 149, 156–57, 159, 164, 170, 172–73, 176, 180–82, 184–87
Syntactical compounds, 136–37, 183
Synthetic languages, linguistic processes, 129, 152–53
Systems (four, of verbs), 79, 95–101

Tatpuruṣa (tappurisa), Tatpurusha (Dependent Determinative) compounds, 131–33, 183
Tenses (of verbs), 14–16, 79, 89–90, 93, 95, 106, 108, 115, 118, 154–55, 162, 164–66, 168, 173–74, 181, 183–84
Transitive and/or intransitive verbs, 13, 18, 21, 43, 77, 96–97, 158, 171, 173–75, 184–86

Verbs, 12–16, 18, 31–33, 50–51, 75–119, 124, 136, 149–50, 154–59, 162, 166–68, 170, 172–76, 181–87
Vocative case, 13–14, 18–19, 31, 37, 42, 50–51, 56, 59
Voice, 78–79, 89, 93–94, 130, 162, 174–75, 186–87
Voiced/voiceless consonants (surds/sonants), 2–3, 7–8
Vowels, 1–8, 12, 75, 85, 135–36, 141, 154, 171, 176

www.ingramcontent.com/pod-product-compliance
Lightning Source LLC
Chambersburg PA
CBHW030826230426
43667CB00008B/1396
9789749511138